THE PROBLEM OF EVIL AND INDIAN THOUGHT

The Problem of Evil and Indian Thought

ARTHUR L. HERMAN

MOTILAL BANARSIDASS PUBLISHERS
PRIVATE LIMITED • DELHI

First Edition: Delhi, 1976
Second Edition: Delhi, 1993
Reprint: Delhi, 2000

ISBN: 81-208-0753-7

Also available at:
MOTILAL BANARSIDASS
236, 9th Main III Block, Jayanagar, Bangalore 560 011
41 U.A. Bungalow Road, Jawahar Nagar, Delhi 110 007
8 Mahalaxmi Chamber, Warden Road, Mumbai 400 026
120 Royapettah High Road, Mylapore, Chennai 600 004
Sanas Plaza, 1302 Baji Rao Road, Pune 411 002
8 Camac Street, Calcutta 700 017
Ashok Rajpath, Patna 800 004
Chowk, Varanasi 221 001

Printed in India
BY JAINENDRA PRAKASH JAIN AT SHRI JAINENDRA PRESS,
A-45 NARAINA, PHASE-I, NEW DELHI 110 028
AND PUBLISHED BY NARENDRA PRAKASH JAIN FOR
MOTILAL BANARSIDASS PUBLISHERS PRIVATE LIMITED,
BUNGALOW ROAD, DELHI 110 007

FOR HELEN

PREFACE TO THE SECOND EDITION

This book intended to do two things in 1976: First, provide a critical history of Western and Eastern theodicies; and second, provide a solution to the theological problem of evil through a Hindu, specifically Śaṅkarian, theodicy. The book used "theodicy" in precisely the sense defined by Immanuel Kant:

> By theodicies one means defences of the highest wisdom of the Creator against the complaints which reason makes by pointing to the existence of things in the world which contradict the wise purpose. One calls such a defence a "plea for God's cause."[1]

It is human suffering, as well as animal and angelic suffering, of course, that "contradicts the wise purpose", and it is the "plea for God's cause" that will constitute the attempted solutions to the problem of that suffering.

The book presented, analyzed and refuted from the Western tradition some twenty-one historical solutions to the theological problem of evil. It then turned to the Eastern tradition and to Hinduism and Śaṅkarācārya in order to examine the "rebirth solution". Analysis revealed that the rebirth solution will solve the problem provided that several additional assumptions about both the "Creator" and about "things in the world" which would contradict the Creator's wise purpose were accepted. It concluded by focusing on several additional problems and questions raised by the rebirth solution to the theological problem of evil. These additional assumptions as well as these additional problems and questions appeared to limit the joyful acceptability of the rebirth solution as either a theoretical, or a working practical, solution to the theological problem of evil.

It has been over fifteen years since *The Problem of Evil and Indian Thought* was first published. During that time a great deal of new thinking and research has occurred concerning the central question raised by this book, viz., Is there a solution to the problem of evil?

1. Immanuel Kant, "On the Failure of All Attempted Philosophical Theodicies (1791)", translated by Michael Despland in his *Kant on History and Religion* (Montreal: McGill-Queen's University Press, 1973), p. 283.

PREFACE

This is an extensive study of a problem that has, as I shall argue, plagued Western, but not Indian philosophy. It's length is, I hope, excusable on the grounds that both Western and Indian philosophers have had a great deal to say about the elements that both generate and dissolve the puzzle; hence any commentator, if he is to come at all close to success in analyzing the problem, must of necessity look to that great bulk carefully, and also lengthily.

Acknowledgements ought to be made to a vast number of people who have helped covertly and overtly in the preparation of this work. But to avoid any extended autobiograpnical undertaking, let me simply express my deep and sincere gratitude to the following few persons who have read the manuscript, in whole or in part, and made helpful comments and corrections on it : D. Burnham TERRELL and Keith GUNDERSON of the University of Minnesota, who were both extremely helpful in their comments; David WHITE of macalester College, St. Paul, Minnesota, who can discover misprints beyond the senses of all other souls on earth; and Karl H. POTTER of the University of Minnesota who patiently and wisely guided me, and this work, around inconceivable blunders and errors. Penultimately, to my colleagues at Wisconsin State University who have over the years been invaluable in keeping me on straight philosophic paths, I owe more than I can express. In particular, the greatest help came from Professors John P. ZAWADSKY, John BAILIFF, John BILLINGS, and Joseph CHULER, who gave unstintingly of their patience, kindness and gentle but goading words. Finally, to BARBARA, my wife who typed and retyped drafts and revisions of the manuscript while simultaneously providing an invaluable running gloss to nearly every paragraph, I owe an unpayable debt.

A. L. HERMAN

Stevens Point, Wisconsin U.S.A.
June, 1971

TABLE OF CONTENTS

INTRODUCTION

Among the many perpetual problems which bother philosophers in both the East and the West, there is one curious puzzle that they do not share: the so-called problem of evil in at least one of its formulations. Thus while Europeans and Indians alike have philosophized and anguished over the problems of God, freedom, and immortality, the puzzles of perception, universals and meaning, Indians have been strangely silent about what has become a traditional western puzzle, the problem of evil. I dare say that Europeans and Indians could, without loss of concern, share the same introductory textbooks in philosophy, and that, by and large, each would feel pretty much at home in the other's philosophic classics, save a few oddities here and there which might be more theological than philosophical. But it is precisely two of these oddities, peculiar to Indians on the one hand and Europeans on the other, that will provide the subject-matter for this present study; and I have in mind the doctrine of rebirth, an oddity to European philosophers, and the problem of evil, an oddity to Indian philosophers. To be truly accurate, I should of course say that these two curiosities are oddities for certain European philosophers and certain Indian philosophers, for no doubt it is a truth as old as Thales and Yājñavalkya, that for every odd philosophic doctrine, there is always an odd philosophic defender.

The general thesis of this study will be that these two oddities, the problems of evil and rebirth, under proper analysis, can be brought together to yield what has heretofore proved to be doctrinally difficult for most European philosophers, viz., an acceptable philosophic solution to the problem of evil. That "proper analysis" will lead us into more specific details. I want to show that the problem of evil has at least three quite distinct formulations, each of which has proved to be a challenge to European philosophers and theologians. Similarly, the doctrine of rebirth has at least two quite distinct formulations, and it will be necessary to separate and analyze these formulations in order to carry out the intent of this study which is to state the philosophic conditions under which the problem of evil can be/would be considered solved or dissolved, and what such a solution or dissolution would look like given the Indian doctrine of rebirth.

That my interest in the problem is philosophical and not sectarian or casuistic will, I hope, be made clear as we proceed. I desire merely to explore the problem as it has developed for European philosophers, remarking on the moves and attempts made toward its solution as those steps appear acceptable or unacceptable to reason and common sense. In applying Indian philosophical standards to this problem, I wish no more than to show what a possible solution might look like, without making the reader feel that he is being proselytized or persuaded to accept any general philosophic or theological position. A disclaimer such as this is made necessary for two reasons: First, to console the reader that simply because a philosophical puzzle is being treated with non-European tools, and at least one of these tools is certainly a stumbling block to Europeans and foolishness to most philosophers, is no reason to panic; the intent of the present study is neither one of missionizing nor sermonizing for any particular belief system. Second, to impress upon the reader the purely philosophical intent of the study: he is being challenged for his philosophic attention alone. The task of the philosopher with respect to traditional philosophic problems, as I see it, is simply to explain as clearly as possible what that problem is, what an acceptable solution to it would look like, what kind of attempted solution would be unacceptable, and what is entailed by all three of these moves. This will be the concern throughout this study, and no other is intended. The rule I follow most closely has been summed up admirably by Henry David Aiken when he says about his analysis of the problem of evil:

> "My present interest in the problem is philosophical: I desire merely to consider what sort of problem it is and to determine the significance of the various theological or ethical moves that have been made in coping with it".[1]

Let me very briefly sketch out the plan of the book. I begin by a discussion of the problem of evil (hereafter "P.E.") in Part I; Part II is concerned with the nature of rebirth; and Part III concludes by relating these two earlier parts, indicating that a solution to the puzzle analyzed in Part I can be developed from the concept analyzed in Part II.

More specifically, Part I is divided into the following four chapters:

I. *The Historical Background.*

I want here to give a historical context to the philosophical puzzle of P.E. The puzzle was generated because of certain intellectual conditions and it will be important to detail these conditions as they arose in the West. Our investigation will reveal some twenty-one attempted solutions.

II. *The Problem of Evil.*

From the historical milieu we concentrate our attention on the theological P.E. The theological P.E. has three quite separate formulations. These I call the theological problems of 1. superhuman evil, 2. human evil, and 3. sub-human evil.

My primary attention will be directed to the second of these theological P.E., the theological problem of human evil. Hence an analysis follows of each of the four premises necessary or needed to generate this specific problem:—

1. God is all powerful.
2. God is all knowing.
3. God is all good.
4. There is evil.

Expressed in more informal terms the theological P.E. comes to this:

> "Why is there any misery at all in the world ? Not by chance surely. Form some cause then. Is it from the intention of the Deity ? But he is perfectly benevolent. Is it contrary to his intention? But he is almighty".[3]

III. *Attempted Solutions to the Theological Problem of Human Evil.*

Whatever solutions there may be to P.E., they must attempt to make the four premises of II consistent. Of the twenty-one attempted solutions, all can be reduced to eight basic types. It will be shown that none of these solutions can be adequate to solving P.E., but that all miss the mark somehow and for reasons to be detailed in IV.

IV. *Conclusions.*

I close with a general discussion of the attempted solutions and with some remarks on the logical nature of the theological P.E.

Part II is divided into the following chapters:—

V. *The Historical Background of Saṁsāra.*

I want here to lay a foundation within the history of Indian thought for the doctrine of rebirth, together with other philosophical concepts that arise within the Indian philosophical frame and that are necessary to that doctrine. The Indian P.E., such as it is, will also be developed.

VI. *The Assumptions of The Rebirth Thesis.*

I will then give an analysis of the rebirth doctrine showing what the logic of the doctrine (the rules for its employment) must be, and at the same time show what varying notions the Indians have held with respect to this doctrine. With regard to this latter point, I want to show that at least two quite distinct notions of rebirth exist: the first to be called "transmigration" and the second "reincarnation"

VII. *Conclusion to Part II.*

I close with some general remarks about these two notions of rebirth. Part III relates P.E. puzzles of Part I with one of the rebirth notions of Part II, and is divided into the following three chapters:

VIII. *The Indian Assumptions to the Theological P.E.*

I want to show specifically in Part III how the Indian doctrine of rebirth in one of its formulations, (a basically Hindu notion) can be used to meet the theological P.E. in all three of its formulations. I begin by showing that the theses necessary to generate the theological P.E. can be found in the Indian philosophical and religious literature.

IX. *Two Indian Solutions to the Theological P.E.*

Having shown in VIII that the theological problem of evil can be generated in the Indian context, I go on to show two of the solutions open to Indians for solving this P.E. I devote the most attention to a presentation and analysis of transmigration as a solution to P.E. and the puzzles that are entailed by accepting it as such.

X. *Conclusion to Part III.*

I close with a few general remarks on the metaphysical pilgrimage undertaken in this study.

Briefly put then the aim of the present work is to show that the theological problem of evil, in all three of its formulations, can be solved by the Indian doctrine of transmigration.

PART I

PHILOSOPHY AND PROBLEMS OF EVIL

Chapter I

THE HISTORICAL BACKGROUND

To sketch out the history of P.E. in the West, it might be well to understand just what it is that we are looking for. Consequently let me give a tentative rendering of the problem, realizing the while that there is much in it that is vague and loose. In Ch. II below we shall see to the necessary tightening and straightening of the elements in the premises, but for the present let us lay on with an intuitive grasp of the problem only, and then see to refinements later.

Whatever else it may have been, P.E. arises because of the felt inexplicability of evil. Through his agony and suffering, reflective man has from time to time raised his head to ask "Why?', and it is during these reflective moments that P.E. has evolved. Whether or not there would be a P.E. without man is a question we reserve for studies below, i.e., whether with, for example, suffering animals and angels, if there be animals and angels who suffer, there would be a P.E., that we leave aside for the moment. It is sufficient now to say merely that in the history of man on the planet there is abundant historical evidence that he has reflected on the apparent inexplicability of evil, on the felt suffering and waste and pain, that his flesh is heir to.

The most frequent, and probably the most poignant, form that P.E. has taken is the theological one, arising when in the course of reflecting on human suffering (as opposed now to super-and sub-human suffering, if such there be), and violence and death, it is recalled that there is, together with this evil (if such it be), a deity or deities with powers to prevent that evil. Thus P.E. becomes a theological P.E. when deity, with certain properties, omniscience, omnipotence, and benevolence, perhaps, exists, and simultaneously with human evil. For those who believe that there is such a God, and that there is evil which that deity could overcome if He wanted to, for such persons P.E. becomes especially distressing. Indeed the disappointment that such a deity does not act is reflected in the oldest expression of the theological P.E. that has come down to us, the dilemma probably first formulated by Epicurus (341-270 B.C.) and quoted by Lactantius (260-340 A.D.):

> "God either wishes to take away evils and is unable; or He is able, and is unwilling; or He is neither willing nor able, or He is both willing and able. If He is willing, and is unable, He is feeble, which is not in accordance with the character of God; if He is able and unwilling, He is envious, which is equally at variance with God; if He is neither willing nor able, He is both envious and feeble, and therefore not God; if He is both willing and able, which alone is suitable to God, from what source then are evils ? or why does He not remove them"?[3]

The point to be made about the dilemma is that while the entire argument appears to be valid, one can still say that it may not be a sound argument for the premises may not all be true. More on this to follow.

Before Epicurus, Plato had taken up the problem in what William Chase Greene has called "the first distinct statement in Greek literature of the problem of evil."[4] Socrates is speaking, and absolving Zeus from all wrong doing in the ills that befall man:

> "Neither, then, could God, said I, since he is good, be, as the multitude say, the cause of all things, but for mankind he is the cause of few things, but of many things not the cause. For good things are far fewer with us than evil, and for the good we must assume no other cause than God, but the cause of evil we must look for in other things and not in God".[5]

The history of the problem from this point on becomes a history of solutions. Indeed, we can deduce from Plato's perfunctory jab at the puzzle that God cannot be the cause of evil because God is all good, and as every good Greek knows (*pace* Homer) a good God could not cause evil. But then the puzzle looms all the larger. For if God, who is good, didn't produce the evil, and if God, who could presumably stop the evil, doesn't, we have two questions to ask, and each is tied to the other to haunt the theist who puzzles about human suffering: First, where did evil come from ? and second, why doesn't God stop it, lessen it, or make us able to bear it ? Thus we are back again to the dilemma raised by Epicurus; and there the matter seems to have lain in the sense that no serious work was done on the problem until it was taken up with a vengeance by Aurelius Augustine (354-430 A.D.). The problem and the solutions to P.E. really commence with Augustine, and we will begin our historical investigations with him, having now discovered in a somewhat desultory manner what it is that we are searching for and should be worried about.

The plan throughout Ch. I will be to take representative Western thinkers and attempt to discover how they conceived of P.E. and how they thought the problem could be solved. Thus we will be looking at puzzles as well as solutions in this historical sketch with a view to preparing the ground for a more careful analysis of P.E. in all its ramifications in Ch. II below and of the representative solutions that will be presented in Ch. III below. I hope to show that the Western thinkers that we shall discuss present a fairly wide list of possible solutions to P.E. Our method will be to simply discuss the various statements of P.E. and then note the solutions offered. The history we are presenting is more logical than chronological, since our intention is merely to note actual and possible representative solutions rather than to completely and exhaustively survey the history of a problem in Western literature.

1. Saint Augustine (354-430 A.D.)

Whatever else may have driven Aurelius Augustine in his theologically voluminous life, the problem of evil must rank first. Unlike Leibniz, who surely saw P.E. as an interesting philosophical puzzle to be handled with logic and a cool brain, Augustine saw it as one of the major challenges to his and apparently to all Christians' belief in God. Consequently, he deliberately eschews the niceties of systematic argument, and as often as not, writes and argues with white hot passion and a frenzy that leads this reader to the conclusion that solving the problem of evil was the most significant theological event in the good saint's entire life.

The principal sources for our discussion of Augustine's understanding of and attempted solutions to P.E. are : *Divine*

Providence and the Problem of Evil[6] composed shortly after his conversion to Christianity in 386 A.D.; *The Free Choice of the Will* (*De libero arbitrio*)[7] from about 395 A.D.; *Confessions*[8] written some time around 400 A.D.; *The City of God*[9] composed from 413 to 426 A.D.; and finally *Faith, Hope, and Charity* (*Enchiridion*)[10] written in 421 A.D.

Augustine gives us, in these works, what seems to be a nearly complete list of all future possible solutions to P.E., some of which he rejects, such as the Manichaean doctrine of two opposed Powers, one malevolent the other benign, fighting for control of man and the world, others which he accepts. Thus it is fair to say, I think, that Augustine's treatment of P.E. becomes the paradigm for all future philosophical handling of the problem, both in fact, because all the major figures who took P.E. to their bosoms relied on Augustine for advice and solace, as well as in theory, for nearly all future solutions to P.E. can be pinned down and located somewhere in the writings of Augustine (the few exceptions will be noted). For this reason we shall be spending not a little time in our own searchings into the Bishop of Hippo's work. And because we are fairly confident about the dates of the five texts to be investigated, it will prove helpful to proceed chronologically with these texts. There are three formulations of P.E. that we will find operating in these texts, for if there is evil to be explained in the creation, and the creation consists of three parts, then there will be three formulations of the problem to deal with. These are not treated systematically in any sense by any of the authors we shall be discussing but I think it will facilitate our research if we make clear at the outset that there are three such levels, and that, consequently, three subproblems of P.E. can be said to obtain. So we distinguish the three creative levels of the superhuman, (angels both fallen and unfallen), man, and finally animals. All three are of concern to Augustine and consequently to us as well.

a. *Divine Providence*

In Book One of *Divine Providence*, Augustine sets forth the problem of evil as a dilemma, reminiscent of the dilemma proposed previously by Epicurus:

"Wherefore, those who ponder these matters are seemingly

> forced to believe either that Divine Providence does not reach to these outer limits of things [where evil is] or that surely all evils are committed by the will of God. Both horns of this dilemma are impious, but particularly the latter . . . . [For] the imputing of negligence is indeed much more pardonable than the charge of ill will or cruelty".[11]

Let me call the first horn of this dilemma 'the negligence horn' and the second 'the cruelty horn'. If P.E. is generated by assuming that God is all-powerful, what in Ch. II below will be called 'the omnipotence thesis,' and that God is all good, what will be called 'the ethical thesis', and by assuming and then denying one or the other of these theses, then I think it is plain that Augustine's formulation of the dilemma attempts precisely that, viz., the negligence horn attacks the omnipotence thesis and the cruelty horn the ethical thesis. Either way we produce P.E.

The solution proposed to explain the presence of evil under the very nose of an all powerful, all good deity (for that is what P.E. comes to in the end) is the start of Augustine's theodicy; it comes essentially to saying, both here in *Divine Providence* as well as throughout the other writings, that the evil we see is seen narrowly and myopically. We need but apprehend the whole creation to realize three things: first, that while the separate parts of the creation may here and there be apparently evil, the whole is nonetheless good; second, that tremendous good comes out of evil; and third, this evil is necessary to the full harmony and goodness of the whole. Thus in Book Two of *Divine Providence*, these three solutions are proposed, and are worth quoting both for the historical interest they afford, i.e., here are some challenging solutions to P.E., and further, for their narrative colorfulness that lightens an otherwise burdensome tale. Augustine begins with what I shall call 'the-whole-is-good solution', or 'the aesthetic solution':

> "Thus it happens that whoever narrow-mindedly considers this life by itself alone is repelled by its enormous foulness, and turns away in sheer disgust. But, if he raises the eyes of the mind and broadens his field of vision and surveys all things as a whole, then he will find nothing unarranged, unclassed or unassigned to its own place".[12]

Augustine follows this by showing that good arises within the whole and for the whole by the presence of these separate evils; and we might call this 'the good-comes-from-evil solution' or 'the teleological solution'. His example is quotable and entertaining:

> "What more hideous than a hangman? What more cruel and ferocious than his character ? Yet he holds a necessary post in the very midst of laws, and he is incorporated into the order of a well-regulated state . . ."[13]

Finally, Augustine seems to argue that the evils present in the society, the particular whole that he chooses in analogy with the universe, are necessary in order to prevent greater evils that could come about without them. The upshot seems to be, if the analogy is consistently applied, that God approves the evils we get because the alternatives are far worse, call this 'the-evils-are-necessary-to-prevent-greater-evils solution' or 'the prevention solution'. Augustine's delightful example follows:

> "What can be mentioned more sordid, more bereft of decency, or more full of turpitude than prostitutes, procurers, and the other pests of that sort ? Remove prostitutes from human affairs, and you will unsettle everything because of lusts . . ."[14]

Finally, in *Divine Providence*, there is one other solution proposed, which will have important defenders later in the history of P. E. Augustine speaks of a barnyard cock fight in which one of the combatants emerges battered, torn and bloody. While this might fall under the category of animal evil, it is plainly meant to apply, again by analogy, to the struggle for good going on within, and finally emerging from, the whole. The production of good wouldn't be good unless there were evil, i.e., the struggle itself. Thus beauty exists by contrast with the ugly. Call this 'the evil-is-needed-to-contrast-with-the-good solution', or 'the contrast solution':

> "And yet, by that very deformity [of the barnyard cock beaten in a fight] was the more perfect beauty of the contest in evidence"[15]

In this rather hasty review of *Divine Providence*, then, at least four solutions to P.E. emerge, viz., the aesthetic solution, the teleological solution, the prevention solution, and the contrast solution. We must delay any analysis of these solutions as 'solutions' and a general discussion of their nature and relationships, until Ch. III below.

b. *Free Choice of The Will*

In *Free Choice*, the problem receives its shortest formulation. The dialogue between Augustine and one Evodius opens with the latter asking : Tell me, please, whether God is not the cause of evil ? But it is not until Book Three, some 100 pages later on, that the question is answered. In Book One, however, Augustine distinguishes two kinds of evil, which will have important applications in the later literature :

> "Augustine....we usually speak of evil in two ways : first, when we say that someone has done evil; second, when someone has suffered something evil".[16]

Now, the evil that man does is, for Augustine, sin (*peccatum*), and the evil that man suffers is punishment (*poena*).[17] I will return to this theme shortly and at greater length in Ch. II. But we have at this stage a distinction later to be called "moral evil" as opposed to "physical evil", respectively.

In Book Three a number of new solutions and themes predominate along with ones already introduced. P.E. is complicated, first of all by the introduction of a new premise, the omniscience of God. Following the distinction between sin and punishment as two meanings of evil, we can introduce two causes of evil, one of which might even be taken for a solution to P.E. Thus if sin is the evil that man does, then surely man is the cause of evil, i.e., if man is free to do the evil that he does, then man is the cause of evil and not God. Call this solution 'the man's-free-will-is-the-cause-of-evil solution' or simply 'the man is free solution'. But the solution runs into trouble if God is all knowing, i.e., trouble develops if the omniscience assumption is added to the omnipotence thesis and the ethical thesis as we shall shortly see. But for the present it is enough to say that Augustine argues that God is all knowing in the sense that He knows events that have happened, that are happening, and that will happen; call this in turn 'the omniscience thesis' for P.E. But keep in mind, as Augustine is at pains to point out, that there is a seeming contradiction between the man is free solution and the omniscience thesis. A second cause of evil, evil as punishment, would seem to directly implicate God in the production of evil; so whether we understand evil as sin which man does, and involve God indirectly as the Knower of what sins I would do, or understand evil as God's punishment for sin, and involve God directly, in either case God emerges as a causer, at two removes or at one remove, of evil, and Augustine has, indeed, his work cut out for himself.

We turn first to the difficulties raised by the omniscience thesis and the man is free solution. Augustine leaps right in with a statement of the puzzle before him, viz., there is a problem

> "...as to how these two positions are not mutually opposed and incompatible, namely, that God foreknows all future events and yet we sin freely and not of necessity".[18]

By 'free' Augustine says he means what is 'in our power', and since the will is in our power it must be free.[19] Further, God may know what my future is but He does not make that future happen as it does: my future is a result of my will. I freely cause my future events and God knows those events as a witness, but not as a cause. Hence, God is not responsible for my sin-events, but I am:

> "There is nothing in our power except that which is present while we are willing. Unless then it is within our power, our will is no will. Furthermore, it is because the will is in our power that it is free. What is not within our power, or cannot be, does not come under our freedom. Accordingly we do not deny God's foreknowledge of all things future, and yet we do will what we will. Since God has foreknowledge of our will, its future will be such as He foreknows it."[20]

But the power is mine, therefore, since He knows the power is mine. Therefore I am proven free by the knowledge that God must have of my freedom:

> The power, then, is not taken from me because of His foreknowledge, since this power will be mine all the more certainly because of the infallible knowledge of Him who foreknew that I would have it.[21]

There is, of course, a grand begging of the question here. If will is defined in terms of power, and free will is power that is mine, one assumes what one is trying to prove if one says, as Augustine does, that the will is in my power: that's the very point at issue: "power" is ambiguous, and can mean either what is really in my power or what is only apparently in my power; Augustine assumes that it is the former that applies to free will and not the latter. Surely, furthermore, if God knows what I will do tomorrow, there is a sense in which I cannot do differently than what God knows I will do, else God is not omniscient. And if I can't do differently than I must do, one wonders how much power I really have. While God does not compel these events, the very fact that they are foreknown ought to give an Augustinian pause. The upshot for Augustine then is that knowing the future and compelling the future are quite separate, and consequently God is not implicated in my sin. In a startling passage, Augustine moves from speaking about God as relieved from implication in my sin to God as wholly involved in the punishment of that sin; once again we are plunged into P.E. with God as sin's Avenger:

> ". . . so God does not compel events of the future to take place by his foreknowledge of them . . . . He is not the cause of all that He foreknows. He is not the cause of evil deeds, but only their avenger."[22]

It is important to keep in mind just where we are at this juncture. First, we are speaking about the problem of human (as opposed to superhuman or subhuman) evil. Second, we are involved with human evil as evil done by (sin) and that done to (punish) humans. Augustine has attempted to solve the first part of this second point (with its omniscience thesis) by appealing to a distinction between future events as known and future events as caused. This distinction is made to absolve God from implication in human sin and pin the blame on man. Our critical discussion of this issue must await our general analysis in **Ch. II** again, where we will develop further the implications of the omniscience thesis together with the omnipotence thesis. Augustine is now committed to the man is free solution, that men and not God cause evil, and also the thesis that the evil that men suffer is the result of their freedom. This brings him up against the hard case of suffering children, a theme that will appear with a vengeance in our later discussion In the writing of, e.g., FYODOR DOSTOIEVSKY and NIKOS KAZANTZAKIS, this theme of innocent suffering receives a poignant statement, and I think that it might be to our advantage to show briefly what these later writers say about the suffering of the apparent innocent in order to compare and highlight Augustine's solution all the more.

In FYODOR DOSTOIEVSKY's novel, *The Brothers Karamazov* Dimitri (Mitya) relates a dream that he has had, a dream in which he saw peasants starving and their children dying. In the passage below, he describes the sufferings of a small child. P.E. in Western literature receives its classic formulation here:

> 'But why is it weeping?' Mitya persisted stupidly, 'why are its little arms bare? Why don't they wrap it up?" The babe's cold, its little clothes are frozen and don't warm it.'
>
> 'But why is it? Why?', foolish Mitya still persisted. 'Why, they're poor people, burnt out. They've no bread..'
>
> 'No. No.' Mitya, as it were, still did not understand. 'Tell me why it is those poor mothers stand there? Why are people poor? Why is the babe poor? Why is the steppe barren? Why don't they hug each other and kiss? Why don't they sing songs of joy? Why are they so dark from black misery: Why don't they feed the babe?'[23]

In a different mood, but one that focuses the responsibility for the suffering of the innocent squarely on the deity, we have Nikos KAZANTZAKIS: his hero Zorba says,

> "I tell you, boss, everything that happens in this world is unjust, unjust, unjust, unjust, ! I won't be a party to it! I Zorba, the worm, the slug! Why must the young die and the old wrecks go on living?Why do little children die? I had a boy once—Dimitri he was called—and I lost him when he was three years old. Well... I shall never, never forgive God for that, do you hear? I tell you, the day I die, if He has the cheek to appear in front of me, and if He is really and truly a God, He'll be ashamed! Yes, yes, He'll be ashamed to show himself to Zorba, the slug"![24]

To this Augustine, who had also lost a son, answers:

> "A more serious complaint, almost compassionate in tone, is frequently voiced concerning the bodily suffering which afflicts young children . . . . they are without sin . . . What evils have they done . . . that they should undergo such sufferings ? . . . But God accomplishes some good in reforming the lives of older people when they are chastised by the suffering and death of their little ones so dear to them. Why should this not happen since, once it is over, it will be as if it never happened for those who suffered it ?"[25]

This may seem unnecessarily callous, for surely Mitya and Zorba would not feel assuaged by such an argument, or rather series of arguments. Tucked into this explanation of child suffering there are a number of quite separate theodical answers. First, Augustine stays with his main theme that sufferings are sent by God to punish the wicked. Hence wicked parents are punished through their children, and the punishment they receive they apparently deserve (the man is free solution). But further, in being 'chastened' their lives are thereby bettered, they become stronger through the discipline of suffering and their characters are reformed; thus they are punished because they are wicked, but they are strengthened in their character thereby. This latter point provides another explanation for the existence of evil as suffering, and it becomes a solution for Augustine to P.E.; call this 'the evil-that-we-get-strengthens-us-disciplines-us, and-builds-our-character solution', or 'the discipline solution'. Augustine seems to pooh-pooh the suffering of the children, since in comparison with this greater good of character disciplining what's a little suffering ?, for once it's over it's as if it never happened.

Augustine goes on to say, in line with this same point, that evil is a goad to the good in compelling man to 'live more righteously' and turn his desires towards 'life eternal'. But there is an added fillip for the suffering child, and this brings us to the last of the new solutions from *Free Choice*. Augustine holds out the possibility of the Kingdom of Heaven as a reward to the suffering children as a recompense for their moment of torture and pain:

"Besides, who can tell what good recompense God, in His hidden designs, has in store for these children . . ."[26]

Thus evil can be explained in the face of an all good, all powerful, and all knowing deity by the solution that says that in Heaven the sufferers of that evil will be adequately compensated. This solution is a species of the teleological solution (that good comes from evil), certainly, but we will treat it separately for the time being, and get on with whatever reductions may be necessary later. So, call this "the innocents-suffering-now-will-be-rewarded-in-Heaven-later solution", or 'the recompense solution'. Again, whether or not this is a "solution" must wait an analysis of that concept, but that it is an acceptable way out of P.E. to Augustine is evident I think from the text. Further, it should be noted in a preliminary way that while the Augustinians may not have much trouble with light, easy sufferings, they will be sore-pressed with what we might call hard, extraordinary suffering. A legitimate question to pose to the Augustinians is simply: Granted that evils do all the things that the aesthetic, teleological, discipline and recompense solutions claim, why is there so much evil, such excessive suffering? Penultimately, a theme appears in *Free Choice* that will carry us into a totally new facet of P.E., and this is animal suffering. This problem will worry theodicists in the West until our own time, and no theodicy can be considered complete unless it takes into account the suffering in the subhuman creation. For purposes of terminological convenience, let's assume that up to this time in Augustine we have been concerned with the theological problem of human evil, that is to say, with the problem of justifying or making consistent certain characteristics of the deity (our ethical thesis, omnipotence thesis, and omniscience thesis) with the fact of human evil in the world, whether it be sin or punishment. And the whole notion of what constitutes a solution to P.E. is bound up with, first, accepting those characteristics together with that fact, and second, finding some justification or explanation for being able to thus accept them. Our concern will now shift from *that* theological problem of human evil to the theological problem of animal evil in the world.

Presumably, though Augustine does not take up the theme of 'nature red in tooth and claw' animals are capable of sin (causing suffering to other animals); but the theme that predominates in *Free Choice* is animal suffering: and animal suffering cannot be mitigated by an appeal to the discipline solution (that it will discipline their character), to the recompense solution (they will be rewarded in Heaven) nor to any of the other solutions open to solving the theological problem of human evil:

> "What evil have even these deserved, they ask, or what can they hope for in the way of good that they should suffer such distress ?"[27]

The creation for Augustine, as for most of the theologians who were to follow him, was man-centered. The world was the stage on which 'the drama of salvation' was to be played. The creation, consequently, could be used or employed by God to call man to his first duty which was, it seems, to attain salvation for his soul. All else in the creation was or became subordinate to the urgency of this first duty. To this end the Creator has written in letters bold His own personality into that creation, and sensitive souls can decipher this signature throughout nature, even in the animal kingdom.

> ". . . all the beauty and movement of those creatures which come to man's attention speak words of instruction for us . . . they proclaim and cry out that we should recognize their Creator."[28]

In this Kingdom, God's unity is given temporal expression among the animals, and their sufferings and distress are taken by Augustine as a sign of their striving to attain unity, and thereby imitate the unity of God. Animals suffer, but as we see them this is justified by the fact that man is made aware by being witness to their suffering of the nature and even the presence of God :

> "The very fact of their suffering makes it quite clear how much these souls strive for unity in ruling over their bodies and imparting life to them. . . . Except for pain in the animal, we would have no evidence of the intense desire for unity in the lower living things... [and] we would not be made sufficiently *aware* that all these have been constituted by the supreme, sublime, and unspeakable unity of the Creator."[29]

Obviously, this is no solution to the theological problem of animal evil: for, he seems to say, animal good can't come from animal evil. But for man good can come from animal suffering, Augustine says. The solution brings us back again to the discipline solution and the teleological solution but with no surcease from the problem of subhuman evil. One might try, though Augustine doesn't, to open the doors of Heaven to them in compensation, a sort of animal recompense solution; or argue that pain builds their character or their species along evolutionary lines with a kind of discipline solution. But neither of these solutions is open to Augustine, perhaps because of the belief that animals are after all inherently irrational and mere pawns on the world's salvation-oriented chess board.

Finally, one other theme appears in *Free Choice*, but only fleetingly, that it will be well to mention. This is the theological problem of superhuman evil, i.e., the problem of how a beneficient, all-powerful and all-knowing deity can be made to stand consistently with the presence of superhuman evil, the sufferings and tortures, presumably, of angels, fallen and unfallen. There is merely a casual remark about the devil in *Free Choice*, but it poses a problem that must be answered if the solution to P.E. is to be a complete solution. Augustine says:

> ". . . how was it suggested to the devil himself to pursue wickedness and to fall from his place on high ?"[30]

In the *Confessions*, Augustine gives classic expression to the theological problems of human and superhuman evil in a single passage. And while we are not treated to a solution of the latter, superhuman problem, the passage is worth mentioning:

> "But, again I said: Who made me ? Surely it was my God, not only Good but Goodness itself ? Whence, then, my ability to wish evil and to refuse the good ? . . . Who placed this in me and planted the seedlings of bitterness in me, since my whole being is from my most sweet God ? If the Devil is the originator, then what is the source of the Devil ? If he, too, by a perverse act of will turned from a good angel into a devil, what is the source . . . when he was made completely an angel by the best Creator ?"[31]

In the *Enchiridion*, among other places, he again brings up the topic, but nowhere, as far as I can discover, does he treat the issue in any systematic way. In the *Enchiridion*, he simply notes that certain angels out of their (free ?) pride and (free ?) impiety deserted God, and that they were subsequently "...cast down into the lowest darkness of this air of ours, the remaining angels abided with God in eternal blessedness and sanctity"[32] Later, in that same work, Augustine implicates God in all that is done, good or evil, and thereby implicates him directly in animal and angel suffering. Given that, I think we can say that not only is the theological problem of human evil a puzzle for Augustine (and his successors and followers) but in addition the theological problems of sub-human and superhuman evil are also going to be puzzles standing in need of explanation. On the previous point Augustine says in *Enchiridion*:

> "Nothing, then comes about unless God wills it so, either through permitting it to happen or Himself performing it. There is no doubt that God does well even in permitting to happen that which happens ill. For He permits this only through a just judgment, and surely everything that is just is good. Therefore, although those things which are evil, insofar as they are evil are not good, still it is good that not only good things exist but also evil. For, unless it were good that evil things also exist, they would never have been permitted to exist by the Omnipotent God . . ."[33]

Thus not only does God permit all that does happen, the good and the bad, but what does happen is, really, ultimately just and good; if not just and good now, why then in the long run, in the outcome. This is another species of the teleological solution that we have seen previously. We can assume, therefore, in closing this topic, that falling angels and suffering animals are permitted by God because they lead to that final ultimate good. We will be returning to this topic later.

c. *Confessions*

In the *Confessions*, P.E. is peremptorily treated but one theme that will subsequently predominate Western theodicies is mentioned, however briefly, viz., that evil is the privation of good. The problem of human evil is expressed much as heretofore; God is all-good and superior to his creation. God's omniscience is not mentioned, but perhaps assumed. How significant the omniscience thesis is anyway to P.E. will be decided in **Ch. II** shortly. Augustine states P.E. as follows:

> "Here is God and here is what God has created. God is good . . . and by far superior to these things. Yet, as a good Being he created them good . . . . Whence then, is evil ?"[34]

Earlier he had responded to P.E. in the *Confessions* by resorting to the now familiar aesthetic solution, e.g.,:

> ". . . while the higher things are better than the lower still I decided by a sounder judgment that all things together are better than the higher things alone".[35]

That is to say, evil and the good are better together than the good would be alone: That whole is better than either of its parts then. But rumbling through this aesthetic solution treatment of P.E. there is another theme which follows from the aesthetic solution together with the statement, ". . . Thou hast made all things good . . . . very good."[36] It is the theme of the illusoriness of evil. It arises most sharply in the following:

> "To Thee there is no evil at all: not merely to Thee, but to the totality of Thy creatures . . . . Now, in its parts, certain things may be considered evil because they are not in agreement with certain others."[37]

I don't wish to impute an illusory-evil doctrine to Augustine; in fact it is contrary to his own most professed beliefs regarding the reality of evil, e.g.,:

> "[Evil is Real for] where there is nothing to fear, we fear none the less. For that reason, either the evil which we fear does exist, or the fact that we do fear it is evil."[38]

But his own doctrine regarding evil as a privation certainly comes close to what I shall call a solution to P.E. by the illusoriness of evil; call this 'the-evil-is-unreal-or-an-illusion solution', or 'the illusion solution'. Even if Augustine doesn't hold it, it can be found by implication in the aesthetic solution; thus if the whole is good then one might say that the evil parts are not really "evil"; or perhaps one might distinguish hard evil from soft evil in some intuitive sense, and thereby conclude that the evil talked about in the aesthetic solution is really instrumental or soft evil, hence not hard evil which is really evil; thence soft evil is illusory evil compared to hard evil; consequently the illusion solution can be gotten from the aesthetic solution with a little work and manipulation. We will return to this again, of course; suffice it for the present that the illusion solution is indeed another kind of possible solution to P.E. and that something like it lurks in the *Confessions*. But the illusion solution is more securely insinuated in another solution put forward in the *Confessions* and this is the famous doctrine of evil as the privation of good, probably gleaned from Plotinus as we will shortly demonstrate. Augustine states, however briefly;

> "I did not know that evil is but the privation of good, even to the extent that evil does not exist at all".[39]

This insinuation grows into a full-fledged commitment in the *Enchiridion* where he says:

> "Now what is the so-called evil but a privation of the good . . . animals [afflicted] with diseases and wounds is nothing other than privation of health . . . For a wound or disease is not a substance but a vice of the fleshly substance; the substance, surely something good, is flesh itself, its accidents being the aforementioned evils, that is, privations of that good which is called health. In like manner evils in the soul are privations of natural good".[40]

I will contend later that the real thrust of this privation theme is the illusory theme of the illusion solution, for if there is no evil, then quite plainly there cannot be a P.E. of whatever variety; whether this entails a *bona fide* solution to P. E. is yet another matter. I am not concerned with the problem of why Augustine felt obliged to wrestle with a privation theme, and why he couldn't come out wide-eyed and brave and manfully accept the illusion solution; that discussion would necessarily involve us in Manichaean and Christian theology. It is, thus, no doubt true that he was in retreat from that prior Manichaean position which obliged him to hold to some hard evil thesis. He says of this older struggle in virtue of which he ultimately turned to Christianity:

> "Since my piety, such as it was, forced me to believe that a good God had not created any bad nature, I set

up two mutually opposed masses, both infinite, but the evil smaller, the good larger"[41]

This hard evil doctrine, wherein evil emerges as a matter, mass, or substance, as with Plotinus, too, is given up in preference to a soft evil thesis where evil comes dangerously close to not being real at all. I think that if we see the privation doctrine against the background of this dilemma, viz., if I make evil hard I risk a substantial dualism, and if I make it too soft I risk an illusionism, then we can see the privation theme slipping between the horns of that dilemma. To this extent then Augustine avoids the Manichaean dualism and the mystical nothingism with regard to evil. (See below the treatment of these themes in JOSIAH ROYCE).

Thus in the *Confessions* the privation thesis emerges as yet another possible solution to P.E. It argues that evil is simply, merely, a privation of good, and then looks to that privation as standing in need of explanation. Call this 'the there-is-no-evil-but-only-the-privation-of-good solution' or simply 'the privation solution'. Much will be made of this doctrine later, for example in St. Thomas. It attempts to solve P.E. by changing the vocabulary a bit, and solves it specifically by shifting the language from "evil" to "privation of good": But it then would seem that we have a problem of the privation of good and nothing is really solved. We will return to this also.

Another solution has been introduced in the *Confessions* as well; that is the Manichaean dualism theme, and while Augustine abjures it, it is a solution and we must note it. Call this "the cause-of-evil-is-another-substance (mass, matter, power) solution", or 'the impersonal substance solution', wherever the substance is impersonal; and where the substance is personal, i.e., where we have as an opposing personal evil force to God's good force, we would have a form of di-Theism, call this 'the cause-of-evil-is-another-evil-God (Devil, Tempter, Wicked Personal Power) solution' or 'the personal substance solution'. It is obvious why Augustine would reject the former as well as the latter, for while both solve P.E., they do so by limiting the power of God, i.e., they argue that there are forces in the universe, whether impersonal or personal, which bring about evil, and God is unable to stop these forces. These positions thus employ the hard evil thesis and a polytheistic thesis that Augustine, it would seem, must avoid if he is to escape the charge of heterodoxy.

Finally, it should be mentioned that Augustine in the *Confessions* returns to the man-is-free-solution established earlier. After all, if you're going to steal pears as a boy, and feel guilty about it ever after, suffer over it ever after, who else can you blame but yourself. On the general man-is-free doctrine he says :

> "What is more innocent than Thou since the things which injure evil men are their own works".[42]

But problems with this solution will develop on a double front; for on the one hand there is the puzzle of squaring sin with divine foreknowledge, taken up again in *The City of God*, below; and on the other, the puzzle of squaring punishment with that good and innocent Thou, for God does punish :

> "...that the free choice of the will is the cause of our committing evil, and thy right judgment the cause of our suffering it".[43]

This notion of God's "right judgment", His justice, will be taken up next.

d. *City of God*

In the gigantic *City of God*, written between 413 and 426 A.D., Augustine reiterates themes previously developed, e.g., the theme that good comes out of evil, and that the whole is better with its evil parts than without:

> "God would never have created a single angel—not even a single man—whose future wickedness He foresaw, unless, at the same time, He knew of the good which could come of this evil. It was as though He meant the harmony of history, like the beauty of a poem to be enriched by antithetical elements."[44]

But one theme is given broader treatment within the aesthetic solution mentioned above, and this is the theme of man's will, which must face the dual problem of God's foreknowledge on the one hand and its own freedom on the other, a puzzle dealt with previously in *Free Choice*. Thus, what about man's sinful will in the total universe. Augustine returns to the aesthetic theme :

> "....and not even the sinfulness of a will refusing to preserve the order of its nature can lessen the beauty of God's total order....For as the beauty of a picture is not dimmed by the dark colors, in their proper place, so the beauty of the universe of creatures, if one has insight to discern it, is not marred by sins even though sin itself is an ugly blotch".[45]

But the question remains, why did God create human ugly blotches, why not leave the extra-human creation blotched up, and the human without it? In other words, why did not God create man free of sin and suffering? One answer appears through the aesthetic solution and the teleological solution, i.e., that things, the whole, in the long run, just look better that way. Another is, as we have seen, that man himself causes some evil, sin, and others are sent to him by God as punishment. The former is a solution to P.E. of sorts and we called it 'the man is free solution'. The latter has not been named yet, i.e., the thesis that God punishes us justly for the sins we do and makes us suffer, but again justly:

> "Here we have an answer to the problem why God should have created men He foresaw would sin. It was because both in them and by means of them He could reveal how much was deserved by their guilt and condoned by his grace, and, also, because the harmony of the whole of reality which God has created and controls cannot be marred by the perverse discordancy of those who sin."[46]

Thus through the evil of human suffering, Augustine seems to be saying, two things are accomplished; first, God punishes man for his guilt or sin, and this is justly done, for man deserves that suffering; and second, 'by means of them' God could show his own grace to man at the same time. It's as if Augustine were saying that God through human suffering reveals His vengeful and benign aspects, simultaneously, to man. If this is the case, then once again great good will, supposedly, come from this justice, and we have a species of the teleological solution. However, it can be separated from that solution and stand as a solution by itself, or at least Augustine seems to think so. Call this new solution 'the-evil-men-receive-is-part-of-God's-justice solution' or 'the justice solution'.

The same theme is present once again in the *Enchiridion*:

"Whatever evil they freely do through blind and unbridled concupiscence, and whatever they unwillingly suffer in punishments manifest or concealed, pertain to the just wrath of God".[47]

Thus in all three works, *Confessions*, *The City of God*, and the *Enchiridion*, we find Augustine appealing to the justice solution as a solution, or possible solution, to P.E.

This justice solution appears to take two forms in rationalizing evil. Thus on the one hand the suffering we get is deserved, (because God is an avenger, i.e., just) and on the other, the suffering we get could be worse but isn't (because God is fair, i.e., just). Thus God's anger and mercy, His revenge and His grace, Augustine seems to say, condone the suffering that befalls man: This is precisely what the justice solution comes to.

But a lingering problem remains and that is the puzzle of human freedom and divine foreknowledge. Once again Augustine argues that man sins freely because while God knows the future he does not make that future:

Now, all this was so accomplished that nothing in the future escaped the foreknowledge of God, yet nothing in the foreknowledge compelled anyone to sin.[48]

This puzzle we will return to in our discussion of the man is free solution below in **Chapter III**. For that future discussion however we must note a cramp of sorts in Augustine's argument. For he believes that God is not only all-knowing but a lso all-powerful. And while this knowledge and this power lead to a teleological solution of sorts, it will prove troublesome on analysis. Thus in *The City of God*, he says:

"God who both foresees all things and can do all things, when he distributes to each of His creatures their appropriate endowments, knows how to turn to good account both good and evil".[49]

And while the teleological solution may stand, problems about "endowments" will arise, e.g., why is one man endowed with arms and legs, and another not? Does this contribute to the good of the whole? Further, if God is both all-powerful and all-knowing, then isn't he responsible, in some sense of that word, for what He knows? For surely if someone knows that some real misfortune (and this is the problem, are there real misfortunes? is there hard evil? unredeemable, gratuitous evil?) will befall you, and he can prevent it, and doesn't, we say of that person that he is responsible (he could have acted) and blameable (he didn't).

e. *Enchiridion*

In the fifth and final work that we are surveying, the *Enchiridion*, written about 421 A.D., there are the usual references to the teleological and man-is-free-solutions which I will not quote extensively; throughout, the theme is generally that "....even out of evil He can do good":[50]

> "....nor would He who is good permit evil to be done unless in His omnipotence He could turn evil to good".[51]

But amid this is the theme, again, that evil is necessary to contrast with good, in which it seems plain that the contrast solution is implied by the aesthetic solution since there could be no aesthetically beautiful whole in Augustine's sense, unless the parts, good and evil, beauty and blotches, harmony and antithetical elements, somehow contrasted with each other. And this in turn implies the teleological solution. They are all bound together here:

> "In this whole even that which is called evil, well regulated and confined to its own place, serves to give higher commendation to the good, making it, in comparison with the evil, more pleasing and worthy of praise".[52]

But now another notion emerges, viz., that not only are these contraries dependent on each other, but further that the one, evil, would not exist without the other, while, oddly, good can exist without evil:

> "Yet, although there is no doubt that good and evil are contraries ("in no thing can two contraries exist at the same time"), not only can they exist together, but evil without good and in anything that is not good cannot exist at all; good, however, can exist without evil" [52a]

This leads us around again to the privation solution, and dangerously close to the theory that evil is an illusion, i.e., dangerously close to the illusion solution:

> "Accordingly that which is called evil does not exist if there is no good....only what is good can be evil, since every being is good nor could there be an evil thing if the thing itself which is evil were not a being. Nothing, then, can be evil except a good".[53]

That Augustine realizes that he is close to the brink of heterodoxy results in his immediately quoting *Isaiah* just in case anyone should accuse him of confounding good and evil.

> "Woe unto them that call evil good and good evil : that put darkness for light, and light for darkness...."[54]

and he repeatedly enunciates his belief in the reality of evil, but not its ontological equality with nor superiority over the good. Of God he says :

> "He judged it better to bring good out of evil than not to permit evil to exist at all".[55]

Augustine has a problem with evil, however. For on the one hand he wants to admit that evil is real, and on the other a privation of good, only. How can these be reconciled? Further, and it seems to me this is a problem stemming from the above taciturnity, he wants to say that man's nature is, not neutral, but basically good, and that he chooses freely to sin or not to sin:

> "But from the being of man, which is good, can arise either a good will or an evil; nor was there any possible original source for an evil will but the nature of angel or man which is good".[56]

Again he enunciates this same thesis, placing man and the angels on the same ontological footing with respect to inherent goodness:

> "....the cause of the good things in which we are concerned is none other than the goodness of God, while the cause of evil things is a desertion from the unchangeable good on the part of the will of the changeable good, first in the case of angels and then in the case of man."[57]

But with this thesis there stands the Christian doctrine of original sin, that "in Adam sinned we all". Thus how good is that race which has as Augustine holds, because of its rebelliousness, been condemned entire by God? How good can man be if his fall were immanent (and known) and how good can man be if he thus stands totally condemned? It would seem Augustine has a problem with "good" wherein it can mean "not-so-good":

> "For if a man does not understand these things, who is he to reply to God? If he does understand them, he finds no better ground for replying. For, if he understands, he sees the whole human race was condemned in its rebellious head by so just a divine judgment, that if no one were to be freed from it, no one could rightly blame the justice of God."[58]

Augustine wants the wicked-nature thesis (it's demanded of him, doctrinally and ontologically, since man is not God but a created being) but he also wants the good-nature thesis (it's demanded of him doctrinally, for God created this all and found it good, *Genesis* 1:31 says so), and for the sake of meeting P.E.: Thus if man has a wicked nature, then the man is free solution is out as a solution, and God can be blamed for evil. This ontological problem is summed up by Augustine when he states that man was created good, as were all natural beings, but not supremely good:

> "All natural beings are good, since the Creator of every one of them is supremely good; but because, unlike their Creator, they are not supremely and unchangeably good, their good is capable of diminution [an evil] and increase".[59]

His solution to this difficulty about evil comes down to saying that God made man good, but time passed and that good diminished. It sounds suspiciously like a Ford Motor Company salesman explaining why the car you own wore out, and one knows with car salesman that when they use words like "good" we have to beware of the user. Similarly, Augustine equivocates with respect to ontological good for God, man, and the angels. He can have his good as it were and eat it too: All are good, only some are better than others. But this can't mean that those which are less than the best are bad or evil! Augustine seems to fudge here, and to commit the sin of equivocation to save the goodness of all, yet have evil possible in it, and have both present from the beginning. This problem, 'the problem of creation', let's call it, is present in Augustine, will haunt the other theodicies that we will mention as well.

f. *Conclusion*

In conclusion to the brief discussion of the five texts we have chosen from Augustine, I might mention what we were about. To facilitate our later discussions about evil, God, and solutions in Chapters II and III below, we are following the historical trail of P.E. as that trail wound through early Western thought. One important result of the investigation to this point is the isolation and identification of some twelve solutions to P.E. It is important to remember that not all the solutions are really "solutions" (for we have yet to analyze that notion), nor are all these solutions acceptable to Augustine as solutions (we can't hold him responsible for anything more than merely mentioning the personal substance, impersonal substance and illusion solutions) nor are all these solutions distinct from one another (we shall see that many are interdependent and that our list can be considerably shortened). Let me very quickly, in closing this discussion of Augustine, tabulate our solutions to date:

TABLE I

Name	*Description*
1. Aesthetic Solution	The aesthetic whole is good, though the parts are evil.
2. Teleological Solution	Good comes ultimately out of evil.
3. Prevention Solution	The evils we have are necessary to prevent greater evils.
4. Contrast Solution	Evils are necessary in order to contrast with and point up the good.
5. Man is Free Solution	Man with his free will is the cause of evil.
6. Discipline Solution	Evil disciplines us and builds our character.
7. Recompense Solution	Evils such as unjust suffering will be recompensed in Heaven.
8. Illusion Solution	Evil is an illusion.
9. Privation Solution	Evil is merely the privation of good.

10. Impersonal Substance Solution	Evil is caused by an impersonal, wicked substance, e.g., matter.
11. Personal Substance Solution	Evil is caused by a personal, wicked God, e.g., Satan.
12. Justice Solution	Evil is God's just punishment of man's sins.

About these solutions the following impressions can be drawn with regard to Augustine :

First, he favors the aesthetic and the teleological solutions in the sense that, to this reader at least, he spends more time mulling over these two solutions than any others.

Second, he recognizes the problems inherent in the man is free and the privation solutions, for he spends much time attempting to reconcile the difficulties inherent in these solutions together with God's omniscience and the reality of evil: And to most commentators he does his least acceptable work with regard to these solutions.

Third, he seems to get the most joy out of contemplating the discipline solution on the one hand and the justice solution on the other, as if to remind himself of the dual nature of God as the loving Father who sends no more evil than the soul can bear, while at the same time reminding himself that that Father is a just Avenger for all sins committed by his children.

Fourth, and finally, he completely rejects, at least *prima facie*, the illusion solution, and the impersonal and personal substance solutions, and this because they could not be made consistent with Christian orthodoxy.

2. *Interim*

St. Augustine stands astride two other philosopher-theologians who also dealt with the problem of evil, Plotinus and Dionysius, the latter, called the Pseudo-Areopagite, by some, and the Areopagite, alone, by others. In this section I want to treat very briefly this Plotinian and Dionysian tradition that feeds into and then streams out from Augustine, and conclude with a comment or two on St. Thomas Aquinas on P.E. These four figures are essential elements, I think, to an understanding of the necessary ingredients to P.E. and its solutions in the West.

a. *Plotinus* (205-270 A.D.)

In the First *Ennead*, eighth tractate, Plotinus sets forth his doctrine of the nature and source of Evil. The ontological system that Plotinus has established is a system wherein the first-metaphysical principle, the Good, produces or creates by a process of emanation. From it flows the Intellect, and from the Intellect emanates Soul. Further, from Soul there comes individual souls and the universe as we understand it. While the Good is beyond the descriptive predicates like good, beautiful, true, and so on, those two metaphysical principles below it are said to exist and to be describable by certain favored honorific predicates. These three divine entities, Good, Intellect, and Soul, are without Evil, and wholly good only:

> "Such is the untroubled, the blissful life of divine beings, and Evil has no place in it; if this were all, there would be no Evil but Good only, the first, the second, and the third Good."[60]

But this isn't all. Evil enters somehow and the problem then becomes one of determining whence it came and what it is.

From the outset I think it is evident that the P.E. presented here is a species of the theological P.E.; that is to say, while the supreme power of the universe is not a personal God with certain honorific properties, it is still an impersonal metaphysical principle with such properties. Thus the problem is similar to the problem faced by Augustine, viz., how to make that supreme power consistent with the world's evil.

Plotinus continues by discussing the nature of Evil, and concludes that Evil cannot have a place among Beings (Intellect and Soul) nor in the Beyond-Being, for these are good.[61] Hence Evil must be Non-being. Non-Being, for Plotinus, is, following in part Plato and Aristotle, potency, the formless, or Matter. And insofar as the Soul has entered into that potency or Matter, it becomes Evil:

> "The bodily kind, in that it partakes of Matter, is an evil thing.... It is, we read, the Soul that has entered into the service of that in which soul-evil is implanted by nature....

> ....such a Soul is not apart from Matter....because it is merged into a body made of Matter."[62]

Further this Non-Being which is Matter, constitutes a Primal Evil or Evil absolute, a Power that stands at the lowest end of the plenum that constitutes all-that-is. Plotinus rejects the notion that Evil is a lack of good, a relative notion, and declares that Evil is an absolute lack. Thus merely falling short of the Good is not what makes Evil, but rather the actual presence of that Evil Absolute, itself; in the cases under discussion, this Primal Evil is Matter. Thus for Plotinus, unlike Augustine, this Evil is Non-Being (but not non-existent) hence a real ontological entity. Augustine, on the other hand, appears to treat evil as a species of the good, i.e., a mere lack of it.

But if this is the nature of Evil, pure Non-Being, where does it come from ? It is produced by necessity, Plotinus argues, by the necessity of a plenum in the great chain of Being itself:

> "But why does the existence of the Principle of Good necessarily comport the existence of the Principle of Evil ? Is it because the All [the plenum] necessarily comports the existence of Matter: Yes: for necessarily this all is made up of contraries: it could not exist if Matter did not".[63]

Here the contrastive explanation of evil is introduced, but with a stronger stress on the *necessity*, perhaps logical or ontological rather than an aesthetic necessity, as in Augustine. That is to say, Augustine had argued that evil was necessary in order to highlight or point up and contrast with the good; he doesn't seem to assume, as Plotinus does, that there is a logical necessity such that you can't in principle have one without the other: Augustine even says that the good can exist prior to and in absence from the evil. Not so Plotinus :

> "If all this be true, we cannot be ourselves, the source of Evil, we are not evil in ourselves; Evil was before we came to be...."[64]

Not only was Evil before we came to be but it had to be :

> "Given that The Good is not the only existent thing, it is inevitable that, by the outgoing from it or....the continuous downgoing or away-going from it, there should be produced a Last....this will be evil."[65]

And again,

> "As necessarily as there is Something after the First, so necessarily there is a Last: this Last is Matter, the thing which has no residue of good in it: here is the necessity of Evil."[66]

This Evil is contrastive alright, but to argue that it is simply that alone would be to miss the force of Plotinus' entire metaphysical system. In answer to the question What is Evil?, we have seen that it is Matter or Absolute Non-Being; in response to Why is there Evil?, the answer is that it is entailed by the nature of the All—wherever there is a First there must be a Last. Evil is necessary, metaphysically and logically (in virtue of the meaning of the metaphysical concepts) necessary to the whole. This answer to a sort of metaphysical P.E. in Plotinus, the solution regarding the origin of evil in a system that has Good, Intellect and Soul as its all-good sources, can be called 'the evil-is-necessary-whenever-good-exists solution' or 'the necessary solution' where necessary is understood in both its metaphysical (where one stuff is, the other must be) and logical (wherever "good" has meaning, "evil" must also) senses.

The question as to whether this explanation is a justification and not simply a description is another whole question. To justify the existence of Evil in the face of all that Good is a problem that would take us into a discussion of plenum-metaphysics. We note here, however, that in Plotinus it is far from clear that his description of the origin of evil and his explanation of the relation of Evil to the Good, is far from being an adequate justification for the existence of Evil. We called this "the problem of creation" in Augustine, and it will be with us from now on.

b. Dionysius (Late 5th century A.D.)

In Book IV of *The Divine Names*, Dionysius leans strongly towards what Josiah Royce has called 'the mystical explanation of evil', i.e., the view that evil is unreal. He introduces his subject with questions regarding the problem of superhuman evil as we have called it. In tones reminiscent of Plotinus he asks:

> "....how is it that the company of the devils desires not the Beautiful and the Good, but being inclined to-

> wards matter and fallen far from the fixed angelic state of desire for the good, becomes a cause of all evils to itself and to all other beings....?"[67]

More specifically,

> "How is it that the devils, having been produced wholly out of the Good, are not good in disposition ? Or how is it that, if produced good from out of the Good, they became changed ? What made them evil, and indeed, what is the nature of evil ?"[68]

Dionysius is loathe to identify the Good with God, and even though he writes half inside the neo-Platonic Plotinian framework and half within the Christian, he trails enough clouds of the former into the latter to warrant our saying that he has like Plotinus a species of the theological P.E. on his hands.

Dionysius argues that evil is double edged in its capacities: On the one hand it is a destructive force in itself, causing misery and suffering wherever it touches; but it is also productive through the reaction of the good. Suppose we speak then of destructive evil, which totally lacks being and gives none; and productive evil, which has being and confers it on others.[69] But productive evil is dependent on the Good, and receives its potency from that source. In itself, destructive evil "hath neither being, goodness, productiveness".[70] It is, further, this destructive evil that is pure evil, and undoubtedly parallels Plotinus' Absolute Evil: For when the Good is absent from evil, "evil is Non-Existent",[71] or in Plotinus' terms, it is "Non-Being".

The metaphysical problem of human evil is then raised and Dionysius concludes that evil in human creatures cannot come from the Good; he then proceeds to jump from talking about the Good to talking about God: Suddenly we are involved with the theological P.E. :

> "And so evil is not in God, and is not divine. Nor cometh it of God. For either He is not good, or else He worketh goodness and bringeth good things unto existence."[72]

But we are still left wondering what then is the source of evil ? Dionysius begins to catalogue the ontological areas where evil does not originate. Thus it cannot originate with God (above) nor the creations of God, angels, devils, brute beasts, nature as a whole, our bodies, or matter[73] which all have degrees of order, beauty, and form. Thus evil is inherent in none of these. Whence is it then? Productive evil is from the Good:

> "In fine, Good cometh from the One universal Cause; and evil from many parti l deficiencies. God knows evil under the form of good, and with Hi the causes of evil things are faculties productive of good."[74]

Further,

> "The Good must be the beginning and the end even of all evil things. For the Good is the final Purpose of all things, good and bad alike."[75]

Dionysius escapes the charge that would make the Good or God the cause of evil, next, by denying that evil has any substantial being.

> "Hence evil hath no substantial being, but only a shadow thereof. . . ."[76]

And,

> "Unto evil we can attribute but an accidental kind of existence. It exists for the sake of something else, and is not self-originating."[77]

Thus productive evil, which had being and produced being, is not really evil at all; the concept of productive evil either is engulfed by the Good since productive evil rides pig-a-back on the Good and is nothing without it (recall Augustine on this point, that evil as privation depends on the good and is ontologically nothing without it), or the concept of productive evil collapses into destructive evil and is in itself non-existent and beingless. It would seem, that is to say, that insofar as productive evil is productive it is part of Good and not evil; and insofaras productive evil is evil it is destructive and non-existent. The upshot is at any rate that evil is illusory and non-existent. But what then of destructive evil? More anon.

Dionysius concludes his discussion in Chapter IV with a statement reminiscent of Plotinus (he talks about the impersonal "good") but switches over to a content with the theological P.E. (he talks about a rather personal "providence" that "cares individually for each particular thing in all the world"):

> "How can evil things have any existence at all if there is a Providence"?[78]

And he answers, with destructive evil plainly in mind,

> "Only because evil (as such) hath no being, neither inhereth it in things that have being. And naught that hath being is independent of Providence; for evil hath no being at all, except when mingled with the Good."[79]

Then it follows that evil is illusory, for if no thing is without a share in the Good, and no thing is utterly destitute of Good, then "the Divine Providence is in all things."[80] From this it follows that

> "Evil is nowhere qua evil; and it arises not through any power but through weakness. Even the devils derive their existence from the Good, and their mere existence is good."[81]

The thesis that emerges from this discussion of Dionysius' work is that P.E. in its theological form, can be solved for humans and superhumans, Dionysius seems to believe, by simply denying reality to evil. We emerge consequently with a species of the illusion solution to P.E. Dionysius seems to be doing what Plotinus could not (without risking the plenum and his neo-Platonic heritage) and Augustine would not (without risking his realistic position with regard to evil, perhaps inherited from the good Plotinus), viz., deny reality to evil as destructive evil. Like Augustine, however, he can admit that productive "evil", can be turned to good account by God, and he thereby furnishes himself with a teleological solution to P.E. :

> "Yea, even the evil effects that arise are turned by Providence to a kindly purpose, for the succour of themselves or others (either individually or in common), and thus it is that Providence cares individually for each particular thing in all the world."[82]

Thus from the double strand of productive evil and destructive evil (and we assume this exhausts the possibilities of evil for Dionysius), we can generate two P.E., a theological productive evil problem, and a theological destructive evil problem. The first is handled by a solution already familiar to us from Augustine, the teleological solution; the second is handled by a solution acknowledged by Augustine but unacceptable to him, but certainly borrowed from the non-being-of-evil thesis in Plotinus, viz., the solution that says that evil is illusory or unreal.

We will be meeting this notion of evil as productive and

destructive later in this book. Thus in Chapter II below I will want to distinguish ordinary evil from extraordinary evil arguing the while that ordinary evil presents no real problem for P.E. since we are all willing to accept a certain amount of suffering, and pain for all sorts of trivial or significant reasons, e.g., toothache, appendicitis pains, labor pangs, heartburn, perhaps even death at the right time, and so on. But it is destructive or extraordinary evil that is wholly gratuitous that presents problems. It is, in other words, the theological problem of destructive evil that will be a major concern to us in the later parts of this book.

Finally, to treat evil as illusory if that is what Dionysius does, is as JOSIAH ROYCE will shortly point out, wholly unacceptable to the plain man. But a complete discussion of this point must also await further developments.

c. St. Thomas Aquinas (1225-1274 A.D.)

Our treatment of St. Thomas will be necessarily short for he is essentially repetitive of Augustine's solutions. Thomas argues that God is the cause, directly and not through matter or intelligent agents, of the world. Further, the created world is good (*Genesis* 1.31), and best as a whole:

> "It is the part of the best cause to produce an effect which is best as a whole; but this does not mean that He makes every part of the whole the best absolutely, but in proportion to the whole."[83]

But this best universe possesses inequalities, and these have been placed there in order to enhance the perfection of the whole; the heirarchical principle of creation, the Plotinian plenitude, is emphasized by both Thomas and Augustine : "For the universe would not be perfect if only one grade of goodness were found in things"[84] But what then, it might be asked, is the nature and role of evil in this all good plenum? Evil, Thomas says, is neither a being nor a good, and he quotes Dionysius' arguments on this point to the effect that what has being is good and vice versa, and that evil as the non-good must have no being.[85] But the perfection of the universe demands that this non-being be present so that all grades of being, for perfection's sake, may be represented.[86] And evil consists here in the fact that a thing fails in goodness.[87] This is familiar enough in Augustine where we saw that evil as the privation of good leads to a solution for P.E.[88] Coupled with this is the solution stated above but now elaborated that the whole is good while the parts may not be:

> "God and nature and any other agent make what is better in the whole, but not what is better in every single part, except in relation to the whole. . . ."[89]

The reason again is that, for these plenitude or plenum Philosophers, the more variety of goods that there are the better the whole will be; and while there may be a logic here that escapes the contemporary reader, there is no doubt that Thomas held it without exception :

> "And the whole itself, which is the universe of Creatures, is all the better and more perfect if there be some things in it which can fail in goodness and which do sometimes fail without God preventing it."[90]

The reasons, again, are aesthetic: The whole poem, the whole painting is made all the more perfect by the presence, as Augustine would say, of cacophany and blotches, of counterpoint and nuance, shading and light, than without. While, indeed, the aesthetic solution may hold to such a doctrine, it is worth exploring the analogy between created plenums and canvases. There is also a further, nagging question, a limiting question in STEPHEN TOULMIN's sense[91] which can be applied to all such solutions: Why did the Creator create in the first place ? This becomes a peculiarly gnawing question when one faces the perfection of the Creator and the relative imperfection of the created plenum. For if the object of creating plenum$_m$ rather than plenum$_n$ is that plenum$_m$ has more perfection than plenum$_n$, then why create at all since the Creator Himself has more perfection than any and all plenums, whatever their perfection ?, the point being that any created plenum as created is imperfect. So why would God create an imperfect thing however good it might be. We are back once again with the problem of creation: Plenum$_m$ may be better than plenum$_n$, but it still falls short of perfection. Question: Why couldn't God create plenum$_l$ that would be perfect ? Thomas continues from the theme of the aesthetic solution to the theme of the teleological solution:

> "Augustine says, *God is so powerful that He can even make good out of evil.* Hence many good things would be taken away if God permitted no evil to exist; for fire would

> not be generated if air was not corrupted, nor would the life of a lion be preserved unless the ass were killed."[92]

Thus leaning heavily on Augustine, Thomas brings forth three, at least three, solutions that his predecessor had developed: the privation, aesthetic and teleological solutions. Other sections in Thomas appear to be variations of these three themes. These solutions or minor variations of them, appear to have lasted until the present day, and represent one of the most significant tendencies in solving P.E. Of this tradition JOHN HICK has said,

> "....the theodicy developed by Augustine and later restated by Aquinas has remained essentially unchanged and is still being presented today by Catholic writers."[93]

This being the case, we can turn ahead a rapid five hundred years to "the golden age of theodicies" as HICK puts it[94] and look at the King of that golden age, G.W. LEIBNIZ, and that most golden of all theodicies, his great *Theodicy*.

3. *G.W. LEIBNIZ* (1646—1716)

Leibniz, like Augustine before him, sets forth a panoply of solutions to P.E., most of which are imitative in intent and content to those of his theodical predecessor. Our purpose in looking to Leibniz' work is not simply to repeat what has already been catalogued but to determine three things:

1. How many similarities are there between formulations of P.E. and the solutions to it, in the two theodicies of Augustine and Leibniz? Our conclusion will be that there is a vast similarity in both formulation and solutions, showing that to a large extent Western philosophy had made certain invested commitments to this problem by the 18th century.

2. What differences are there between the two theodicies? Our conclusion will have to show where emphases have been placed rather than to reveal any overt differences.

3. What fresh insights, distinctions, new terminologies will the latest theodicy display?, i.e., what new philosophical techniques have been developed to enhance understanding of P.E. and its solutions? Here we shall find new terminology, but just how useful it will ultimately be remains to be seen.

a. *Theodicy*

Leibniz begins *Theodicy* by boldly stating in its Preface what he intends :

> "I show how it is possible for everything to depend upon God, for him to cooperate in all the actions of creatures, even, if you will, to create these creatures continually, and nevertheless not to be the author of sin."[95]

And more specifically, and most importantly he expects to show,

> "That it has been possible for God to permit sin and misery, and even to cooperate therein and promote it, without detriment to his holiness and his supreme goodness: although, generally speaking, he could have avoided all these evils."[96]

Leibniz' thesis rests upon three well known assumptions: First, God is most perfect and all wise; second, out of his infinite wisdom and goodness He chose this world from an infinite number of possible worlds; finally, this world is the best that God could have chosen, because He is perfect in the above senses; hence this world is called 'the best of all possible worlds'.

> "....God, having chosen the most perfect of all possible worlds, had been prompted by his wisdom to permit the evil which was bound up with it, but which still did not prevent this world from being, all things considered, the best that could be chosen."[97]

Two things need, perhaps, to be noted at this stage: on the one hand Leibniz' God could not, given His nature, have chosen to have a world different from the one we have: God was in a sense limited by His nature to producing the best; on the other hand, His best was none too good, the critic might say, for given what is possible in the way of worlds, God was limited by what was ontologically available; thus "the most perfect of all possible worlds" does not mean "the most perfect." VOLTAIRE and PANGLOSS were quite misled on this point. Leibniz does not say this is "the most perfect world", but rather "the most perfect of all possible worlds" Thus, in a sense, God was limited (prevented from doing differently) by his choice *and* the possible worlds available: The world we got is none-too-good, perhaps, but you should have seen the others.

At this stage of the development of his thesis, we have a new solution to P.E. It would seem to say that God hates evil but approves of the evil we have because the alternatives are far worse. Call this "the-evils-we-have-now-are-better-than-those-God-could-have-chosen solution', or 'the worse alternatives solution'. This seems to be borne out in the following apology:

> "Now this supreme wisdom, united to a goodness that is no less infinite, cannot but have chosen the best. For as a lesser evil is a kind of good, even so a lesser good is a kind of evil if it stands in the way of a greater good: and there would be something to correct in the actions of God if it were possible to do better....there is an infinitude of possible worlds among which God must needs have chosen the best, since he does nothing without acting in accordance with supreme reason."[98]

The point is that that "lesser evil is a kind of good" assertion, becomes the justification of the world we have with its lesser evils, which are still evils, compared to the world we could have had, with its greater evils, i.e., with its less good. Hence a justification exists for finding the worse alternatives solution in the *Theodicy*.

Leibniz anticipates the objection 'Why couldn't God have found a better world?', and his answer to the objection reinforces our previous point that God was limited by what remained in the realm of possibility:

> "Some adversary not being able to answer this argument will perchance answer the conclusion by a counter-argument, saying that the world could have been without sin and without sufferings; but I deny that then it would have been *better*....Thus if the smallest evil that comes to pass in the world (wherein "the universe ....is all of one piece, like an ocean") were missing in it, it would no longer be this world; which....was found the best by the Creator who chose it."[99]

Two comments on this passage: First, Leibniz is in direct opposition to St. Thomas Aquinas on this issue of whether God was necessitated or compelled to produce this world; specifically on the question as to whether or not God could have made a better world, Thomas and Leibniz would be at odds on the first sense of "better" distinguished by Thomas:

> "When it is said that God can make better things than He does, if better is taken substantively, this proposition

> is true. For He can always make something else better than any individual thing....If, however, better is taken as an adverb, referring to the mode of God's activity, then God cannot make anything better than He makes it...."[100]

Thus in the adverbial sense of "better" Leibniz has already argued that since God is perfect, what he does, his activity, must also be perfect. But the possible worlds, preformed by logic, eternally set, are beyond the possibility of bettering. Not so for Thomas :

> "Yet God could make other things, or add something to the present creation; and then there would be another and a better universe."[101]

My reason for lingering over this issue is to point out another solution of sorts to P.E., a solution that would be totally unacceptable to Leibniz because it would imply a limitation of God's power, but a kind of solution none-the-less. It will recur in the theodicy, such as it is, of John Stuart Mill. It attempts to explain and justify the coexistence of God and evil by simply stating that God is not all-powerful. In the present case, God is overwhelmed by the logically possible worlds open to Him. In Mill's case He is overwhelmed by the creation itself. In both cases this limited God needs help and, as Mill will point out, this is where man comes in: To help a not all-powerful Creator care for His creation. Again, I don't wish to impute this solution to Leibniz. Call this 'the-evil-we-have-is-the-result-of-a-limitation-in-the-choosing-power-of-the-Creator solution', or 'the Creator limitation solution'. The fact that God's choices can be limited by forces over which He has no control means of course that God is no longer all-powerful. Thus just as the impersonal and personal substance solutions attacked the goodness of the Divine in attaining a solution of P.E. previously, so now the Creator limitation solution attacks the power of God in bringing about its solution. Like the worse alternatives solution mentioned above the Creator limitation solution is a direct assault on the nature of God's power. These four apparent solutions then are distinguished from our other solutions in the fact that they are all the result of directly denying some traditionally accepted aspect of the Divine's nature: Its goodness or

Its power. Hence, as we shall point out below, none of them can really be *bona fide* solutions to P.E.

On the basis of the recognition of the inherent imperfection of this present possible world, together with the more traditional Augustinian notions of sin (doing evil) and suffering (undergoing the consequences of sin), Leibniz draws his famous tri-partite division of evil :

> "Evil may be taken metaphysically, physically, and morally. *Metaphysical evil* consists in mere imperfection, *physical evil* consists in suffering, and *moral evil* in sin. Now although physical evil and moral evil be not necessary, it is enough that by virtue of the eternal verities they be possible. And as this vast Region of Verities contains all possibilities it is necessary that there be an infinitude of possible worlds, that evil enter into divers of them, and that even the best of all contain a measure thereof. Thus has God been induced to permit evil."[102]

In summary, we find here at least four notions: We can see the familiar Plotinian plenitude concept; a doctrine of the necessity of evil given the possible worlds doctrine (the kind of necessity we previously found in the necessary solution, might or might not enter here; Leibniz is conceiving of necessity on a far grander, i.e., cosmological, scale than was implied in the necessary solution where we merely contrasted good with evil, and held whenever the former obtained, the latter had to); the doctrine of the permission of evil by God as opposed to the causing of evil by God; and finally the doctrine of the three evils. Of the latter, he says:

> "It is again well to consider that moral evil is an evil so great only because it is a source of physical evils, a source existing in one of the most powerful of creatures.. One single Caligula, one Nero, has caused more evil than an earthquake. An evil man takes pleasure in causing suffering and destruction....But God....it is impossible that in him there be fault, guilt, or sin; and when he permits sin, it is wisdom, it is virtue."[103]

Three comments on this passage: First, in arguing that moral evil is a source of physical evil, and that moral evil is man-caused, Leibniz introduces the man is free solution, arguing that man is the cause of evil in the world; second, there is a subtle shift in the classification of evil from sin and suffering to moral and physical evil. This shift is important because later philosophers, as we shall see, interpret moral and physical evil as man-caused suffering and nature-caused suffering, respectively. Leibniz with his distinction thus stands astride a tradition that is changing from a theological orientation with regard to evil (sin and the suffering occasioned by man) to a more naturalistic orientation (suffering that is man-caused and nature-caused): and finally, the introduction in the last passage of what appears to be the teleological solution, that the permission of sin is virtuous (not merely necessary now) and good, because of what it must lead to—greater perfection. He has alluded to this previously in arguing:

> "Thus we see....that a sequence of things where sin enters in may have been and has been, in effect, better than another sequence without sin."[104]

But not only does God permit sin in order that it might lead to better consequences but it is permitted in order to show off the good, display it by contrast, all the more. This contrastive solution is also familiar to us by now:

> "Do men relish health enough or thank God enough for it, without having ever been sick? And is it not most often necessary that a little evil render the good more discernible, that is to say, greater?"[105]

Let me say a word about metaphysical evil. It will lead us into an array of further solutions. By metaphysical evil, Leibniz tries to get his meaning as close to the Christian concept of original sin, and the Plotinian notion of Matter as he can. Metaphysical evil is an evil which is inherent in man, part of his nature, notwithstanding that God made all that he did and found it good. In that original disobedience, in that stuff farthest down the great chain of being, in the Creation itself, there is a certain intransigency, a certain flaw that renders the creature imperfectable: Thus Leibniz asks, whence evil? and brings us around to the problem of creation mentioned previously:

> "The answer is, that it must be sought in the ideal nature of the creature....original imperfection in the

> creature before sin, because the creature is limited in its essence...."[106]

Thus the creature may be good; but falling short of the essence of God renders the creature imperfect. There is a dilemma here for the Creator which we shall return to later, and it bears directly on P.E. When the Creator begat, He could begat in two ways: Either He could have begat another or others like Himself; they would be perfect, since they would be God-replicas, and no P.E. would ever arise; or He could have begat another or others ontologically different from Himself, they would be imperfect, and P.E. would arise. As we have seen since Plato and Plotinus, the latter interpretation is the interpretation chosen by Western Christian theologians. It would seem, consequently, that given the Creator's dilemma, there is no way out of the problem that metaphysical evil is bound to generate. The problem of creation leads inevitably to the Creator's dilemma.

This brings us then to a version of the man is free solution which held that evil was caused by man because of the misuse of his free will. The present version, however, is that evil is brought about because of a basic flaw in man's nature. But then it really isn't a doing of man or on man's part. For on the metaphysical evil thesis, evil is bound and fated to happen in the creation because the creation is flawed in some way by being limited in its essence, i.e., the creation *qua* creation is evil to begin with. What we have here would seem to be an instance of the Creator limitation solution, where God is limited by the possibilities of creation and thereby prevented from limiting evil. That metaphysical evil is a direct consequence of the choice of possible worlds by Leibniz's creator is, I think, evident from our discussion of the Creator limitation solution above. And yet it is also evident, I think, that the limitations imposed by metaphysical evil are limitations after the fact of creation, and not before that fact. Thus the Creator limitation solution dealt with the limitations imposed by the logical possibilities which lay outside God; what we have here, with metaphysical evil, is a limitation inherent in the very stuff of creation. The solution to the problem of metaphysical evil, then, is simply to explain that evil. Call this 'the-evil-in-the-creation-is-there-in-virtue-of-the-inherent-imperfection-and-intransigency-of-the-mutable creation-itself solution' or 'the metaphysical evil solution.'

Thus while the existence of moral evil and physical evil may be explained, say, by the man is free solution and the contrast solution, respectively, we can now, with the metaphysical evil solution and some assistance from the Creator limitation solution explain metaphysical evil as well.

Next Leibniz takes up Augustine's old problem of God's foreknowledge and human free will. Leibniz's answers are unsatisfactory, but he argues, as Augustine before him that foreknowledge "does not make truth more determinate" in the sense that what is true is true because it is foreseen; rather what is foreseen as true is true independently of its being foreseen.[107] In other words, God is a seer but not a causer of events:

> ". . . . that predetermination be taken as not necessitating. In a word, I am of opinion that the will is always more inclined towards the course it adopts, but that it is never bound by the necessity to adopt it. That it will adopt this course is certain but it is not necessary."[108]

Just why this is "unsatisfactory" must await analysis below in Chapter II, but for the nonce it is enough to say again that what God knows will happen, if He knows that it will happen, cannot logically, theologically or what-have-you, fail to happen. Surely that makes it necessary, logically, theologically, or what-have-you. In a remarkable passage later in the text, Leibniz appears to argue that even if the future be determined we can't know it, and since we can't know it, why bother about it as a problem at all: Tend your garden and be at peace. This entire passage strikes this reader as a grand giving-up over the problem of free will and godly omniscience:

> "The whole future is doubtless determined, but since we know not what it is, nor what is foreseen or resolved, we must do our duty, according to the reason that God has given us and according to the rules that he has prescribed for us; and thereafter we must have a quiet mind, and leave to God himself the care for the outcome."[109]

Thus it's small comfort to be told by one of the fore-most thinkers of the 18th century *Aufklārung*, to relax and leave philosophical concerns to God. I mention this somewhat heatedly here, because it is an element of irrationalism or anti-intellectualism that creeps in from time to time in dealing with P.E., itself. We shall find a species of it in our examination of John HICK's theodicy later.

Leibniz continues his catalogue and I might mention one or two of the passages where he pulls out all stops and comes forth munificently with all sorts of justifications for evil,

> "And as for evil, God wills moral evil not at all, and physical evil or suffering he does not will absolutely. Thus it is that there is no absolute predestination to damnation; and one may say of physical evil, that God wills it often also as a means to an end, that is, to prevent greater evils or to obtain greater good. The penalty serves also for amendment and example. Evil often serves to make us savour good the more; sometimes too it contributes to a greater perfection in him who suffers it. as the seed that one sows is subject to a kind of corruption before it can germinate...."[110]

The instrumental explanation of evil, here, is familiar to us as the teleological solution, as well as a combination of the contrast solution, together with the discipline solution. Further, God's willing evil for punishment of sin is familiar as the justice solution under the Augustinian theodicy: suffering is the display of God's justice for man's sin.

Other solutions are repeated as well. How, for example, does God in his justice permit the wicked to prosper and good people to fall into misfortune? The answer is that they will be rewarded in heaven for their unjust suffering;

> "....the remedy is all prepared in the other life; religion and reason teach us that...."[111]

This theme is repeated later when Leibniz turns from his discussion of moral evil to the misfortunes of physical evil:

> "....these sufferings [of which we are not the cause] prepare us for a greater happiness. But one must believe that even sufferings and monstrosities are part of order; and it is well to bear in mind not only that it was better to admit these defects and these monstrosities than to violate general laws...."[112]

Thus at this point, Leibniz re-emphasizes the notion that he has pushed from the beginning and on which his whole case rests:

If we had fewer evils in our world, it wouldn't be our world; if we had fewer evils we'd have to have different natural laws; but we couldn't have a different world with different natural laws because it would never have been actualized from the realm of possible worlds. Why not? Because the Great Actualizer, God, is perfect, and could have created nothing but the best: This world is the best, despite its evils, and despite the fact that it's none-too-good.

Leibniz introduces another new solution to P.E. when he says in a passage with elements of the aesthetic solution and the man is free solution:

> "Yet he [God] allows men to fall....perish....where is his affection....goodness....power? Vain objections, which suppress the main point, which ignore the fact that it is of God one speaks. God takes care of the universe, he neglects nothing, he chooses what is best on the whole. If in spite of all that someone is wicked and unhappy, it behoved him to be so."[113]

If it is "of God one speaks" what then? Presumably, and I think this is the force of the utterance, things said about God have to be said in special ways. When I attribute *affection*, *goodness* and *power* to God, what am I attributing? Well, human predicates of course, i.e., predicates that name human properties. Can I do this? Can I use this language to apply to the majesty of God? Is "the main point" here that such language cannot be used about God? or if it is used is it simply symbolic or metaphoric in some very special way? Some philosophers as we shall see when we come to John Stuart Mill, have taken this approach in solving P.E. Call it 'the language-we-use-to-talk-about-God-is-metaphorical-or-symbolic-only solution' or 'the metaphor solution'. Thus God is not *good*, *all-knowing* and *all-powerful*, but perhaps He is Good, All-knowing, and All-powerful, the uppercase, initial letters serving to illustrate the special symbolic nature of the language about God. Hence we have no P.E. It has been "solved" with a rather violent move.

Another solution proceeds from Leibniz's optimism about this best of all possible worlds. It is an optimism that is born of a kind of detachment from the problems and evils of the world that serves to set the German genius apart from the Bishop of

Hippo. John HICK has struck on this point well when he says:

> "....one feels in reading Leibniz's Theodicy that the problem of evil was for its author an intellectual puzzle rather than a terrifying threat to all the meaning that he had found in life."[114]

This is partly expressed in Leibniz's optimistic calculations about good; thus Leibniz says, following a brief section about animal suffering :

> "I would dare to maintain that even in this life, goods exceed evil, that our comforts exceed our discomforts. ......" [115]

And later he sounds more or less the same optimistic note from God's vantage point when he says:

> "....it is enough where God is concerned that there is incomparably more good than evil in the universe."[116]

I don't believe this is a trivial point at all. For there is certainly a solution to P.E. here, provided that one stretch it a bit and tighten some terminology. For if evils are outweighed by goods sufficiently, and if evils are outweighed to the near vanishing point (if one has to go that far), then obviously there is no P.E. The optimism of Leibniz can pooh-pooh evils into near extinction, and without evils, suffering at the least, what would be left of sin or moral evil ? If one had no measurable effects of evil, like suffering, I would imagine it would be hard to convince anyone even of the existence of metaphysical evil and sin. When soft evil, constructive or ordinary evil, becomes too soft, the P.E. is solved. Call this 'the goods-so-far-outweigh-the-evils-that-evils-become-of-no-consequence solution' or 'the outweighs solution'. J.W.N. SULLIVAN has commented on the vanishing of suffering in the modern world, and that comment has bearing here:

> "To the modern mind suffering is essentially remediable. Suffering is primarily due to physical and moral maladjustment, and with the spread of science and correct social theories we shall be able to abolish it. For an increasing number of people suffering is already practically abolished. They may go through life without meeting one problem they cannot evade until they reach their death bed...."[117]

Enlightenment philosophy can lead to optimism of the sort expressed by statements such as this. And Utopian literature from Plato on has been a reflection of this optimism. That it does present a problem for theologians who adhere to metaphysical theories of sin, guilt, and evil is obvious. That it does point to a possible "solution" to P.E. I think is also obvious.

The solutions that seem to be most favored by Leibniz, if one is going to count sheer repetition as a sign of favoritism, are the aesthetic solution and the teleological solution. Here are some typical examples:

> "Thus the apparent deformities of our little worlds combine to become beauties in the great world, and have nothing in them which is opposed to the oneness of an infinitely perfect universal principle: on the contrary, they increase our wonder at the wisdom of him who makes evil serve the greater good."[118]

That he is in accord with Augustine on these most favored of solutions can be seen from what he says himself about his eminent predecessor. Here he is replying to an argument which concluded by saying that God did not choose the best course (because He made a world in which there was evil). We may note the aesthetic solution, the teleological solution, and the man is free solution, all after the manner of Augustine:

> "....I would justify [my] denial by pointing out that the best course is not always that one which tends towards avoiding evil, since it is possible that the evil may be accomplished by a greater good....I have followed therein the opinion of St.Augustine, who said a hundred times that God permitted evil in order to derive from it a good, that is to say a greater good; and Thomas Aquinas says (in libr. 2, *Sent. Dist.* 32, qu.1, art. 1) that the permission of evil tends towards the good of the universe.. it was consistent with order and the general good for God to grant to certain of his creatures the opportunity to exercise their freedom, even when he foresaw that they would turn to evil....a world with evil may be better than a world without evil."[119]

Two final matters before we close our discussion of Leib niz. He mentions one other solution of a sort but does not stay for an analysis of it. In the course of discussing how it is that the soul could be infected with original sin, metaphysical evil, without God's justice being impugned, he has occasion to mention three theories of the soul. The last two, traduction and Creation, do not concern us, but the first does. It is the theory of pre-existence, about one version of which we shall make much-to-do in Parts II and III of this book. Leibniz says:

> "The first difficulty is how the soul could be infected with original sin, which is the root of actual sins, without injustice on God's part....This difficulty has given rise to three opinions on the origin of the soul itself. The first is that of *pre-existence of human souls* in another world or in another life, where they had sinned and on that account had been condemned to this prison of the human body, an opinion of the Platonists which is attributed to ORIGEN....HENRY MORE....advocated something like this....Some of those who affirm this pre-existence have gone as far as metempsychosis. The younger VAN HELMONT held this opinion [and]....WILLIAM WANDER...."[120]

Calls this 'the man-is-responsible-for-evil-because-of-sinning-in-a-previous-existence solution' or 'the rebirth solution'. Pre-existence and metempsychosis are not the same as Leibniz recognized. "Rebirth" is meant by me to stand for rebirth or pre-existence theories in general, and we will have to leave the distinctions necessary for a clear understanding of the rebirth solution until later. Suffice it to say, the rebirth solution in any of its forms is not taken seriously by any of Leibniz's predecessors for the solving of P.E., and even the English Platonists seem to urge it only in a limited way, i.e., outside P.E.

Finally, let me turn from the theological problem of human evil to the theological problem of subhuman evil. Leibniz has a theodicy for it, however brief, and it is to all intents and purposes the same solution offered in the theodicy of John Hick, to be discussed below. Leibniz says that it is no doubt true that animals suffer (even Augustine had agreed with that) but that their pleasure as well as their pain is not as keen as it is in man:

> "....for animals, since they do not reflect, are susceptible neither to the grief that accompanies pain, nor to the joy that accompanies pleasure."[121]

Eschewing the sort of solution we found in Augustine, that animals suffer for our benefit, Leibniz chooses a solution rather like the outweighs solution above, only now the argument seems to be that there is no real problem of evil for them because they can't really feel pain, not in the Cartesian sense, but in the Leibnizian sense that animal pain is not human pain for it is not as keen as human pain. This is obviously not a solution of the problem of subhuman evil, but simply an explanation of the nature of animal pain. If Leibniz had gone on to say that they don't suffer, or that their pain is illusory, perhaps we could have listed a solution for this problem here. The wiser course will be to wait upon John Hick who analyzes the theological problem of subhuman evil more completely and pin a solution label on him once he has presented his case.

b. Conclusion

I think it is obvious that Leibniz has carried on the doctrine that evil is real but that it serves a larger good, a doctrine that we found partly in Plotinus and more fully in Augustine and Thomas. Evil has taken on three forms for Leibniz, metaphysical evil bound up with the necessary finitude and imperfection of the creation, moral evil or sin, and finally physical evil or pain and suffering. Leibniz has attempted to show that metaphysical evil is necessary in this best of all the possible worlds that could have been chosen, and that God allows or permits moral and physical evil because the world we have is better as a whole with them than without them.

In our search for classical theodicies, we turn next to a work that is not thought of as classical and at times not even a theodicy, John Stuart Mill's *Three Essays on Religion.* As a bridge to that work we might mention what Mill says about his predecessor, the illustrious optimist of the 18th century; Mill's comment seems a fit conclusion to our discussion of Leibniz. Mill has just spoken of many theodicists' inability to believe that God was all powerful, such that when faced with a choice between accepting God's goodness or His power, they will invariably elect His goodness over His power:

> "[This] nowhere shines forth so distinctly as in Leibniz's famous Theodicee, so strangely mistaken for a system of optimism....Leibniz does not maintain

> that this is the best of all imaginable, but only of all possible worlds.......and though his pious feelings make him continue to designate that power by the word Omni-potence, he so explains that term as to make it mean, power extending to all that is within the limits of that abstract possibility."[122]

Mill leaves no doubt in the reader's mind that Leibniz has indeed forsaken the omnipotence thesis with respect to God.

I conclude by listing in Table II the new solutions to P.E. found in Leibniz's *Theodicy*. They are, many of them, repetitive to be sure but this repetition will be resolved shortly.

TABLE II

Name	*Description*
13. Necessary Solution	Evil is logically and metaphysically necessary for the existence of good.
14. Worse Alternative Solution	God hates evils but approves of what we get for the alternatives are far worse.
15. Creator Limitation Solution	The evil we have is the result of God's choices being limited at the time of creation.
16. Metaphor Solution	The language describing God is merely metaphorical.
17. Outweighs Solution	Evil is not so bad, for the good in the world always out-weighs the evil.
18. Rebirth Solution	Man, as a consequence of his previous births, is the cause of evil and is responsible for evil.
19. Metaphysical Evil Solution	Evil in creation is caused by the imperfections of the creation itself.

4. *John Stuart Mill* (1806-1873)

a. *Three Essays on Religion*

In the first of his essays, *Nature,* in the book *Three Essays on Religion*, John Stuart Mill begins with a discussion of what we have called the problem of subhuman evil. Like David Hume and Baron Paul Henri d'Holbach before him, Mill challenges the doctrine that there is in nature evidence for Divine purpose and design. The principal thesis, however, which Mill seeks to explode is the notion that if only man would behave naturally or act according to nature, all would be well. Mills' criticisms of the teleological argument and the act-natural thesis need not concern us. What does concern us is what Mill has to say about P.E. and about solutions to it.

He states the problem of subhuman evil, i.e., evil in *nature* ("....a collective name for all facts, actual and possible"):

> "For however offensive the proposition may appear to many religious persons, they should be willing to look in the face the undeniable fact, that the order of nature, in so far modified by man, is such as no being, whose attributes are justice and benevolence, would have made, with the intention that his rational creatures should follow it as an example."[123]

Thus it would seem that a certain set of facts are imbued, however improbably, with what we shall call 'evil'. The theme is familiar to us now: a being who is good and powerful, has left behind a creation that is evil and imperfect. How does one explain this?

> "In sober truth, nearly all the things which men are hanged or imprisoned for doing to one another, are Nature's every day performance. Killing....protracted tortures ....all this, Nature does with the most supercilious disregard of both mercy and of justice...."[124]

Mill details some of the solutions that have been offered to explain nature's ways in the presence of a benevolent creator: The aesthetic solution and the teleological solution. For example, to the defense that good will come from evil, Mill says :

> "It is undoubtedly a very common fact that good comes out of evil....But in the first place, it is quite often

> true of human crimes, as of natural calamities [that] they are crimes nevertheless. In the second place, if good frequently come out of evil, the converse fact, evil coming out of good, is equally common."[125]

If the defenders persist, and hold that ultimately, in some tremendous ultimate resolution all will be justified and all these things we see as evil now will be turned to wise and good ends, Mill replies,

> "I must remark that whether they are so or not, is altogether beside the point"[126]

for they are evils, nonetheless. Mill concludes his critique by adding :

> "If the maker of the world can (do) all that he will, he wills misery, and there is no escape from the conclusion."[127]

He follows then with a ringing denunciation of theodicies like Augustine's and Leibniz's, and in the course of it leads us directly into the theological problem of human evil :

> "Every kind of moral depravity is entailed upon multitudes by the fatality of their birth; through the fault of their parents, of society or, of uncontrolable circumstances, certainly through no fault of their own. Not even in the most distorted and contracted theory of good which ever was framed by religious or philosophical fanaticism, can the government of nature be made to resemble the work of a being at once good and omnipotent."[128]

Mill's own solution to the theological problem of evil then follows:

> "The only admissible moral theory of creation is that the Principle of Good *cannot* at once and altogether subdue the powers of evil, either physical or moral...."[129],

i.e., God is not all powerful.

Two comments on this final passage: first, Mill speaks about "the only admissible moral theory", as if there were only one solution, his own, to P.E. This is a bit strong, considering our own cataloguing of solutions. Second, Mill's solution to P.E. is now laid bare: It is that God is not all-powerful. The remainder of the essays are taken up with expanding and reworking this solution. Thus *Three Essays* is, after all, a theodicy.

Mill's "only possible" solution is, of course, similar to ones we already have, viz., the Creator limitation solution, the metaphysical evil solution and possibly the worse alternatives solution. But none of the others is as explicit as Mill's, and while some reflection will show that these three mentioned solutions are species of Mill's solution, i.e., can be reduced to it rather obviously, the latter is nonetheless worth mentioning in its own right. Call this 'the God-is-not-all-powerful solution' or 'the not all-powerful solution.'

Mill contends, that in the history of religious theodicy, philosophers have generally been willing to forego God's omnipotence in order to save God's goodness. Thus, he implies, that what he is doing is merely making explicit what is already implicit in the subject and thereby possibly saving many theologians from intellectual or theological hypocrisy or embarrassment.

> "There is no subject on which men's practical belief is more incorrectly indicated by the words they use to express it than religion....But those who have been strengthened in goodness by relying on the sympathizing support of a powerful and good Governor of the world have, I am satisfied, never really believed that Governor to be, in the strict sense of the term, omnipotent. They have always saved his goodness at the expense of his power....They have believed that he could do one thing, but not any combination of things: that his government, like human government, was a system of adjustments and compromises; that the world is inevitably imperfect contrary to his intention."[130]

The proof for a limited deity argument lies, Mill argues, in looking at nature itself. The imperfect and the striving to become perfect in the natural world is a sure sign, Mill says, that its Maker is also limited and imperfect.[131] Man's task when faced with such a world and such a Creator is to amend that world, not imitate it.[132] Mill's argument on the former point is a bit obscure but seems to be something like this: Because it took wisdom to make the world, this implies a limitation of God's power. If God was really powerful, the argument seems to say, He could have done what he did without wisdom. And since constructing the world out of matter and force required wisdom,[133] God must have been limited in his power. Mill, therefore, seems to have two arguments to prove God's impotence; first, the nature of the imperfect world, and second, the clash between the two powers of God, His wisdom and His potency, such that if He needs wisdom, He lacks potency. The two arguments at first sight seem to contradict each other. For if God had wisdom (argument two) then He wouldn't have created such a botched up world (argument one). So that if argument two is right, argument one must be wrong. On the other hand, if He lacked wisdom, and that's why He created such a mess (argument one), then there's no reason to suppose a clash between His powers, wisdom and potency (argument two). I don't think Mill meant the arguments to work in such a fashion. He means to give simply an empirical argument for God's lack of power (argument one) and a logical, ontological argument for the non-compresence of wisdom and potency as attributes of God (argument two). It would seem that Mill could equally well have concluded from the second argument that, if these two attributes cannot be compresent in God and one has to go, it could equally well be wisdom that goes. But the empirical argument supports the contention that it is potency that goes, and wisdom (limited or unlimited) stays. On this last point, whether God is omniscient, Mill stays loose and open, i.e., if omnipotence goes, this may or may not affect omniscience:

> "[This does] not, in the same manner, exclude omniscience: if we suppose limitation of power, there is nothing to contradict the supposition of perfect knowledge and absolute wisdom. But neither is there anything to prove it."[134]

We will return to these puzzles again when we discuss the nature of God and P.E. in Chapter II.

Mill summarizes his findings regarding the nature of God based on the logical, ontological argument noted above:

> "These, then, are the net results of Natural Theology on the question of the divine attributes. A Being of great but limited power, how or by what limited we cannot even conjecture; of great, and perhaps unlimited intelligence but perhaps, also, more narrowly limited than his power...."[135]

b. Conclusion

The conclusion that Mill draws from his discussion is a moral one, viz., that given a creator who possesses the attributes that limit his power, and given the creation with its base imperfections, and given, further, the good intentions of this limited deity, man's duty to himself, other men, and God is to help the Creator to perfect the creation:

> "One elevated feeling this form of religious idea admits of, which is not open to those who believe in the omnipotence of the good principle in the universe, the feeling of helping God—....a battle is constantly going on, in which the humblest human creature is not incapable of taking some part...."[136]

Mill's call to moral arms is, I fancy, quite appealing. There is a kind of optimism, surely, in the call itself: "Come on men, if God is on our side who can be against us." In fact, much of 19th century imperial British optimism can, of course, be explained by this religious moral posturing. But while it lacks the pessimism of original sin—*cum* metaphysical evil—there lingers in it, nonetheless, an agonizing question: If God, with all His wisdom, and goodness, and even limited power, if God who is so much greater than man couldn't do it, how can man be expected to do it ? But that's perhaps a sluggard's and a laggard's question. It could only be asked after two world wars, and after multiple I.C.B.M.'s, M.I.R.V.s, and the like. Mill would no doubt have replied in a quick, light Kiplingish tone "Well, come on, lads, anyway let's try."

Looking ahead to our analysis in Chapter II however, the reader is forewarned that Mill's not all-powerul solution is not a *bona fide* solution to P.E. For once again in place of accepting the theological premises regarding the perfect nature of God together with the fact of evil, it attacks one of those premises, and thereby avoids P.E. rather than solving P.E.

5. *Josiah Royce* (1855-1916)

a. The World and the Individual

Josiah Royce's, *The World and the Individual* contains a number of valuable solutions to P.E., some familiar, some not. Royce approaches P.E. by designating three separate positions with respect to P.E., each of which provides views on the nature of evil and a theodicy to explain that evil. The three positions are the mystical, the realist, and the idealist. Before coming to those, it might be well to say something about the nature of evil as Royce understands it. Royce says:

> "An evil is, in general, a fact that sends us to some Other for its own justification, and for the satisfaction of our will."[137]

But it is clear from the discussion that follows that the paramount element in a situation or in a person in a situation that makes the situation evil is the dissatisfaction produced in our will:

> "Any temporal fact, as such, is essentially more or less dissatisfying, and so evil."[138]

This dissatisfaction or frustration of the will is expressed in the defeat of purposes which the will designs and proposes:

> "But death—and above all, not our own death nearly so much as the death of our friends—is an evil insofar as it appears in our experience as a temporal defeat of the purposes of human love, and the need of the human world for its good men."[139]

Having explained evil as a function of a frustration of will, Royce goes on to detail three views that have been taken with respect to explaining this evil.

The first view involves a mystical theodicy, and entails the mystic's saying that evil is without reality or Being—an illusion, a dream a deceit. We have seen already that Dionysius leans in this direction, and that even Plotinus, who holds that evil is Matter hence absolute Non-Being, tends towards this direction (though Plotinus saves himself as Dionysius apparently does not, by maintaining however inconsistently that Non-Being exists and has effects). To those who contend that evil is merely finite error, and here one might suppose that he has Augustine and the not all-powerful solution or the metaphysical evil solution in mind, Royce challenges:

> "If evil is merely called finite error, this finite error remains none the less, as a fact of human experience, an evil. One has only changed the name. The reality remains what it was."[140]

To those who contend that evil is simply an illusion, and here one might suppose that he has Dionysius in mind, (though he explicitly mentions ECKHART, "Hindoo" mystics and ANGELUS SILESIUS as philosophers who contend that the Godhead or Absolute Self knows neither good nor evil) and the illusion solution also in mind, Royce says:

> "The mystic first denies that evil is real. He is asked why then evil seems to exist. He replies that this is our finite error. The finite error itself hereupon becomes, as the source of all our woes, an evil. But no evil is real. Hence no error can be real. Hence we do not really err, even if we suppose that evil is real. Herewith we return to our starting point."

The escape from this is found,

> ". . . . by asserting that it is an error to assert that we really err. . . ."[141]

Royce takes a final swipe at the mystics by stating that their doctrine is impractical if not immoral for:

> ". . . . it is equally obvious that this simple denial of the reality of evil makes an end of every rational possibility of moral effort."[142]

The second view that he criticizes involves a realistic theodicy. It is plainly an attack on theologians like Augustine and Leibniz and the man is free solution:

> "According to this view real evil is entirely due to the free will of moral agents who are essentially Independent Beings, and who have their existence apart from one another, like all the entities of Realism."[143]

Royce condemns this view also, and he uses the reply that realism as explained here cannot handle the sufferings (physical evils) that seem to fall upon the innocent. The realist can of course counter, as Royce demonstrates, with the view that the righteous man has secretly sinned, if not in this life, then as with "the popular doctrine of the Hindoos", in some previous life.[144] Royce responds rather weakly to this realist's response, and without clarification of his position:

> The result is here indeed a moral fatalism, of an unexpected, but nonetheless inevitable sort.[145]

Unsatisfactory as this reply is, perhaps Royce can be forgiven, for in his haste to lay out his own idealist theodicy and explain all the facts commonsensically, he has failed to lay a proper ground for his realist's response; with the consequence that any reply he, Royce, gave would probably be inappropriate. Moral fatalism or no, his failure to meet the Hindoo challenge may have other reasons behind it than haste and improper ground laying: It is possible that the rebirth solution cannot be challenged within the idealist's framework at all. But more on this in Part III of this book.

Royce, of course, plumps for an idealist theodicy that will explain real evil but explain that real evil within a nexus of interlocking relations among the agents, the world, and God. First, this evil is real for Royce, and it defines itself as moral and physical evil:

> "Every ill of human fortune....is ....either directly due to the magnitude and ideality of our finite plans, or else is more or less directly the expression of the morally defective intent of some human or extra-human moral agent...."[146]

Earlier, Royce had made this distinction between moral evil or sins connected to human conduct (like embezzlement), and natural evils, evils that happen to us (like death). We will have occasion to comment in Chapter II on the change that is occurring with respect to this terminology throughout the history of P.E. The upshot is that, for Royce, evil is real, not illusory. Second, that in this order of being in which we are caught all are bound to all, not only through the nexus of logical internal relations, but also through the nexus of physical-moral internal relations. My suffering, consequently, may be totally undeserved, but I will suffer as long as you sin and as long as you and I are bound ontically together in this vast idealist system: All are bound to all, all are responsible for all, all suffer for all and by all:

> "It follows that in our moral world, the righteous can suffer without individually deserving their suffering, just because their lives have no independent Being, but are linked with all life."[147]

The justification for all my suffering is that ultimately we have "the assurance of the divine triumph in eternity lighting up the whole."[148] Thus the evils I suffer now all men suffer more or less, but the justification lies in the final reward for all, a species surely of the recompense solution, though with an absolute idealist twist. It is with this as a ground that Royce can also say:

> "All finite life is a struggle with evil. Yet from the final point of view the Whole is good,"[149]

a view which we found in Augustine as the aesthetic solution; and this view receives further confirmation when Royce argues that the "longing in Time" is necessary in order that there is "peace in Eternity."[150] The whole travail is necessary in order that the Divine will be accomplished and not frustrated, wherein the final goal will be my ultimate fulfilment in the Absolute:

> "Through this my tribulation the Absolute triumph, then, is one. Moreover, this triumph is also eternally mine. In the Absolute I am fulfilled."[151]

But the Absolute is not an impersonal, emotionless entity—Royce is neither neo-Platonist nor Hegelian in that sense. God knows sorrow and human tribulation, for if He did not He could not know the highest good, which is "the overcoming of sorrow."[152] Thus human will, constantly frustrated on earth, doomed to disappointment and despair, receives its highest reward in Eternity where itwill be worthy of its absolute reward; the purpose of evil, it would seem then, is to try, test, mold and perfect man:

> ". . . . through the endurance and the conquest over its own internal ills the spirit wins its best conscious fulfilment."[153]

We must "consent to endure. . . . for the sake of the spiritual beauty that we thereby learn to contemplate"[154] for man is ennobled through suffering, prepared through evil, disciplined by pain. We have also seen this solution before, and called it the discipline solution. Another familiar solution is also proffered by Royce, when he admits that the presence of evil is a condition of the perfection of the eternal order. Since Oneness alone is nothingness, the Absolute needs and demands this other, this "presence of ill." We have a combination here of the contrast solution together with the necessary solution, the view that evil is logically and metaphysically necessary to the perfection of the whole or the presence of good.

But aside from these by now familiar solutions there is one more that is new. It relates back to a remark we made earlier in regard to Leibniz regarding the anti-intellectual or irrational strain one frequently finds rumbling through these theodicies. And it comes out in Royce:

> "In regard to the question: Whence and by whose deed or defect came just this ill-fortune?—we have indeed seldom any right to venture upon any detailed speculations. For since the Internal Meaning of the processes of nature is, in general, hidden from man, we do well....to observe how best to adjust our skill to the actual ways of Nature, than to waste our time in a practically vain blaming of unknown hostile agencies...."[155]

If "vain blaming" is just that, *vain blaming*, then obviously it is a waste of time. But much thought-out, well-reasoned blaming is the very work of those philosophers who would challenge the various theodicies we have been engaged with. And who has more right "to venture upon detailed speculations" into those matters hidden from man than the theodicist after all ? That this does indeed border on an intellectual giving-up is seen, finally, when Royce comes as close as he ever does to discussing P.E. directly, but at the last, turns, dodges and runs:

> "....such sorrow [degrading ill fortune, pain, etc.] seems in no wise ennobling ....Can such sorrows be justified ? He [man] cannot now know the ideal meaning of the vast realms of finite life in whose fortunes he is at present mysteriously doomed to share."[156]

This is a "solution" to P.E. of sorts, but it violently removes the problem from discussion by saying that there is no solution knowable now. It solves by denying. Call this 'the presence-of-evil-cannot-be-justified solution' or 'the mystery solution'.

We shall meet it more fully with our final author, John Hick, and I leave it for discussion until that time, for surely as the mystery solution stands now it is either tantamont to having no solution at all, or else having a solution but in virtue of doing violence to what we would intuitively understand by "solution" That is to say, it cannot be called a *bona fide* solution to P.E.

b. Conclusion

Briefly then, Josiah Royce adopts the belief that evil is real enough and necessary to the grand design of the Divine Will. That Will seeks its own total perfection through the trials and perfectings of its various parts. But in order that the Whole can share in the final triumph of the sought-after perfection wherein

Will is no longer frustrated, it now shares with the creation the consciousness of the ills and evils that beset that Creation.

Royce's God is a suffering compassionate God that can be looked upon as the origin as well as the end of the world's tribulations. Royce's system is not an Absolute, impersonal idealism then, and his P.E. is a theological one. He avoids the unacceptable-to-commonsense view of the mystics that evil is illusory, while remaining aloof from the realist view that each man's suffering is his own fault. Thus he can explain the real evil suffered by the innocent as a consequence of his metaphysical idealist system of moral and ontic internal relations: No evil deed is lost in the whole; all suffer when one suffers; the creation groans in agony at each moral slight, at every human plight.

But in the face of the attempt to justify hard evil, extraordinary suffering and gratuitous pain, Royce rings down a curtain of mystery. It seems as if there must come a point, a degree of human suffering, such that beyond it no known human explanation suffices. It is on the rack of such human sufferings that human theodicies are stretched and broken.

It might be useful to catch up our list of possible solutions to P.E. from our discussions in Mill and Royce. Both the not all-powerful solution and the mystery solution will become clearer from our discussion in Hick. Recall once more the *caveat* introduced above that awaits explanation in Chapter III, viz., that neither will be acceptable as a *bonafide* solution to P.E.

TABLE III

	Name	*Descriptions*
20.	Not All-powerful Solution	God is limited in his power and needs help in combating evil.
21.	Mystery Solution	The presence of evil cannot be rationally justified.

6. *John Hick*

a *Evil and the God of Love*

John Hick's *Evil and the God of Love* is a theodicy in the style of Leibniz's work. For in it we find a catalogue of solutions to P.E. with certain favorites emerging. Unlike Leibniz but more akin to the philosophic spirit of Mill (and David Hume, of course), Hick is critical of many theodicies. We shall turn to his criticisms in part, here, but only insofar as they affect his own Christian theodicy. To understand that theodicy is the principal task before us in this final section, as well as laying down any new solutions to P.E. not yet mentioned in our own catalogue.

Hick puts forward and defends a number of traditional solutions to P.E., notably the aesthetic, teleological, contrast and recompense solutions, as well as a form of the mystery solution. In our recounting of Hick's theodicy we will be pointing to these solutions and to a curious inconsistency within his own theodicy. To lead up to this point let me first state P.E. as Hick understands it; say a few words about his conception of evil; and then go on to a more specific detailing of his theodicy.

The problem of evil receives two formulations in Hick. The first is familiar, and loose, the second is new and tighter. The difference between them is the way in which the nature of evil is apprehended and developed. The approach to P.E. that Hick takes is to see the problem resting on the deprivation or privative notion of evil, a notion going back as we have seen, at least as far as Plotinus, Augustine and Dionysius:

> "Evil is thus loss and lack, a deprivation of good....it tends, by its inherently negative character towards nullity and non-existence. As a characterization of evil within the framework of Christian theology, this privative definition must be accepted as wholly sound. It represents the only possible account of the ontological status of evil in a universe that is the creation of an omnipotent and good God."[157]

The problem arises, Hick urges, only for a religion which "insists that the object of its worship is at once perfectly good and unlimitedly powerful."[158] While this may not be enough to generate the theological problem of human evil, it will nonetheless start us on the road to it. Coupled with this deprivation notion of evil is the familiar concept of sin from which concept Hick developes his own idea of P.E.:

> "And because sin thus belongs to our own innermost nature and is at the same time the source of so many forms

> of evil it has usually, and surely rightly, been seen as constituting the heart of the problem of evil."[159]

Given the fact of sin, then, and it is a concept again familiar to us since Augustine, Hick states the problem:

> ". . . . the theodicy problem ["at this point, consequently"] takes the form: Why has an omnipotent, omniscient, and infinitely good and loving creator permitted sin in His universe ?"[160]

But the one characteristic difference between Hick and the other theodicists so far discussed (save Mill), is that Hick treats P.E. as a problem involving not ordinary evils like Royce's embezzlement, and undeserved suffering,[161] but rather what he calls dysteleological evil. Hick's insight at this juncture challenges the rather silly solutions like the outweighs solution in our list of possible solutions, where that solution treats lightly the evils that do exist. A word now on the types of evil. Hick uses the distinction already present in Leibniz, between moral evil, and physical or natural evil:

> "Moral evil is evil that we human beings originate: cruel, unjust, vicious, and perverse thoughts and deeds. Natural evil is the evil that originates independently of human actions: in disease bacilli, earthquakes, storms, droughts, tornadoes, etc."[162]

And adds, following Leibniz' metaphysical evil:

> ". . . . metaphysical evil . . . . the basic fact of finitude and limitation within the created universe. The Augustinian tradition . . . . traces all other evils, moral and natural, back to this as their ultimate cause. . . ." [163]

So far there is nothing startlingly difficult to separate Hick from his predecessors, other than his willingness to recognize rather bravely the existence of hard evil. But it is this hard evil, manfully recognized, that will prove fatal to Hick's own rational theodicy.

Next Hick distinguishes two theodical traditions in the West, the Augustinean and the Irenaean. The former sees evil primarily as a privation of good resulting from misused freedom on the part of man and the fallen angels. The creation is good, as we have seen in Augustine and hence God is not responsible for the evils found in it. This view is aptly represented by that Augustinian tradition running from JOHN CALVIN to

KARL BARTH, and its principal doctrines would seem to focus directly on the utter absolute depravity of man, i.e., metaphysical evil with a vengeance, and the utter goodness and majesty of God. Hick criticizes this Augustinian theodicy rather decisively, saying to God:

> "For if He chose to make creatures who are bound sooner or later to fail (even though they do so without external compulsion), He cannot reasonably complain when they do fail. He must have foreseen that they would fail if He made them, and He must nevertheless have decided to make them. This consideration points to a fatal contradiction within the Augustinian-Thomist theodicy."[164]

The principal source of this difficulty lies in the notion of evil as metaphysical non-being, Hick feels. He says:

> "Instead of construing evil as metaphysical non-being, we must see it primarily as a failure in personal relationship. Instead of upholding the perfection of the universe as an aesthetic whole, we must think of it as perfect in the rather different sense that it is suited to the fulfilment of God's purpose for it. And instead of invoking the juridical principle of moral balance, we must see God's free forgiveness at work ultimately transforming sinners into citizens of His Kingdom."[165]

As an alternative to this Augustinian tradition which locates evil in sin and creatures, Hick offers what he calls the Irenaean tradition which he traces through IRENAEUS (130-202 A.D.) and the Eastern Church. Accordingto the general Christian view man was created "finitely perfect" but in his freedom rebelled against God, and ever since he has been under a Divine condemnation. We are, the general view continues, born as sinners and our nature is bound to lead us into further sin—only by God's grace, free and incomprehensible, are some saved. We have seen this as the man is free solution in the catalogue of solutions to P.E. But now Irenaeus appears:

> "Irenacus suggests that man was created as an imperfect, immature creature who was to undergo moral deve-

> lopment and growth and finally be brought to the perfection intended for him by his Maker."[166]

Thus man's inherent sinful nature is a weakness worthy of pity and not an offence to be condemned.[167] Hick identifies this doctrine as "soul making" and traces the tradition itself through SCHLEIERMACHER (1768-1834),

> "In his teaching that sin and evil are ordained by God as the preconditions of redemption, SCHLEIERMACHER has sponsored the thesis that evil ultimately serves the good purpose of God,"[168]

and F.R. TENNANT (1866-1957),

> "And so TENNANT concludes that physical evil is inevitable in a world governed by general laws and inhabited by embodied creature. Since it is only in such a world that moral personality can develop at all, the Creator's goodness is vindicated."[169]

It is with these theodical optimists that Hick places himself:

> "....we have adopted the Irenaean view that God is gradually forming perfected members of the humanity whose fuller nature we glimpse in Christ."[170]

This Irenaean view entails what Hick calls "soul making" :

> "Rather this world must be a place of soul-making."[171]
>
> "....our theodicy must still enter upon the soul-making process that we believe to be taking place within human life."[172]

This is a familiar notion to us also, for it was bound up in the discipline solution: The evils that man receives build and form character in order to make us all worthy of God's love, Heaven, Grace, or what-have-you. Soul making or character development as an explanation of evil falls on difficult times, however, when faced with dysteleological evil. And Hick is hard put to square his Irenaean position with the existence of hard evil. He tries a number of ploys. He makes it clear that the world was never intended to be a palace of pleasure:

> "Such critics as Hume [who thinks of God's relation to the world on the model of a human building a cage for a pet to live in] are confusing what heaven ought to be as an environment for perfected finite beings with what this world ought to be, as an environment

> for beings who are in process of becoming perfected."[173]

and conceives of the world and its relation to God instead on a child-parent analogy:

> "I think it is clear that a parent who loves his children, and wants them to become the best human beings that they are capable of becoming does not treat pleasure as the sole and supreme value."[174]

But all this is quite beside the point when one looks World War II straight in the face. And I think that it is with this look that Hick's theodicy runs into trouble. First comes the retreat from the discipline solution. Hick has earlier stated what the intention of his theodicy must be:

> "Given the conception of a divine intention working in and through human time towards a fulfilment that lies in its completeness beyond human time, our theodicy must find the meaning of evil in the part that it is made to play in the eventual outworking of that purpose; and must find the justification of the whole process in the magnitude of the good to which it leads,......a Kingdom which is yet to come in its full glory and permanence."[175]

And he now asks, in effect, can this stand up to the test, to take his first examples, of Hiroshima and World War II? His response is weak; if there were no Hiroshima to complain about, then we'd complain about Rotterdam; if God had prevented World War II, then we'd have to complain about World War I or the Civil War:

> "There would be nowhere to stop, short of a divinely arranged paradise in which human freedom would be narrowly circumscribed, moral responsibility largely eliminated, and in which the drama of man's story would be reduced to the level of a television serial. We always know that the rugged hero who upholds law and order is going to win the climactic gun fight. ....the struggle for righteousness and human dignity would become unreal."[176]

But while the discipline solution or soul-making may become impossible for the victims of war and disease, it is still possible,

Hick claims, for those of us who witness their tragic deaths, to be ennobled and ensouled. Thus in a world built after Utopian hopes and desires,

> "In such a [just] world misery would not evoke deep personal sympathy or call forth organized relief and sacrficial help and service....It seems, then, that in a world that is to be the scene of compassionate love and self-giving for others, suffering must fall upon mankind with something of the haphazardness and inequity that we now experience. It must be apparently unmerited, pointless, and incapable of being morally rationalized....No undeserved need would mean no uncalculating outpouring to meet that need."[177]

In such a world, morality would fail for there would be no doing of the right for the sake of the right:

> "Further [elimination of unjust suffering, etc.]would mean that there would be no doing of the right simply because it is right and without any expectation of reward.....good will....which [KANT] said [was] the only intrinsically good thing in the world or out of it would be excluded." [178]

Whether dysteleological evil must exist in order to save a Kantian ethics is debatable to say the least. But more important is the question whether or not such a saving is worth the price. That is to say, while there is certainly no guarantee that excessive suffering inevitably leads to a right for right's sake morality, it is highly questionable whether it is worth the price. What suddenly makes KANT's ethical principle so terribly important to Hick ? I think there is a serious flaw in his theory at this point, for no ground has been laid for this deontological position, hence the need to salvage it is without support. It seems like a desperate move for a theodicist in obviously desperate straits. Hick continues by saying that those who have suffered undeservedly will however receive their perfection and reward:

> "....in the final accounting be no personal life that is unperfected and no suffering that has not eventually become a phase in the fulfilment of God's good purpose. Only so, I suggest, is it possible to believe

> both in the perfect goodness of God and in His unlimited capacity to perform His will."[179]

This sounds like the recompense solution though Hick, in denying the existence of Hell[180] also denies that this present view is a classical reward-in-Heaven view. However that may be, whether a recompense or an aesthetic solution, one or the other or both are certainly present when he continues,

> "....these sufferings....will in the end lead to the enjoyment of a common good which will be unending and therefore unlimited...."[181]

But Hick's own discipline solution with its inherent optimism comes a cropper as he himself admits, against the example of the extermination of four to six million people in Europe from 1942-1945:

> "Was this in any sense willed by God? The answer is obviously no. These events were utterly evil, wicked, devilish and unforgivable; they are wrongs that can never be righted, horrors that will disfigure the universe to the end of time....It would have been better—much better—if they had never happened."[182]

It is interesting to read this together with an appeal to a teleological solution made earlier:,

> "[Evil turns to good] As the supreme evil ["the murder of the divine Son"] turned to supreme good ["the occasion of man's salvation"], it provides the paradigm for the distinctively Christian reaction to evil."[183]

The inconsistency seems obvious. Further Hick admits, inconsistently again, I think, that God's purpose for the world was retarded by the above atrocity. For this is tantamount to holding that if no purpose was served by this event, and if the event was contrary to God's own wishes, and it wasn't stopped, then it couldn't be stopped. We are left with the not all-powerful solution as the only solution, though Hick takes, perhaps another way out as we shall see. For these four to six million sufferers and in compensation for their sufferings, Hick brings in a final reward. Again this is inconsistent with his earlier apparent denial of the recompense solution, apparent but not real.[184]

"In the realms beyond our world they are alive and will

have their place in the final fulfilment of God's creation."[185]

Why does Hick's moral, but not theological indignation, rise to such heights over the issue of this mass extermination ? Was it the manner of their death ? of their bodies' disposal ? of the fact that innocents, women and children, were involved? But wouldn't he feel the same if it were only one million that were killed ? or a hundred thousand ? But then how can he wax wroth at this number and not at ninety and nine or even one ? And why not rise up in moral indignation, and theological indignation to boot, at *any* instance of dysteleological evil, in place of speakingof theodical compensations such as are implied in the recompense and the aesthetic solutions ? There is a kind of myopia to suffering, present here, that many would find difficult to understand because it seems plainly inconsistent: The theologian who can see trouble for his theodicy only when four to six million die at one fell swoop, but is unable to see the same trouble when one dies miserably and wretchedly.

I think Hick in some way sees this inconsistency and I think that's why he runs from the problem in an irrational move that we called 'the mystery solution' in our discussion of Royce. Here is an example of what I mean :

> Our 'solution', then, to this baffling problem of excessive and undeserved suffering is a frank appeal to the positive value of mystery....The mystery of dysteleological suffering is a real mystery, impenetrable to the rationalizing human mind.[186]

The only problem of course is that either Hick has been inconsistent in trying to penetrate the mystery (the entire book is such a probe) or he has been misleading the reader into believing that soul-making together with the aesthetic, teleological, discipline and recompense solutions are indeed viable solutions to P.E. in a viable theodicy. It is interesting to speculate on the sort of alternative that the mystery solution provides, and the reasons behind moves of this sort. We will return to this in time and discuss it in the light of what Stephen Toulmin has called "limiting questions". It might very well be that Hick has reached the end of his intellectual tether in attempting to treat of dysteleological evil. It sounds as if, judging from Hick's discussion that, as Toulmin has said in another context,

> ". . . . a point was reached beyond which it was no longer possible to give 'reasons' of the kind given until then; and eventually there came a stage beyond which it seemed that no 'reason' of any kind could be given."[187]

On the final issue I want to take up, animal suffering, Hick like his predecessors, seems once more peculiarly inconsistent. He cites the existence of the problem :

> "To some, the pain suffered in the animal Kingdom beneath the human level has constituted the most baffling aspect of the problem of evil."[188]

Hick himself rejects animal pain as a problem for theodicy, since (1) death is really not a problem for them as it is for us since they cannot anticipate it and feel anxiety about it, and (2) they are incapable of worrying over the future dangers that could happen to them.[189] Thus on grounds of psychological suffering alone, Hick argues in effect, that animals don't suffer. Their physical suffering he appears to justify in virtue of the fact that the creation is man's to use for his own salvation: The stage for the drama of salvation, as we saw with Augustine, is this world, and insofar as the animals aid and abet man in his struggle against evil and in the perfection of his soul, then their suffering will be justified:

> "If, then, the animal Kingdom plays its part in this 'eighth day of creation', the process must be justified by its success. The problem of animal pain is thus subordinate to that of human sin and suffering . . . ."[190]

It may be subordinate but that does not mean it does not exist. To imply that physical pain and suffering are less important than psychological pain, and thereby resolve or excuse animal suffering is to dodge the very obvious truth that pain is pain, whether psychological or evil. To treat animal suffering in this manner is to open the door to treating infants, the mentally ill, and the mentally deformed in like manner. Hick's position can be reduced to absurdity once one finds other creatures who satisfy the criterion that Hick's animals satisfy, viz., of not being able to anticipate the future, and thereby not being able to suffer that kind of anxiety.

b. *Conclusion*

Enough has been said already about Hick's solutions. Suffice it to say that when faced with dysteleological evil, Hick turns to mystery and drops out of the discussion. He is unable to answer the problem of extraordinary evil save to take refuge in the mystery solution. All his theodicy comes to focus, finally and ultimately, on this solution and as we shall see in Chapter III below, it is really not an adequate solution at all to P.E.[191]

7. *Summary of Chapter I*

Hick together with the other figures discussed in this brief section has supplied us with a list of possible solutions to P.E. Our concern here in Chapter I has been simply to garner such a working list and from time to time offer justifications for these solutions, and to criticize them where that seemed advisable. In concluding this chapter it might be well, then, to list in order all of the solutions which we have mentioned in the course of this historical review. In the chapters that follow, but especially in Chapter III, we will have occasion to refer back to this list. There may be repetitions; indeed the list of twenty-one solutions we shall see in the third chapter below can be substantially reduced. Furthermore, as we have stated repeatedly, a number of these "solutions" will later be rejected as not *bona fide* solutions to P.E. It might be pointed out once again that since any genuine solution to P.E. must justify real evil in the presence of certain properties of God, any "solution" which denies the existence of those properties or that evil cannot be a *bona fide* but only a spurious solution to P.E. Thus the list in the following table can be considerably shortened not only by performing certain reductions on obvious repetitions but also by excluding certain spurious solutions to P.E., e.g., the not all powerful solution and its equivalents which patently reject one of the premises necessary to generate what we shall call "the theological problem of evil'. We shall return to this topic again below in Chapter III. For the present our list of representative solutions runs as indicated in Table IV.

TABLE IV

Name	*Description*
1. Aesthetic Solution	The aesthetic whole is good though the parts are evil.
2. Teleological Solution	Good comes ultimately out of evil.
3. Prevention Solution	The evils we have are necessary to prevent greater evil.
4. Contrast Solution	Evils are necessary in order to contrast with and point up the good.
5. Man is Free Solution	Man with his free will is the cause of evil.
6. Discipline Solution	Evil disciplines us and builds our character.
7. Recompense Solution	Evils, such as unjust suffering, will be recompensed in Heaven.
8. Illusion Solution	Evil is an illusion, and not ultimately real.
9. Privation Solution	Evil is merely the privation of good.
10. Impersonal Substance Solution	Evil is caused by an impersonal, wicked substance, e.g., matter.
11. Personal Substance Solution	Evil is caused by a personal wicked substance, e.g., Satan.
12. Justice Solution	Evil is God's just punishment of man's sins.
13. Necessary Solution	Evil is logically and metaphysically necessary for the existence of good.
14. Worse Alternatives Solution	God hates evil but approves of what we get, for the alternatives are far worse.
15. Creator Limitation Solution	The evil we have is the result of God's choices being limited at the time of creation.

Name	*Description*
16. Metaphor Solution	The language describing God is merely metaphorical.
17. Outweighs Solution	Evil is not so bad for the good in the world always outweighs the evil.
18. Rebirth Solution	Man, as a consequence of his previous births, is the cause of evil and is responsible for evil.
19. Metaphysical Evil Solution	Evil in creation is caused by the imperfections in the creation itself.
20. Not All-powerful Solution	God is not omnipotent and needs help in combating evil.
21. Mystery Solution	The presence of evil cannot be rationally justified (one must give up reason, have faith, see the mystery in evil, etc.)

CHAPTER II

The Problem of Evil

In this chapter I want to cover very briefly two things:

1. Introduce the problem of evil and show precisely under what conditions it is a problem, or can be said to be a problem.

2. Analyze the premises (four of them) of the theological problem of evil.

1. *Introduction*

The problem of evil, i.e., the theological problem of evil, arises when one assumes two things: First, that there is evil in the world, and second, that there is simultaneously a God who has certain describable properties, viz., omnipotence, beneficence, and possibly others as well. Thus when this latter assumption is combined with the assumptions that evil is real, we generate the theological problem of evil.

The theological problem of evil can be further subdivided, depending on the type of evil under discussion. Thus supposing that we have an intuitive grasp of the concept of evil and understand that somehow or other, it means suffering, pain, and the like; also suppose that the realm of beings capable of experiencing pain and suffering is full, i.e., includes grades of being from the highest beings to the lowest as described in our plenum philosophies in Chapter I, then we can generate at least three layers of beings in this plenum, superhumans (God, gods, angels, archangels, dominions, thrones, powers, virtues and whatever else is included traditionally in that realm, but including especially fallen angels); humans, the old, the middle, the young; and subhumans (animals and conceivably plants). Hence we can generate theological problems of evil (abbreviate this now 'T.P.E.') for all three realms, viz., a T.P.E. for superhumans, a T.P.E. for humans and a T.P.E. for subhumans. The questions raised by each in general would be 'Why would a good and powerful God make (or allow) beings, e.g., devils, men, or animals (to) suffer?' Our particular puzzle with T.P.E. will be with humans rather than with angels or animals, but all three will be brought to bear on the various solutions to be offered in Chapter III below.

2. *The Theological Problem of Evil*

T.P.E. is brought about by the conjunction of certain necessary assumptions. First there are certain assumptions about God, call these 'the theological theses'; second there is an assumption about evil, call this 'the evil thesis'. Let me take the theological theses first and see what they contain, and then turn to the evil thesis last.

a. The Theological Theses

There are three parts to these : (1) the ethical thesis, (2) the omnipotent thesis and (3) the omniscience thesis. I will treat each one separately in what follows. The entire discussion, of course, is predicated on the deity being a person, and all that that entails. HENRY AIKEN says, regarding such an attribution:

> "In short, there is already built into the notion of personality a characteristic normative function which prescribes a certain comportment toward those to whom personality is ascribed and which at the same time imputes to them certain inescapable liabilities and responsibilities."[192]

We have already seen that all of the historical figures we dealt with in Chapter I, even Royce, regarded God as a person, a kind of superman. We shall assume a personality for God throughout our entire discussion. Without such a personality, as a little reflection will show, we can have no T.P.E.

(1) The ethical thesis

A Being exists, this assumption runs, that is all-good. In calling It 'all-good' the intent is to exclude from It certain properties in (a) Its own Being and (b) in Its own making, and (c) in Its own willing.

(a) This Being has no immoral ontic properties. It has only pro-qualities and is ontologically pure in those pro-qualities It does have. Thus it would seem, contrary to our discussion of the contrast solution and the necessary solution, that God could have in Himself good without any admixture of evil. And this would prove troublesome, in fact an impossibility, to theodicists like Augustine and Leibniz both of whom argued that good without evil would have no meaning. However that may be, the ethical thesis must hold to this kind of ontological purity, and do it with predicates we would all understand, i.e., there cannot be, without becoming obscurantist, an appeal to symbolic or metaphorical meaning. This point bears on the metaphor solution and will be taken up in Chapter III, below.[193] Thus, God must be seen as a superperson throughout this discussion, possessing all the characteristics of a good person; in both what He is and in what He does we must say God is beneficent (a maker of only good things) and benevolent (willing and desiring only the good). Good stands here not only as a term of praise and commendation, but primarily it is ontological in its intent, i.e., it refers to the substance of God which is incorruptible, and 'good' then is predictive of what God could or could not do. Thus 'good' functions ontologically and logically in the first sense; as Augustine states:

> "Why should we say anything more as to the reason why the Substance which in God is not corruptible, for if it were corruptible, it would not be God."[194]

We play on the English 'corruptible', of course, when we say that it follows from the incorruptibility (unchangeableness) of Divine Substance that God would not normally corrupt in his willing or doing. Thus God's nature defines and limits as it were God's possibilities as willer and a doer. Hence we could predict that if God willed or made anything his volition and his creation would both share the character of his nature, they would both be morally uncorrupt, they would be good.

(b) But it is perfectly conceivable, of course, that God has all the ontological goodness possible and be stupid wherein some thing or someone could mislead Him into doing an evil that He Himself was persuaded was good. God might not know the difference between good and evil? Doesn't this raise a problem? This involves a puzzle that goes back to Plato (*Euthyphro*) and that was popularly squabbled about in the Scholastic period of Western thought between the *Volitionists* and the *Intellectionists*, viz., Does God will the good and is that why it's good, or Does God will the good because it's good ?, i.e., is the good dependent on God's will, or separate from it and independent of that will ? Our concern here, of course, is that either way the relation is seen, God could neither will, want, nor do anything that was contrary to the good, whether it be a good He made (hence divinely arbitrary) or a good He looks to or refers to (hence separate from and eternal with God). Thus if God is stupid or simple, and good, He could still not do or will evil. But couldn't He do so inadvertantly, mistakenly ? Would we call a person who makes moral mistakes, but does it in ignorance, 'good' ? We might say, Smith means well, and he's basically a good fellow, but look at the moral mess he's made. If Smith was too simple, I think we'd say he was 'amoral', or even psycho-or socio-pathic. We wouldn't say he was to be praised or commended. Thus if God was stupid or simple it would make no difference to his ontic goodness as long as His willing and His doing, as expressed somehow, were not evil as long as He did good, in other words. Thus it would be quite compatible to have a simple, or even an ignorant deity who was also good, provided only that in His doing, what He did was not immoral.

But suppose He never did anything ? Would we call God good if God just sat and twiddled, amorally, the divine thumbs ? We might say, Smith is good, because he never hurt anybody; Yes, someone might counter, but name someone he has helped; Well, I can't; Then why do you say he's good ? Here the discussion will possibly switch from ethics to ontology, and such a move justifies someone's saying of God, God is good because, although he never interfers in the Creation, it is revealed that He is good. Thus a non-doing, non-effect producing God might still be called good, on ontological, revelatory grounds but not on ethical grounds. Of course one can add that if such a God did do anything what He did would have to be good.

(c) If God is really all-good, then He is benevolent, as well as beneficent (good in all He does), and ontologically moral (good) and wants the best for all. It is still possible, however, for evil, to exist given the characteristics of the all-good being: For this being, good in what It is, makes, and wills, might be nonetheless impotent.

In conclusion, we might say, for those who hold that the

divine personality is all good, certain problems do occur: First, can the divine be all-good without any admixture of evil ?, but then what happens to the contrast solution and the necessary solution as developed by Augustine and Leibniz ? Second, I think it is evident from our discussion that while God may be ontologically good as is implied by Augustine from the very meaning of 'God' in a sort of ontological argument for the goodness of God, there is a question regarding the possibility of God's ethical goodness, His beneficence and benevolence, in the absence of other properties such as wisdom and power: If the road to Hell is paved with good intentions, an all-good but powerless and simple deity could outbid all other contractors for eternity. Finally, what will emerge from this discussion is simply that the three theological theses must hang together in the sense that if one is missing, the other two alone cannot stand. I think this emerges from the discussion above, and will receive fuller treatment below.

(2) The omnipotence thesis

One can treat 'all-powerful' as a noun or as an adjective. Many commentators take it in its noun form and let it go at that. I think it will be helpful to treat it as an adjective, as Augustine does in the *Enchiridion*:

> "For, unless God can do what He wishes and the effective force of His omnipotent will is not impeded by the will of any creature, there is no ground for truly calling Him omnipotent."[195]

It is in His will that God is said to be all-powerful. If all-powerful is taken as a noun it can cover within itself powers unspecified and lead us nowhere, (or everywhere at once). Specifying its adjectival sense will simply facilitate our analysis and keep one other property, omniscience, free for separate discussion below.

To say that God is all-powerful and can do anything has traditionally been hedged upon for there are a number of things which it is denied God can do. Thus Thomas Aquinas has argued, and the tradition has been maintained, that God cannot do the logically impossible, He cannot lift an unliftable stone, or square a circle;[196] and Leibniz, we have seen, argued that God could not do the ethically impossible, he could not make anything but the best possible world, (while Aquinas believed God could have made a better world). Indeed, the presence of God's goodness together with the potency of His will clash over this very issue:

> "If it [the Augustinian tradition of theodicy] insists [with Leibniz] that this is indeed the best possible world, it thereby implies that God was powerless to make a better one, and so denies His omnipotence; but if on the other hand it asserts (with Thomism) that this is not the best possible world, it calls in question God's goodness and love, which were not sufficient to induce Him to will a better one."[197]

There is this problem and defenders of the omnipotence thesis must be prepared to solve it.

To say that God is all-powerful in His will means that God can do anything He wills. But can God will anything? Without getting into a promised regress by answering, He can will it if he wants to, let's assume that God's all-powerfulness relates to what He does will, and let's assume that His willing can be boundless. Now God's doing must be consistent with the ethical thesis, else we run afoul of that first assumption. Thus if God is good in His being, making and willing, God cannot make Himself be wicked, do the wicked, or want the wicked. If we had started with the omnipotence thesis first, then our hedgings must needs still come, i.e., we would have to say, While God is all powerful, and could do, will and be wicked, we must assume that if He is good, what He does, wills and is, will in turn all be good. The point I am driving towards here is better stated by J. L. Mackie in what he calls 'the paradox of omnipotence'. This paradox is best expressed by asking,

> "....can an omnipotent being make things which he cannot subsequently control? Or....can an omnipotent being make rules which then bind himself?"[198]

Whether one answers 'yes' or 'no' to either question, the result is that that being cannot be omnipotent. Thus God is not omnipotent only if He is omnipotent: The paradox of omnipotence. Can God lift the unliftable stone, square the circle, make yesterday come today? In order to *do*, first, the thing-to-be-done must be do-able, i.e., logically do-able. Since as traditionally understood, these three to-be-dones are not really meaningful do-ables at all, they are not to-be-dones in any sense, for they are not possible actions at all. It is not that God's power is limited then, but that these three items are not properly classed as do-ables. We conclude, that God is controlled internally (by his nature) and externally (by logic), and that these limit His doings.

But God might still be all-good and all-powerful, and evil exist and there still be no P.E. Since our task here is to state the conditions for generating P.E., we still lack one such condition. This is significant, for many philosophers and theologians apparently believe the above two theses together with the evil thesis are sufficient for generating P.E.[199] But imagine super Smith who is also good but simple. When a fire breaks out next door super Smith who could stop the fire, and who would want to stop the fire, doesn't stop the fire because he doesn't know about the fire. Who are we to blame? Not simple super Smith. No P.E. can be generated unless we understand that God's goodness and power of will must be accompanied by His knowledge.

(3) The omniscience thesis

If God knows all things, then presumably He knows all events as well, past, present, and future events. A problem arises at this point; for if God can see the future, with all its attendent evils (and goods) all the sufferings and deprivations of creatures, then surely such a God, given his goodness with its attendent sympathy and empathy traits, must be a nervous wreck, wracked with sorrow and pain at what He Himself sees in the future. Thus if super Smith knew who in his town would die, and how and when they would die in the next ten years, and if he was compassionate, loving, empathetic and sensitive, how could he bear the knowledge of those seemingly terrible future events. Super Smith would fly, emotionally, apart, as I suggest would our analogy also if it were based, as it is for most theists who use the theological theses in this way, on such ordinary concepts as *good*, *powerful*, and *knowing*, with a super person as the subject of those predicates. Call this puzzle leading to that emotional cataclysm 'the Cassandra paradox' after that most miserable of seers.

The theist must presumably find ways of limiting his deity such that He will be subject to human-like characteristics, but not to human-like frailties connected with the operation of those characteristics. Thus sensitive super Smith must become detached and cool in the face of all the envisaged suffering—but He must become detached and cool without losing any of the morally approved characteristics attributed to him by the ethical thesis.

Another minor problem would be that super Smith could never come to the point of changing his mind about anything. Thus if Smith knows he will eat hash tonite, because he is all-knowing, then he cannot change his mind, even if he is all-powerful, and eat eggplant instead. It doesn't help to say that Smith would know he was going to change his mind, because that would entail his eating eggplant, and *ex hypothesi* he knows he's going to eat hash.

More seriously, this means that God's knowledge of future events, if "omniscience" does indeed mean that he knows such future particulars, limits his omnipotence, for now God can only will to do those things He knows He will do. But the things He knows He will do, must be things He has the power to do. Hence it seems that God can only will to do the things that He knows He will do, and the things that He knows He will do are those things which He is able to do. His characteristics, power, goodness, and knowledge all interlockingly limit each other. Again, God's freedom of doing, willing and even knowing would appear to be mutually limiting. Call this 'the problem of internal limitations'. A consequence of the problem of internal limitations then is that since God's omniscience limits His power, and His power determines what He will know, then God's omniscience limits what he will know, i.e., it limits itself, in a curious way. This limitation is a sort of intra-divine fatalism. But there may be even more serious problems in calling God good under these circumstances. For if God knows the future and is thereby limited in what He can do by what He knows, in what sense is He good ? Only free beings can be morally good; but beings who have their choices limited in whatever way, beings whose future behavior is compelled because of whatever reason, are surely not free. We say that a man is free under the conditions that if he had wanted to he could have chosen to do differently than he did, and he could have wanted to: He is compelled neither physically nor psychologically. Now quite plainly

God could not do differently than He knows He will do (before the fact). If He does or did differently than He thought He was going to do, then quite plainly He is not omniscient, for He is wrong about something He thought He knew—and plainly God can be no more wrong than He can be wicked or weak. This is a sort of paradox of divine fatalism.

It would seem then that we have what I would call 'the paradox of perfection', where the perfections of all-goodness, omniscience and omnipotence cannot constitute a consistent set of predicates without involving us in a kind of inconsistency where God ends up being either wrong, wicked or weak; or at least it would seem one of the perfect predicates must be inapplicable of God if the others are to be true of God. The problem of internal limitations leads then to the paradox of perfection, and this in turn would seem to point to an inconsistency within the set of predicates attributable to God. The least we can say here, however is that God's personality, His holy and majestic person, is rapidly dissolving, if by 'person' we mean all those things we had intended to mean as mentioned above.

The defender of the theological theses, or the theological position with respect to P.E. must find some way then of handling the paradox of omnipotence, the Cassandra paradox and the paradox of divine fatalism, if he is going to make his position consistent and acceptable: Call these three paradoxes when taken collectively, and when used with reference to the theological theses 'the paradox of perfection'. And indeed the theological defender of the divine perfections has his own solutions to muster in the face of the above puzzles; recall again, e.g., St. Thomas's and our own distinctions about what constituted do-able acts for God or anyone else. Applying the spirit of that defence to the above attacks the theodical defender of the divinely perfect nature need simply retort that certain types of so-called acts, events or happenings are not properly speaking do-able, foreseeable or controllable because those acts, events or happenings, are not *real* do-ables, foreseeables, or controllables. Consequently, for most serious theodicists the above paradoxes and problems connected with the theological theses are not insuperable or insurmountable puzzles.

b. *The Evil Thesis*

Evil must be real, else no P.E. can be generated. Of course, to admit that evil is an illusion is one way of solving P.E. but since we are concerned here in this chapter with the necessary conditions for simply starting that puzzle, we must assume that there is evil. Of the authors that we have examined in thc first chapter, the most overriding forms that evil has taken are sin, the evil that one does, and suffering, the evil that one experiences. Metaphysical evil, which Augustine and certainly Leibniz held to, as the condition of creation itself shot through with limitations, need not concern us: For it is the effects of metaphysical evil (of matter *per se*, for Plotinus, of that original sin in the Garden for Augustine, of the striving, churning, groaning creation which is good but limited for Leibniz, Mill, Royce, and Hick) as sin and suffering that are apparent to us in the world. Thus, for all practical purposes, metaphysical evil is reducible in its working effects, to sin and suffering. Whether there is anything more to metaphysical evil than these effects is beyond the domain of this chapter.

(1) Sin (Deontological evil)

If sin is moral wrong-doing, or transgression of some sort, then there must be some rule or set of rules of an ethical sort that are disobeyed. In the universe, with respect to such doing, there are four possible classes of beings, for our purposes, capable of doing: man, superhuman creatures, subhuman creatures, and nature as the organic world. We can, that is to say, personify each group and say that they are capable of wrong doing with respect to rules Further, each of these four is capable of this sort of personified doing, and their wrongness may be relative to a set of deontological rules and their act which is deemed wrong is wrong in virtue of the act itself being among a set of acts forbidden by the law. Thus if I eat of the forbidden fruit, I am guilty of an act of disobedience simply because it was forbidden to eat that fruit, i.e., the rule says Thou shalt not eat forbidden fruit. I disobey the rule; I have committed, let's say, deontological evil.

I think it is obvious that man and super-human beings possess the capability of disobeying moral rules which are deemed inherently right in themselves (they are, therefore, capable of deontological evil), and they obviously have the capacity to cause suffering to others and themselves. Since both groups, the human and the superhuman, can be aware of moral rules, and can presumably make choices to act on those rules or not, we say that they differ from the subhuman creatures and nature, where choices are instinctive or conditioned (subhuman creatures) or non-existent (nature). Thus all the moral rules, and all the moral cunning and moral persuasion imaginable, won't prevent a squirrel from eating the forbidden fruit, nor prevent a wind from knocking it from its sacred, lofty perch. Consequently, while the subhuman creatures and nature are capable of causing suffering, they are incapable of doing deontological evil.

Now if sin is the transgression of a moral rule of some sort it follows that only humans and superhumans can commit sins or deontological evils. Hence if there is a P.E., and the evil concerned is deontological evil, we can generate only two kinds of P.E. with respect to sin, one for humans and another for superhumans. In its theological form we can then have with regard to sin a theological problem of human evil on the one hand ('Why does an all mighty God permit man to sin ?'), and a theological problem of superhuman evil on the other ('Why did an all mighty God permit Satan to fall into sin ?'). There can be no comparable problem or questions for animals and nature.

(2) Suffering (Teleological evil)

While sin dealt with the doing that is somehow wrong, suffering deals with the effects of doing in general. If a man hits me and I suffer, what he did is *prima facie* wrong. But if a tree falls on me and I suffer, we don't say that what the tree did, was wrong. It just didn't "do" in the sense that it didn't act, but rather was acted upon. But if it was acted upon by wind and certain known casual laws, can we then say that they, the wind and the law of gravity, are wrong for what they did to the tree which the tree then did to me ? No. Obviously not; for what they did was not the kind of conscious, planned doing that is at least one, necessary part of human action. The same must be said about subhuman creatures.

But while subhuman creatures, animals at any rate, cannot be guilty of deontological evil like superhuman and human creatures, they are capable of experiencing suffering, i.e., some people have argued that they do suffer. Thus superhumans and humans can do evil and cause evil, i.e., they can be necessary or sufficient conditions for suffering, for example, and they can do and cause deontological evil by transgressing moral laws, or getting others to sin in this way; further, we will say that subhumans and nature can cause suffering, as necessary or sufficient conditions of suffering among the human and subhuman species, but that they cannot do deontological evil, although they may be instruments in sin, e.g., dogs trained to kill, inorganic and organic poisons, and so on. Further, while superhumans and humans may do evil (sin) and both together with subhumans may cause evil (as conditions for sin and suffering in others), all three are capable of undergoing suffering, teleological evil, let's call it, of experiencing suffering. Nature alone, while it may be a cause in suffering, apparently does not experience suffering. Some would disagree: It is claimed that mandrake roots scream when pulled from the earth, that begonias bleed when cut, that seeds which are hated and plants which are disliked will not grow as well, if at all, as seeds and plants which are loved and fondled, that woodbine twineth round headstones of beloved village vicars, that columbine and morning glory will intertwine in longing and sorrow over graves of star-crossed lovers, that ancient oaks will die in sorrow when ole massa's in his grave, and so on. However, it may be with the botanical world, our concern here will be with the animal, human and angelic universe, since suffering there is most frequently pointed to by those who think ill of theodicies; and, besides, theodicists have enough problems there without being concerned about vines, oaks, and acorns.

Evil as experienced suffering abounds in the triple worlds of damned devils in hell, humans in hell and on earth, and animals on earth. But the suffering that is experienced is of two kinds as we saw from our discussion in Chapter I: ordinary and extraordinary, the justifiable and necessary, and the wholly gratuitous. The form that extraordinary evil takes, the effect it produces on men, is to drive home to man the sheer waste that exists in the universe, the waste that, as Mill pointed out previously, is so rampant in nature. A.C. Bradley has summed up most beautifully what I want to say here, and he does it in the context of Shakespearean tragedy:

> "This [centre of the tragic impression] is the impression of waste. With Shakespeare, at any rate, the pity and fear which are stirred by the tragic story seem to unite with, and even to merge in, a profound sense of sadness and mystery, which is due to this impression of waste. 'What a piece of work is man,' we cry; 'so much more beautiful and so much more terrible than we knew! Why should he be so if this beauty and greatness only tortures itself and throws itself away?' We seem to have before us a type of the mystery of the whole world, the tragic fact which extends far beyond the limits of tragedy. Everywhere, from the crushed rocks beneath our feet to the soul of man, we see power, intelligence, life and glory, which astound us and seem to call for our worship. And everywhere we see them perishing, devouring one another and destroying themselves, often with dreadful pain, as though they came into being for no other end. Tragedy is the typical form of this mystery, because that greatness of soul which it exhibits oppressed, conflicting, and destroyed, is the highest existence in our view. It forces the mystery upon us, and it makes us realise so vividly the worth of that which is wasted that we cannot possibly seek comfort in the reflection that all is vanity."[200]

It is the comfortless, irrational, and inexplicable character of this extraordinary evil that makes it such a challenge to the theodicist. It is the apparently negative character of evil that kills and devours all hope, all solace, all meaning of life:

> "Evil exhibits itself everywhere as something negative, barren, weakening, destructive, a principle of death. It isolates, disunites, and tends to annihilate not only its opposite but itself."[201]

But ultimately it is the waste that haunts us, the destructive, inexplicable, all-devouring waste:

> "We remain confronted with the inexplicable fact, or the no less inexplicable appearance, of a world travailing for perfection, but bringing to birth, together with

> glorious good, an evil which it is able to overcome only by self-torture and self-waste. And this fact or appearance is tragedy."[202]

EDGAR SHEFFIELD BRIGHTMAN strikes a similar note when he says that a difficulty for religion arises when it confronts,

> "....the cruel and irrational waste and the seemingly aimless futility which evolutionary studies have revealed."[203]

This evil, what EDWARD H. MADDDEN and PETER. H. HARE have called "gratuitous evil",[204] serves no apparent purpose, no end, no goal;

> "....unbearable pain and suffering caused either by natural events or the acts of other men, character defects, immoral acts, physical and mental deformity the prosperity of rogues, and the failure of honest men."[205]

And ARTHUR O. LOVEJOY points to the reality of this extraordinary or, as we called it previously, "hard" evil, when he says that the suffering of animals, and the waste when, as WILLIAM JAMES put it, "individual existence goes out in a lonely spasm of helpless agony", these, LOVEJOY says "can never be *aufgehoben*, nullified, or even perfectly compensated."[206]

It is a curious fact, if true, that the reality of these sufferings, this hard evil, may have been, as some authors argue, what first drove men to religion, and at the same time it is what drives others away :

> "Yet the existence of evil is the chief reason for the existence of religion, at least of such religions as promise salvation, and the explanation of evil is the chief problem of all religions and philosophies, and the problem which all alike are conspicuously unsuccessful in solving."[207]

The existence of inexplicable, hard or extraordinary evil, is indeed, cause for giving up belief in the existence of God, as many commentators realize. Thus the author of I Corinthians, 10:13 is wrong when he says, "God is faithful, who will not suffer you to be tempted above that ye are able", i.e., the existence of extraordinary evil, if real, would seem to indicate God is not always faithful, and that God, therefore, isn't the God whom one thought was all good. MADDEN and HARE state the conclusion engendered by this doubt:

> "We are claiming that neither theism nor quasitheism is able both to make sense of the facts of [gratuitous] evil and to have an acceptable concept of God, and that this incompetence constitutes a good reason for rejecting each of them."[208]

And John Hick says:

> "The fact of evil constitutes the most serious objection there is to the Christian belief in a God of love.[209]

Finally, on this same point, HENRY AIKEN comments on this crisis of faith with evil in general when he says :

> "All such ways of overcoming the problem of evil [by making excuses for God, the person] involve, a fundamental breakdown of the monotheistic syndrome or, which comes to the same thing,a fundamental attenuation of the traditional monotheistic faith."[210]

But it is important to remember that it is dysteleological evil, hard, gratuitous evil, extraordinary evil, that leads to such a conclusion. If there is pointless evil, waste, then it would appear that faith in the existence of the traditional good, powerful and omniscient God is a faith in trouble. Any theodicist, of course, worth his weight in apologetics and persuasions, will deny that there is gratuitous, useless, or extraordinary evil. And there's where the philosophical feathers are flying at their thickest.

The problem the theodicist faces, then, is principally one of explaining what to the critics appears as extraordinary evil. He must walk a narrow line, indeed, for if he goes too far to the left, he ends by saying that evil is illusory; too far to the right lands him in the lap of irrationally giving up on explaining evil and resorting to faith. The mystics, according to Royce and as we have seen with Dionysius, take the former way out and hold to the illusion solution; the theologians like Hick take the latter way out and, holding that extraordinary evil is a mystery known but to God, cling to the mystery solution. The philosophic way must be a sort of antinomy of evil, neither ending in the illusion solution nor the mystery solution; a sort of proper distancing of it without losing it or one's reason in the process of distancing. Such a way will, I hope to show, be made evident in our discussion in Part III.

(3) Natural evil and Moral evil

Many critics are inclined to draw a distinction between the evil that man causes, and the evils caused by nature. I think this distincion is superfluous and I want to explain why. The distinction may grow from the dichotomy made by Leibniz between moral and natural evil. But it is used in a slightly different sense by many contemporary writers. The distinction is introduced by them to discredit the man is free solution: If man is the cause of sin and suffering, how then do you explain, for example, the great Lisbon earthquake of 1751. Surely man didn't cause and is not responsible for that? Then the answer involves a distinction between moral evil, suffering caused by man, and physical or natural evil, suffering caused by or through nature. But in Leibniz the matter is more opaque than this. Leibniz, as we have seen, says simply that physical evil is suffering and moral evil is sin,[211] and in this matter follows his mentor Augustine. Further, "Moral evil is an evil so great only because it is a source of physical evils, a source existing in (man) ...."[212] Thus we would seem to be able to conclude that sin causes suffering. But, as we pointed out in discussing these passages previously, this distinction and these conclusions would seem to stand at odds with the contemporary distinction. Leibniz, as we have seen, turns to the teleological solution as a way around apparent evil in nature, and the man is free solution as a way around imputing responsibility to God for sins committed by man in the natural world. But Leibniz' belief that moral evil is a source for physical evil (Would he believe that the great quake of Lisbon in 1751 was entirely due to man's wickedness?) is curious, indeed, but highly useful in showing that current distinctions between moral and physical or natural evil are at most superfluous, and at least misleading. Thus many contemporary philosophers employ a terminology that is distinctly Leibnizian. For instance, Madden and Hare make a rather common distinction:

> "*Physical evil,* we shall say, denotes the terrible pain, suffering, and untimely death caused by events like fire, flood, landslide, hurricane, earthquake, tidal wave, and famine and by diseases like cancer, leprosy, and tetanus—as well as the crippling defects and deformi-

ties like blindness, deafness, dumbness, shrivelled limbs, and insanity....

"*Moral evil*, as we use it, denotes both moral wrong-doing such as lying, cheating, stealing, torturing, and murdering and character defects like greed, deceit, cruelty, wantonness, cowardice, and selfishness."[213]

And MONROE and ELIZABETH BEARDSLEY state :

"Briefly put, *moral evil* consists in wrong actions for which human beings are morally responsible—crime, war, injustice—and *natural evil* is suffering and deprivation."[214]

One can go on to show, and this is the point of the distinction, that natural evils are due to the operation of empirical causal laws, and moral evil is due to human free will, and such laws and such freedom involve God not one whit (we referred to these solutions as the metaphysical evil solution, and the man is free solution, respectively, in Chapter I).[215] CORNMAN and LEHRER follow the same line :

"Moral evil consists of all the evil in the world which is the causal result of those morally responsible agents who exist as part of the world. Natural evil includes all the other evil that there may be.... immense suffering resulting from such natural disasters as earthquakes, floods, draughts, hurricanes...."[216]

And JOHN HOSPERS,

"Natural evils are those that occur in the course of nature without man's intervention: earthquakes, volcanic eruptions, floods, hurricanes, plagues and so on. The catastrophies are not caused by man's activity. Moral evils, however, are those inflicted by men upon other men, such as mental and physical torture, plunder, killing, war."[217]

Finally, JOHN STUART MILL has said :

"These evils ("poverty, oppression and persecution, war") are manifestations of human sin... there remain other sources of pain which are entirely independent of the human will, for example, earthquake, hurricane, storm, flood, drought, and blight."[217a]

My quarrel is simply that in a very real sense physical evils are not independent of human will but quite dependent on it;

they are caused by man's inactivity, and man is as responsible for earthquakes, storms and floods as he is for greed, vanity and avarice. For we must admit first of all that there is nothing inherently evil in floods or earthquakes—it is in the consequences of these natural upheavals that their evil exists. For just as we argued previously that subhuman creatures cannot be said to be capable of deontological evils, so also the inorganic world itself is not shot through in any of its parts with deontological evil, but only instrumentally does it cause others to suffer. But man can control and is learning how to control the forces of nature that cause suffering. That he has not learned to control earthquakes but that he has learned to control floods is a measure of this potential for overcoming the physical 'evil' occurring in nature. When floods occur in the spring or rainy season now, we blame Washington or Delhi and not nature. When a field of grain is destroyed by stem rot, thus causing hunger in a farmer's family, we blame the farmer, not the virus or the rust organisms in the air. Inability to control earthquakes is just as much due to human laziness and inefficiency as is the inability to prevent war, fights in the local saloon, and hangnail.

Thus, as Leibniz wisely saw, moral evil, cupidity, avarice, greed, ignorance and laziness, are the cause or source of physical evils, not "nature" The problem of evil, then, that we are discussing can be treated consequently as a problem of moral evil, where the source of suffering rests in the sins, by omission or commission, of man. This means then, that if this quarrel is resolved in the way proposed, solutions to P.E. must be sought within the human-to-God context and not in the nature-to-God context. Man and man alone is the source of evil. The theological P.E. is considerably simplified by this move for now we have simply to ask 'Why does God permit man to cause extraordinary evil?' Thus 'natural evil' as a designation of the secondary source of suffering may be useful for philosophic purposes (Rule One in philosophy is : When in doubt, make a distinction) but it is highly misleading nonetheless, for it allows man to sit on his heels, blame nature, the sun, the earth, the winds, for his misfortunes, and remain sitting and cursing till Doom's Day : Without the distinction the problem of evil is a problem about man, and the theological problem of evil is a problem about God and man, not about nature. or nature as God-directed.

(4) The kinds of evil

This brings me to a final point then with respect to evil; we have to relate the types or sorts of suffering as well as gratuitous or extraordinary moral evil, i.e., evil caused by man, to P.E. We can, from our previous discussion, assume that suffering of the type we called 'extraordinary' occurs on at least three ontological levels : the superhuman, the human and the sub-human. We can therefore create, as we mentioned in the introduction to this study, at least three P.E. on the theological level, i.e., a T.P.E. for, let's say, angels, man, and animals. Call these

1. 'The theological problem of superhuman evil' (abbreviated "TP SpE"), 2. "The theological problem of human evil' (abbreviated 'TPHE') and finally, 3. "The theological problem of subhuman evil" (abbreviated 'TPSbE').

Since our principal concern has been with moral evil as both deontological and teleological evil, TPSpE and TPSbE will not occupy us at any length, save for one or two passing remarks about them in Chapter III below. But while our principal concern in hunting for solutions in Chap. III will be the concern with TPHE, it is important to consider the significance of both TPSpE and TPSbE in analyzing the theological theses for P.E. in general. Thus if the three theological theses stand and there is eternal suffering in Hell for angels who have fallen there for whatever reason, or there is extraordinary suffering for animals here on earth, then the theodicist must find a way of meeting both TPSpE and TPSbE. Our single concern, however, in noting the solutions that follow in Chapter III will be with their relation to TPHE alone.

3. *Conclusion to Chapter II*

We have now completed the investigation of the theological theses and the evil thesis. A note or two before we proceed. First, given the ordinary meanings as analyzed for "all good", "omnipotent" and "omniscient" and given the meaning of "extraordinary evil" as "wasted suffering", can a case be made for saying that T.P.E. is logically insoluble, i.e., is the set of predicates in the premises of TPE logically inconsistent, such that no theodicy, however ingenious, can possibly salvage from it a God simultaneously existent with evil? I think not. A great deal of time trouble, and effort however, would be saved if one could neatly point to a logical inconsistency amongst the properties of God, such that no acceptable solution would be forthcoming.[218] What might such *apriori* dissolutions of T.P.E. look like ? In general they must turn up an outright contradiction in the divine nature. The most popular form of this is simply to point out that good and evil are ontologically incompatible. That, further, if a Being were to have both properties attributed to Him a logical contradiction would result, such that there could be no such Being, or if there were, it would not be worthy of a disciple's attention. Then what remains is to show the contradictions. We have already dealt with the problems arising for the theological theses' three predicatesof goodness, omniscience, and omnipotence. I don't wish to repeat that here. So let me take the relations ofjuxtapositions between the evil thesis and one or more of the theological theses and attempt to see what possibility for logical contradiction develops when these combinations are looked at separately and severally. There are exactly seven combinations.

1. Evil and Goodness
2. Evil and Omnipotence
3. Evil and Omniscience
4. Evil and Goodness and Omnipotence
5. Evil and Goodness and Omniscience
6. Evil and Omnipotence and Omniscience
7. Evil and Goodness and Omnipotence and Omniscience.

Of these I would contend that the first three, 1, 2, and 3, involve no logical contradictions, i.e., there is nothing to prevent evil in the world and a limited deity from living side by side in logically consistent comfort. Thus for 1, a good but impotent God would presumably hate evil, and live with His frustrations, or create helpers to aid in the overcoming of this uncontrollable evil.[219] For 2, even though the deity were all-powerful he might nonetheless be wicked, and send us rather gleefully the evils we get, and with a spirited but foul heart. As William T. Blackstone has put it :

> "However, the evidence points to at least as much evil and suffering in the world as there is good......and there is even evidence which supports the hypothesis that God, though perhaps omnipotent, is evil and wants living things to suffer.[220]

For 3, it is apparent that all the knowledge possible won't interfere with evil in any logical sense since a wicked, all-wise, or a not all-powerful and all-wise deity is quite compatible with evil in the world.

The interesting analysis, however, comes with the next four combinations. For 4, suppose that there is evil, that Smith, our person who can do incredible things because he has incredible properties, is good or sweet, and all powerful or super. The question is then, can sweet, super Smith be or exist consistently with evil in the neighborhood ? Would we say of sweet, super Smith that he was sweet and super if we knew there was evil ? I think the answer is yes. Smith could be sweet, super but ignorant or simple, and thus live contentedly with an evil he knows nothing about. And if sweet, super, simple Smith can consistently be with evil in the neighborhood, then presumably God could also be or exist without contradiction under analogous circumstances.

For 5, suppose that there is evil, that Smith is sweet and all-knowing or sagacious. The question is then, can sweet, sagacious Smith be or exist consistently with evil in the neighborhood. Yes, I think to a point it is not inconsistent to answer that Smith could exist under such circumstances. But an objection we raised earlier would still obtain viz., that if Smith knew of the existing evils, and the future evils as well, and he was sensitive to them because he was sweet, then he would of necessity fall victim to the Cassandra paradox, doomed to make true prophecies that would never be believed, and doomed to live in anguish and torment because of what is known and what he feels. Thus if sweet, sensitive sagacious Smith falls victim to such torments, presumably a deity with the same personable characteristics would suffer likewise, and thus the paradox; for what kind of deity would one have who lived doomed to impotent anguish ?

An interesting way out of this problem is suggested by NELS F. FERRE, though Ferre uses his ploy as a solution to P.E. The strategy is a species of the personal substance solution, that evil is caused by a personal substance that is wicked, another deity let's say. This sort of Trinity polytheism explains evil for a Christian like FERRE, for only a part of God, the Father, is evil-involved, while the Son, who is all-good, suffers with man and thus, as God, shares man's fate and anguish:

> "The modern world has taken to the idea of a suffering God. It has failed to distinguish between the Father and the Son. It forgets that the Son comes down to bear the Cross *in history*. The idea that the Father suffers with the Son is a heresy."[221]

But FERRE's polytheistic solution, and that's patently what it appears to be, avoids the Cassandra paradox precisely because it is polytheistic. *Our* deity has his sagacity, his sweetness, and his sensitivity all in one lump, and splits and shares with no-one. The price FERRE pays, polytheism, is one few theodicists would be prepared to match.

For 6, suppose that there is evil, and that Smith is super and sagacious. The question is then can sagacious, super Smith be or exist consistently with the neighborhood evil? Again, I think the answer is yes, and precisely because sagacious, super Smith might not be sweet. He might be mean and nasty. He could prevent the neighborhood evil because he's super; he knows all about the neighborhood evil because he's sagacious; but he might not give a damn, Thus there is no contradiction given Smith's properties and the conditicn of the neighborhood. And the same conclusion could be reached about a deity.

As pointed out previously in the paradox of perfection, there is a kind of strangeness in attributing omniscience and omnipotence to a being anyway. Thus God's omniscience puts a limitation on what God will do presumably, for what He knows He will do is precisely what He must do if, indeed, all is known. But when choices are thus limited, when even God cannot do differently than He does do from time immemorial, for eternity, then this 'divine fatalism' as we called it implies a limitation resulting from that omniscience and that omnipotence in juxtaposition.

For 7, suppose that there is evil, that Smith is sweet, super, and sagacious. The question is then, can sweet, sagacious, super Smith be or exist consistently with the evil in the neighborhood? Now we have more or less plugged all the loopholes that we formerly left open. Smith is sagacious, which he wasn't in 4; Smith is super, which he wasn't in 5; and Smith is sweet, which he wasn't in 6. And the neighborhood is torn with suffering and pain. Are Smith's properties consistent with that evil? The puzzle now takes on the shape that it did with Epicurus, and we can produce the famous dilemma mentioned previously. But our question was about properties. Is the property of there being evil consistent with there being properties that know of that evil, would want to prevent that evil, and could prevent that evil? Is existent evil consistent with properties which when combined imply that there can be no evil? Suppose Smith is a sagacious, sweet, super fireman in the town. He hates fire; when he knows that a fire has started and he knows this instantaneously, he puts it out, and he puts it out instantaneously. Everybody has to cook with electricity, no one burns trash, no one lights candles on birthday cakes, no one smokes; strangers who try to light up meet with Smith, red suit and all, in the twinkling of an eye. But suppose one day a fire starts and burns, and Smith doesn't show up. Someone says, Has Smith gone away? Doesn't he care? What's changed him? There seems to be a kind of practical inconsistency, someone might say, between his character and his lack of action. I think one would have to say, further, that the presence of fire in the town we described would seem to have been practically (not logically) impossible given the presence of Smith. Of course, Smith might die or go away. His super powers might not sustain him indefinitely. But these solutions, radical enough to produce a crisis in faith when applied analogically to the cosmos and to our deity, are not a happy way out for the theist, and are consequently rejected. To avoid the conclusion that a logically inconsistent set is present, theodicists, of course, have devised all sorts of schemes and the ways around that conclusion are, of course, notorious. They involve altering, ever so slightly, the characteristics of either evil (fire) (calling it illusory, or "good" for man, or great in the long run, and so on) or deity (Smith) (calling Him a mystery, "super" good not "human" good, a man with a plan, and so on). We have detailed twenty-one or so of these attempted solutions and will turn to them next. It will be our conclusion that TPHE as traditionally put does involve an inherently troublesome though not insuperable problem; more to the point for our purposes here, TPHE cannot be solved by the solutions detailed above in Chapter I; more accurately, given the solutions traditionally open to theists in the West, TPHE is insoluble.

Chapter III

Attempted Solutions to the Theological Problem of Human Evil

1. Philosophical Problems and Solutions

Before beginning on our list of attempted solutions, I think it will be well to ask 'What is a solution to a philosophical problem?' For without an answer to this question we may not know what to look for, nor know when to stop, should we find a solution.

Philosophical problems are notorious, of course, in not having solutions, real solutions. Puzzles of the mind, theoretical puzzles, that are called "philosophical" are frequently given that label precisely because no one has found a universally accepted solution. No one would call "Is 2 plus 2 equal to 4?" a philosophical problem. It's theoretical however in that its solution is not found in any kind of practical activity; neither does it involve an act of faith; but reason alone, given a system of meanings, can answer the question by an appeal alone to those meanings. "Is the house on fire?" is not a philosophical puzzle either, but a practical problem of looking, remembering and acting. For that matter, showing flies the way out of fly-bottles is not a philosophical enterprise either. Ludwig WITTGENSTEIN has his finger on what a problem in philosophy is, though, and what a philosophical solution is like when he says of philosophical problems:

> "These are, of course, not empirical problems; they are solved, rather, by looking into the workings of our language, and that in such a way as to make us recognize those workings: in despite of (*entgegen*) an urge to misunderstand them. The problems are solved not by giving new information, but by arranging what we have always known. Philosophy is a battle against the bewitchment of our intelligence by means of language."[222]

Thus philosophical problems, whatever else they may be, seem to be theoretical puzzles whose resolution must be rational rather than empirical, and always doomed to failure. For when a solution succeeds, the philosophical puzzle ceases to be philosophical. Thus when the Milesians worried over the problem of the ultimate nature of things, whether liquidy or solid or fiery, they worried over a philosophical problem. Science eventually answered the problem for the metaphysicians and now no philosopher puzzles over precisely that puzzle any more. Thus philosophical problems when they get solved cease to be philosophical. It is indeed a puzzle's apparent insolubility by reason alone then, that is one of the necessary characteristics of a philosophical problem. Indeed, P. E. for many theologians is not a philosophical or even a theological problem at all. Evil, they might contend, is necessary to the religious life, a challenge to it, and not a potential threat or refutation of that life. Their solutions we will examine shortly. Rather than attempt to define a philosophical problem any further, rather than try to distinguish it from engineering problems, religious problems, population problems, and so on, I would simply remind the reader that philosophy historically abounds in puzzles, and that whatever they all might seem to share, whatever that is, it must in some way make up the nature of a philosophical problem. If WITTGENSTEIN is right, these problems at least all share the form "I don't know my way about."[223] The solution lies then in learning one's way about and escaping the enchantment thrown upon us by our language.

It is one thing to be enchanted, and another to merely feel enchanted, however. Philosophical problems are not solved when the irritation of doubt disappears, or when the feeling of disenchantment reigns. If this is all a philosophic solution were, then pills and prayers and psychiatry could relieve our feelings, doubts, and irritations in a thrice. Philosophical problems are not subjective, psychological problems that disappear with the sunrise, the full moon, and human or demi-human wiles. The philosopher wants reasons, a standard criterion for being able to say "Ah, there, that's the answer to the puzzle. I see and understand : the solution measures up to the criteria I have set." But though standards are essential we still want to avoid such obvious relative and simplistic standards as those implied by saying as BOYD H. BODE has :

"The whole problem of evil is the problem of reconciling

> divine power with the requirements of what we ordinarily consider to be moral and social standards."[224]

"Ordinarily considered social standards" are too varied and fluctuating to be a standard for much of anything as ethical theorists are at pains to point out, and as young men of draft age soon discover much to their sorrow. Such criteria would mean that one society might indeed solve the problem of evil and another not, simply because let's assume, one society has a high or low tolerance for pain, suffering or evil, and the other does not.

I think a more rationally objective approach is to take criteria which all might be said to agree on, criteria which are not social but, let's say, philosophical.

Three Criteria for Solutions to TPHE

Therefore, I want to propose rather dogmatically that an acceptable solution to any philosophical problem must satisfy three criteria. The criteria are those of common sense, consistency and completeness. Let me briefly explain what I mean with respect to TPHE :

(1) Common sense (A subjective criterion)

The solution to TPHE and to T. P. E. in general, must be couched in non-technical, ordinary language, or where technical terms are employed, they must be defined in that language. Further, while the language must be clear so as to obviate obfuscation and ambiguity, the solution itself must meet standards of naturalness and believability. Thus if someone argues that evil is caused by creepy, pink devils that are everywhere and lets it go at that, while the language is clear insofar as the words are understandable, the thought expressed stretches the standards of justifiable credulity. What I have in mind is the kind of thing MARY BAKER EDDY says about evil in her book, *Science and Health with Key to the Scriptures*, about which JOHN HICK comments :

> In this book, with its confused medley of half-digested philosophical themes, Mrs. EDDY taught 'the nothingness and unreality of evil.'[225]

To avoid such confused medleys, if they are indeed that, we introduce the common sense criterion.

This criterion I also call 'subjective' in that it relies on the educated and enlightened feelings of the critic. We said earlier that the problem of evil arises because of the felt inexplicability of evil (cf. Ch. I-1 above), together with that real evil. This 'felt inexplicability' is of course a subjective notion. When one feels the problem that's the beginning of the problem. One may go on from there surely to develop more formal criteria for showing just why it is a problem. Similarly when one feels that the problem has been resolved, when one feels no longer the bewitchment that only philosophical puzzles can engender, then that is the beginning of the solution to the problem. This subjective criterion merely serves to remind us to follow our intuitions and our hunches and our feelings as a first step in reacting to proposed solutions.

(2) Consistency (A formal criterion)

The solution to T.P.E. must be stated such that there are no internal logical inconsistencies in the solution itself. Thus to say that evil is caused by a God who is all good and all not-good, violates the criterion of consistency. The inconsistency to be tested for must be a logical one involving blatant contradiction.

(3) Completeness (A practical criterion)

The solution, or solutions to T.P.E. must be complete in explaining all the puzzles that could be raised with respect to the problem. Thus if someone uses the argument that evil disciplines man's character, he must also, if his solution is to be complete, similarly explain animal suffering and the pains of the mute and the innocent, if such there be. For a solution to explain only some of the puzzles arising in T.P.E. is to have no solution.

Thus in what follows we shall use the criteria of common sense, consistency, and completeness as standards of measurement in examining the solutions to T.P.E. We can say that any adequate solution must work within the limits or expectancies of the above three criteria, and run afoul of none of them.

Let me begin by referring the reader once more to the twenty-one solutions of Table IV.

2. Some Reductions

The solutions to T.P.E. listed in Table IV are repetitious to say the least. All 1-21, are taken from historical sources. And all, if applied to T.P.E., might seem able to dissolve that puzzle, some satisfactorily perhaps, keeping in mind our criteria of what a solution must do to be an adequate solution, some unsatisfactorily in that they would not pass the test established by our standard. The solutions align themselves under a number of possible heads and a strategy for finding the least common denominator for these solutions might be sought. First, separate those that relate to the theological theses from those that naturally fall under the evil thesis. Following this we could relate those falling under the theological theses to the three separate elements of the theses, the ethical, omniscience and omnipotence theses, and possibly begin our reductions under these headings. I'm going to eschew these approaches for the moment in favor of a more intuitive strategy. I think this more obvious move is simply to get rid of all repetitions, and once that task is finished see where we stand. Keeping the table of solutions in mind let's try this approach.

There are certain obvious reductions that seem to gather around the aesthetic solution, e.g., the contrast solution, that evil is necessary in order to highlight the good; and the recompense solution, that the good that will come in the end, Heaven, makes the evils endured now justifiable; and finally the outweighs solution, that goods outweigh evils, so the evils we have now are not so bad compared with that later good. In all these cases, the end result, the Whole, Heaven, the final good that comes from evil or that is pointed up by evil, is itself better and more rewarding than those collective smaller parts that are evil. Call this syncretized solution that synthesizes the contrast, recompense and outweighs solutions by the single but familiar name, 'the aesthetic solution'.

Next, the discipline solution, obviously includes the teleological solution, that good will ultimately come from evil; further even the recompense solution may be included here on one of the soul-building interpretations, viz., where evil makes us worthy of Heaven by preparing us ahead of time, now, for eternity later. The recompense solution can thus be treated here or under the aesthetic solution above. Call this 'the discipline solution' and recall that it includes the teleological solution and under one interpretation, the recompense solution as well.

Further, the explanation of evil as the work of free will, the man is free solution, can easily be combined with the justice solution, that God sends punishment to man for his sins committed now, or in a past life, the rebirth solution. Call this solution that combines these three solutions by another familiar name, 'the man is free solution'.

Next, the illusion solution, that evil is an illusion, has obvious affinities with the privation solution, that evil is merely privation of good and is in itself non-being. Call the sólution that combines these solutions 'the evil is illusion solution'

Further, the view that God is limited in his power over evil, the world, and man, is represented in the not all-powerful solution which, while not a *bona fide* solution at all as we have argued above should be analyzed further since it has certain obvious similarities with four other attempted solutions. Hence we will retain the category of the not all-powerful solution and treat these four other solutions under it. They are : the impersonal substance solution, that an impersonal, or the personal substance solution where a personal, separate substance causes evil; the metaphysical evil solution that an imperfection in the creation causes evil; the worse alternative solution, that God hates evil but approves of the evils we have because the alternatives are worse; the prevention solution, that evils are necessary to prevent greater evils; and the creator limitation solution, that God's choices were limited by what was possible. So we call the solution that combines all these several solutions 'the not all-powerful solution'.

This bit of cryptic maneuvering can be justified by the fact that in analyzing the eight solutions that now remain we will be careful to include those parts previously separated but now synthesized, where and when treating or analyzing those parts separately is called for. Let me now renumber and redescribe our eight solutions in Table V. The strategy of this Chapter III will be essentially that carried out on a smaller scale by J. L. MACKIE in "Evil and Omnipotence"; commenting later in a review of JOHN HICK's *Evil and the God of Love*, MACKIE summed up that earlier work and took a stab at HICK simultaneously :

> "In a wide-ranging historical survey, and in his own struggle to develop a solution, HICK provides an unintentional confirmation of the claim I made in an article eleven years ago : All the possible solutions of the problem of evil can be grouped under a small number of headings[226] and then can be systematically shown to be inadequate as defenses of orthodox theism."[227]

Three of our previous solutions, however, are not as easily reducible so we include them here (items 6-8) as we found them previously in Table IV.

TABLE V

Name	*Description*
1. Aesthetic Solution	The whole is good because (even though) the parts are not.
2. Discipline Solution	Evil disciplines man, and builds his character.
3. Man is Free Solution	Evil is the result of free will.
4. Evil is Illusion Solution	Evil is not ultimately real, but an illusion.
5. Not All-powerful Solution	God is not all-powerful.
6. Necessary Solution	Evil is logically and metaphysically necessary for the existence of good.
7. Metaphor Solution	The language describing God is merely metaphorical.
8. Mystery Solution	Evil is a mystery.

A few general remarks before we continue with the analysis of these several solutions. First, there are some curiosities in the list; item 5 patently contradicts one of the theological theses and is consequently not a solution at all; item 4, seems to contradict the evil thesis but this is not really the case as we shall show, hence it is a *bona fide* solution candidate; item 7, the metaphor solution leads to a giving up on the puzzle by challenging the language of the entire set of theses needed to generate T.P.E. while item 8, the mystery solution is also the result of irrationally giving up on the puzzle but by undercutting the evil thesis. Second, judging by the literature current on T.P.E., the solutions we have ended with are more or less historically typical; in other words, as will be apparent shortly, our reductions have not, it would seem, thrown out solutions we ought otherwise have dealt with. Third and finally, the list of solutions in Table V does not pretend to be more historically complete than were the solutions in Table IV. I have tried to deal with the most historically typical solutions the literature affords; I have eschewed the typical ones where they appeared obscure or unenlightening. For example here are two : the view that evil is pain and pain warns us of dangers in this world and the next, and thereby bids us change our ways, is a species of the discipline solution; that Christ's resurrection seals evil's docm and destroys all evil is a species of the no-evil solution; but the first of these I find unenlightening, and the second obscure. Other similar examples abound in the literature, but I think from our previous discussion it is obvious that whatever the pretended solution might be it must relate to one or another of the assumptions in the theological theses or the evil thesis itself, or all four together as the mystery solution seems to do. It must relate to the set of these theses in such a way that their apparent practical inconsistency can be explained. The strategy will now be to state the attempted solution, spend some time describing it in the contemporary literature, and then show how it fails of the standard we have adopted for an adequate solution.

3. Eight Solutions and their Analysis

The strategy in this section will simply be to state the attempted solution, try to clarify its various parts where necessary by referring to the more modern literature, and then measure it as a solution against our standard for adequacy. There will be some patently glaring problems with some of the solutions, such that simply pointing out their obvious absurdities, implicit or explicit, will allow us to reject the solution as inadequate. Others again may have to be tortured and manipulated before they give up the ghost of credibility. It should come as no surprise, then, from what has been said here-tofore, that I intend to show that all eight (i.e., twenty-one) solutions fail somewhere, and that all are patently inadequate for solving T.P.E. in general and TPHE in particular :

1. The Aesthetic Solution : The whole is good because (even though) the parts are not.

The position as we have seen is ably represented by AUGUSTINE, LEIBNIZ, and ROYCE. ROYCE seems to sum up the view when he says :

> "The wise man contents himself, as far as possible, with the knowing, in general, that there is an indefinitely vast range of voluntary finite evil-doing which, in the temporal order, has to be endured, and for which atonement must be temporally rendered, in order that the divine will may be eternally accomplished."[228]

And JOHN HICK says of this view in Christian thought :

> "Christian theodicy claims, then, that the end to which God is leading us is a good so great as to justify all the failures and suffering and sorrow that will have been endured on the way to it."[229]

This synthesized solution is formed from the recompense solution and the teleological solution among others, and these three views admit the existence of evil but contend that it is worth the greater good. The greater good is identified in various ways in the literature. It may be Heaven, as we have seen, or it may be some kind of organic whole or unity. G.E. MOORE describes such a unity in his *Principia Ethica* :

> "But, as a matter of fact, I cannot avoid thinking that there are wholes, containing something positively evil and ugly, which are, nevertheless, great positive goods on the whole."[230]

And both this view and the view that Heaven or the extended life of the individual must be taken as part of the whole is stated by ROYCE :

> "All finite life is a struggle with evil. Yet from the final point of view the Whole is good. The Temporal

> Order contains at no one moment anything that can satisfy. Yet the Eternal Order is perfect. We have all sinned, and come short of the glory of God. Yet in just our life, viewed in its entirety, the glory of God is completely manifest."[231]

Thus the view being put across whether ROYCE's or not, entails in essence that the evil suffered now is worth the good that will come from it later. It is consequently a sort of 'jam tomorrow, but no jam today view'.

The aesthetic solution holds on its aesthetic side that the good in the whole is heightened by contrast with the evil in the parts, just as a painting is made more beautiful by its dark and sombre colors contrasted with its lighter, happier tones—the parts are individually dark and foreboding or happy and gay, but collectively the whole is just beautiful. This in essence is what the aesthetic solution comes to then : The whole is better than its parts, and in some way justifies those parts. But some criticisms will have to be met by those who accept the aesthetic solution : The jam-tomorrow argument, as I shall call that aspect of the aesthetic solution which says that the reward will come later when all is revealed, serves to underscore or support the you-can't-see-it-now argument, as I shall call that aspect of the aesthetic solution which says that the whole can't be seen now but only the parts. Both jam-tomorrow and you-can't-see-it-now rest upon the analogy with the painting argument or a scriptural argument that promises a happy future life after this one.

The painting analogy argument differs, of course, from the actual situation in two important respects DAVID HUME in his *Dialogues Concerning Natural Religion* has an attack similar to the one we propose, wherein he goes after the argument from design which had been used to prove the existence of God) :

(1) We have seen paintings, the parts of them and the whole work itself. But who has seen the actual universal whole ? The argument for the aesthetic solution rests on the assumption that there is an organic whole called the Universe, and of course this would have to be proved in some sense. But the you-can't-see-it-now argument obviates such a proof.

(2) Further, while parts that are dark do indeed heigh-

ten the painting's aspect by contrast with the lighter areas, what assurance has anyone that evil heightens the whole by contrast with the good? The argument assumes that good and evil are opposites in the same sense that light and dark are. But while each set is a set of opposites it would have to be shown in what precise way evil and dark are alike in their contrastive abilities with good and light respectively. And finally, even if this could be done what assurance have we that the whole is thereby made better because of evil, since we have not seen the whole. To say 'Wait and see' is no argument. To return to analogies with paintings helps not at all, for it has to be shown in what way paintings are like unseen wholes; and how anything seen can be like that which is unseen, perhaps unseeable, is indeed a puzzle.

(3) If the suggestion is made, as both jam-tomorrow and you-can't-see-it-now seem to do, that scripture is the source for the promise, then we are at once involved in a new discussion, the justification of scripture, which discussion is always notoriously inconclusive.

(4) A final thrust is sometimes made by the aesthetic solution defender, and that is to resort to what I shall call the Have-faith argument. This move is really a species of the mystery solution in which evil and the relation of it to God and man becomes a mystery wherein man must trust in God and knowing that God is all-good, all-wise and all-powerful, he is assured that the outcome will be for the best. But this begs our whole question all over again, viz., if there is evil in the parts of the whole how can God have those properties that are claimed for him? To say, Well, He does, is no argument.

(5) Another devastating counter to the aesthetic solution is simply to ask, Why so much evil? Why must children suffer so? and here the literature dealing with the problem is immense, from ALBERT CAMUS' *The Plague* to FYODOR DOSTOIEVSKY's *The Brothers Karamozov*, to AUGUSTINE himself, as we have seen previously. The question is not a question about soft evil, "Mommy, why does my tooth hurt?", but hard evil, gratuitous evil, or to give the aesthetic solution its due, "apparently" gratuitous evil, what we called "extraordinary evil"; why is there so much? We saw that JOHN HICK in the face of the evidence from the Nazi death camps, resorted to the

mystery solution as the only answer. If just sheer quantity of evil drove one rather hearty defender of the aesthetic solution to the mystery solution, perhaps this is a harbinger of what other aesthetic solution defenders would also do when faced by similar extraordinary evil.

(6) Further you-can't-see-it-now and the jam-tomorrow responses to extraordinary evil look rather ridiculous without the mystery solution. And if all these rest on the mystery solution then we shall have to wait until we get to it for a reply.

Conclusion

It might seem that the aesthetic solution as a solution to TPHE runs afoul of the criteria for an adequate solution. For the reply of the aesthetic solution defender becomes uncommonsensical when he speaks of, or has to speak of, unobservable wholes that one cannot now observe but that can be "seen" someday. The language about such wholes, that is to say, is obscure.

Further, and most damaging, the aesthetic solution cannot explain extraordinary suffering—there is no apparent reason, even if the aesthetic analogy were to hold up, why the divine Artist needed so damned much suffering in His Creation. The aesthetic solution cannot explain satisfactorily, for instance, intense suffering in children; it is consequently incomplete.

Finally, the aesthetic solution would have to show in what way a future good justifies a present evil, under the following circumstances: where that future good is an organic whole whose existence cannot now be described or determined save by questionable analogy; where some present evils are so unquestionably unbearable as to jeopardize any such promised future good. If the individual person is the whole that is being perfected by evil in the manner described, and suppose we are not talking about universes now, then that is a whole we can see. But then we are speaking about the discipline solution so let's turn there next.

2. The Discipline Solution: Evil disciplines man and builds his character.

There is an obvious affinity between the discipline and aesthetic solutions in that both make promises about jam-tomorrow and both rest upon a kind of well-even-if-you-can't-see-it-done-now-its-going-to-happen argument.

We have seen the soul-building argument in JOHN HICK and also in JOSIAH ROYCE. Here is one example of it from J. W. N. SULLIVAN in his book on Beethoven :

> "But to the vast majority of people suffering is still one of the fundamental characteristics of life, and it is their realization that an experience of suffering, pure and profound, enters as an integral part into Beethoven's greatest work, that helps to give that work its unique place in the minds and hearts of men."[232]

Thus suffering is justifiable because of its results in men. Later in commenting on the *Grosse Fuge* and the magnificent *Hammerklavier* sonata, he says :

> "To be willing to suffer in order to create is one thing ; to realize that one's creation necessitates one's suffering, that suffering is one of the greatest of God's gifts, is almost to reach a mystical solution of the problem of evil, a solution that it is probably for the good of the world that very few people will ever entertain."[233]

The German romantic tradition that found sympathetic friends across the world from COLERIDGE and WORDSWORTH to EMERSON, ROYCE, and even DOSTOIEVSKY argued strenuously that man is ennobled through suffering. LEIBNIZ had said,

> "These evils serve to make the elect imitators of their master, and to increase their happiness."[234]

And certainly pain becomes more bearable when it is believed that it is for the soul's ennoblement and preparation for Heaven :

> "The pains He (Christ) had to bear may not give you and me a theory about pain, but they help us to bear pain... He who triumphed through pain is with them in all their darkness and suffering."[235]

Thus both spiritual and manly growth could be expected from exposure to pain and suffering, and it is assumed, of course, that it is pain and suffering undergone oneself rather than pain and suffering administered *a la* Marquis de Sade. It is frequently argued, for example, that man's sympathy and compassion would not be aroused unless there were suffering in the world. Thus NELS F. S. FERRE in *A Philosophical Scrutiny of Religion* argues that evils are spread widely and generally, and not according to merit, just so that man's social nature, which involves the capacity for compassion, love, and sympathy, might develop and flourish.[236]

One might think that if we switch the program from the discipline solution in TPHE to the same solution in TPSbE and ask about animal suffering, that the defenders of the discipline solution might be stopped. But this is not necessarily the case. It is argued by C. S. LEWIS for example[237] that the survival of the fittest through the mechanism of natural selection depends on pain in animals; and AUSTIN FARRER[238] argues that pain is necessary for the simple survival of animals. Two brief comments :

(1) I think such arguments, whether they interpret the discipline solution as applying to fitting animals to survive or man to grow, run afoul of the same conclusion reached in the aesthetic solution: Granted that evil is necessary, important, and worthwhile, why is there so much ? For example, how does the death of a child under the extremist conditions of cruelty and horror help build character or make souls ? But why pick a child ? When anything dies, cruelly tortured and suffering, is there any reason to believe that necessarily souls will be built, that the fit will be driven to survive ?

(2) The defender of the discipline solution is hard put at this point, for he must show that every case of evil must lead to soul building. If he admits to one case of gratuitous, inexplicable evil, e.g., as JOHN HICK did with the victims of the death camp, then the discipline solution as well as the aesthetic solution are both lost. It is wishful thinking, I suspect, and unduly optimistic to assume that all evil does indeed build souls.

Conclusion

Prima facie the discipline solution cannot explain suffering in animals since traditionally they have no "souls" to be disciplined. But the discipline solution can be altered such that what is implied by it is the possibility of survival through pain. While this avoids the difficulty of this solution's being incomplete, it does so in the face of extraordinary evil which must not be called senseless or gratuitous. It seems at this point to violate common sense, for there just seem to be, as JOHN HICK seems willing to admit, inexplicable cases of evil in the world which do not build character or lead to survival : How about glaciers that wiped out whole species of now extinct animals who must have died under excruciating torture from cold and hunger ? If the defender of the discipline solution leaps to a wait-and-see type of argument, then we are back again with the mystery solution. As PETER BERTOCCI has said in a very low-keyed way :

> "It is all too easy to forget that in a given life, suffering, especially to the degree often experienced, is neither merited nor necessary to deepen appreciation."[239]

Evil very often ennobles man's soul, but just as often it is likely to destroy it. And there's the rub.

Finally suppose that evil matures souls, won't it then be to my advantage to rush around doing all the evil I can, producing suffering wherever possible, ennobling souls and building character all over the world ? My good deed would be to do evil deeds: Utilitarians would have to rewrite their books, *Mind* and *Philosophical Review* would be swamped with papers on *The New Immorality*, masochists and sadists might become paragons of public behavior, the outrageous would become the rage.

Defenders of the discipline solution have their work cut out for themselves, indeed.

3. The Man is Free Solution: Evil is the result of free will.

To begin with, the man is free solution is obviously not going to answer TPSbE, nor will it in any satisfactory way settle the problem of suffering in children, for neither animals nor very young children have free will, nor do they always get the suffering they deserve. The man is free solution is incomplete as a theory right from the start. But this solution is worth exploring, nonetheless, for quite recently a great deal has been written about it by professional philosophers, and these people are always enjoyable to watch.

The man is free solution holds essentially two theses: First, the evils man gets are the result of something he did;

Second, the evils man gets are the results of something he is in virtue of something that someone else did. The second view is meant to encompass the belief that in Adam sinned we all, i.e., when original man exercised his own will it was in one instance at least an act contrary to God's will. The result was that suffering entered the world by that act of first disobedience : So just in virtue of being a man I, too, am fallen, depraved, and am now subject to suffering, even though it was not my act but Adam's that was the efficient cause of the fall and the sin and thence the suffering. This view we found in AUGUSTINE and it has been ably represented by JOHN CALVIN in the 16th century.

The first thesis is plainly explained, e.g., by JOSIAH ROYCE when he says :

> "......I can indeed say, in-general, that all ill fortune results from the defects, or at least from the defective expression, of some finite will."[240]

ROYCE's way of putting the problem could account for suffering in children and animals, i.e., they suffer because men let them. If men were conscientious enough in the exercise of their duty, neither animal nor child need suffer anywhere in the world. There is a problem, of course, connected with the state of the world before the arrival of man, and in this sense there is an incompleteness to the man is free solution. But as we saw previously, if physical or natural evil, storms and earthquakes, can be treated as, or reduced to moral evil then there seems to be no *prima facie* reason why man is not responsible by omission or commission, for all evils in the world at least now if not in the human past. H. J. PATON, while not agreeing with the position, has summed it up as follows :

> "The problem of moral evil.... (is) if men are to be good, they must be free; and if they are free, they must be free to do wrong; and it is impossible to separate wrong-doing from wrong suffering."[241]

With regard to the second thesis it might be asked, why didn't God either prevent the Fall, or stop man now from sin, since both lead to such suffering? To this suggestion ALVIN PLANTINGA has answered that it is logically incoherent for God to create beings who would always act rightly, and he defends on grounds such as this the consistency of God and evil.[242]

JACQUES MARITAIN in *God and The Permission of Evil*, returns to the Thomist solution, that while man causes evil, God can only cause good :

> "....we must hold with Saint Thomas that every creature is naturally fallible ; God can no more make a creature, angel, or man, naturally impeccable than He can make a square circle."[243]

Finally, JOHN HICK has stated the logical nature of the argument, hence the similarity of the man is free solution to the necessary solution is disclosed, when he says,

> "In creating God must either produce another reality on the same level of perfection as Himself—in fact another God—or else a creaturely realm which is inferior to its Maker. The first alternative is ruled out as absurd; whence it follows that the creation must be less perfect than its Creator...imperfect."[244]

(1) The obvious challenge to HICK's argument is, Why is the first alternative so absurd? Presumably, as we shall see in a moment, because anything that is created cannot be perfect. But who says so and when? There are surely types of perfection. Why stick with metaphysical perfection ("eternal", "uncreated", and perhaps even "circular"—that latter was a favorite criterion of metaphysical perfection for Parmenides; shall we now include that too)? We are aiming here at moral perfection, anyway, not metaphysical perfection. Surely, unless God Himself is some sort of automaton, man can be morally perfect also without being a machine—if God is morally perfect.

(2) On the one hand, it would seem that God is limited by the logical possibilities of the situation, (see the necessary solution below), or limited internally by His own potential, (see the not all-powerful solution below). But the upholders of the man is free solution want to argue that it's neither a matter of possibilities nor power but instead one of logical contradiction. Thus square circles, if that means squares that are not squares, and perfect creations, if that means perfections that are not perfect, are according to this view both on the same level of contradictoriness. But could God create a being that he couldn't control? It would seem we have a choice between accepting that, as opposed to a being that could never be perfect.

(3) We don't have to go to such metaphysical extremes to see that while God needn't have created a perfect being (couldn't have) he needn't have created such an imperfect one. There is no justification for as much imperfection as there is, as much hard evil as there is as a consequence of free will. Why is the imperfection so damned imperfect?

(4) If God is omniscient and knows all further events, there is a genuine question as to how much freedom His "free" creatures have, for in a very real sense, if I am going to run over a man tomorrow, and sagacious Smith knows it, then I cannot do differently than sagacious Smith knows I am going to do tomorrow. And if I cannot do differently (have no real choice between running-over and not-running over) than Smith knows I am going to do, then that is sufficient reason to say I am not free. To say God permits me to act this way, is quite beside the point. The issue here is not God's involvement with evil, but simply my freedom to have choices and to act on those choices. There is plainly an inconsistency here which the defender of the man is free solution must look to.

(5) There is another dimension of this solution that must be mentioned, and that is this: The evil that occurs, the suffering and the deeds that lead to suffering, may indeed all (moral as well as physical) be due to man. We have assumed this throughout. And we have assumed that this is due to the exercise of his will in this life. But there are certain events involving untold suffering that cannot be laid to the exercise of free will, e.g., those apparently fortuitous events that happen purely by accident; many examples of this class of accidents were formerly referred to as physical or natural evils. Thus Jones gets on the wrong train and it crashes, killing him, and we ask "Why Jones?" Or a flood carries away an entire village and thousands die. I am thinking of those events in which not man but apparent chance plays such an important part. Or take birth defects, those which happen because of quite spontaneous mutations in genes or alterations in the foetus. Why have they occurred to this child or that child, and to them alone? The explanation for this type of seemingly inexplicable evil cannot be held to free will in this life—frequently no will at all is present. The solution we called 'the rebirth solution' has been raised by some philosophers to account for those ex-

amples of seemingly chancy physical evils; I want to treat this whole question later in Parts II and III. For the present it is enough to say that the man is free solution will be hard put to explain such seemingly non-free-willed events simply because no will at all seems to be involved in their production. Again, I am not giving up my previous point that all so-called natural or physical evils can be reduced to moral evil. That argument seems obvious to me and it still stands. What I am suggesting now, however, is that there is a class of events that may be due to chance and that are not in principle caused by human will or design, e.g., spontaneous cell mutation causing organic defects and suffering. It is with this class of events, if there really are any, that the defenders of this solution must make their peace.

Conclusion

The man is free solution will have to answer the charge that it is apparently inconsistent in holding that God, with all His properties, permitted man to be created knowing what He knew, and escape culpability in the result. For it would seem to imply that God is responsible at one remove at least for the evil that goes on, for he created man knowingly.

Baron Paul Henri d' Holbach (1723-1789) in his book, *Le Bon Sens*, translated in 1856 as *Good Sense* by J. P. Mendum, stated the problem as follows :

> "God is the author of all; and yet, we are assured that evil does not come from God. Whence then does it come? From man. But, who made man? God. Evil, then comes from God. If He had not made man as he is, moral evil or sin would not have existed in the world. The perversity of man is therefore chargeable to God."[245]

And we would appear to be involved in the dilemma that if God created man imperfect because He had no choice, (and it is not clear that God could not have made man more perfect, if not wholly perfect, *pace* St. Thomas), then God is not all-powerful; if God created man imperfect and chose to do so willingly, then God is responsible at a second remove for the evil that man does, for God is omniscient and knew what man would do.

A further inconsistency plainly develops between what God knows man will do and the imputation of free will to man : You cannot have free will and antecedently limited choices. Logical incoherence or practical inconsistency plainly develops around joining divine omniscience and human free will.

Finally, this solution is incomplete for it plainly cannot account for suffering in animals or children since, as far as we know, they have no will, i.e., no deliberative power of choice. And so, insofar as they have no will, the man is free solution becomes incomplete when it attempts to solve TPSbE.

4. The Evil is Illusion Solution : Evil is not ultimately real.

The unreality of evil was introduced by ROYCE in his criticism of the mystical view of evil, and is familiar in SPINOZA, certain German Idealists like HEGEL, English Idealists who followed HEGEL's Absolute Idealism, like T. H. GREEN, and, if ROYCE is right, mystics in general in the Western tradition. Thus SPINOZA says,

> "....that all things are necessarily what they are and that in Nature there is no good and no evil."[246]

It is difficult to know what it is that is being denied here. The evil is illusion solution surely violates common sense if it is taken in a bald, open faced form (in fact in its bald form it, like the not all-powerful solution, cannot be a solution to T.P.E. at all). Men suffer and there's an end to it ! BERTRAND RUSSEL says of this view called "mysticism" and its attitude towards evil :

> "The last of the doctrines of mysticism which we have to consider is its belief that all evil is mere appearance, an illusion produced by the divisions and oppositions of the analytic intellect. Mysticism does not maintain that such things as cruelty, for example, are good, but it denies that they are real : they belong to that lower world of phantoms from which we are to be libearted by the insight of the vision."[247]

Thus PLOTINUS and AUGUSTINE, as we have seen, deny metaphysical reality to evil with their privation solution, but neither wishes to deny that man suffers. Thus the metaphysical status of evil need not really concern us. It is with the fact of suffering that we must contend, and men do suffer.

The status of the no-evil solution has been debated in the

literature; thus H. J. McCloskey in "God and Evil" has contended :

> "Some theists seek a solution by denying the reality of evil or by describing it as a 'privation' or absence of good. They hope thereby to explain it away as not needing a solution."[248]

John Hick disagrees with this interpretation of the privative doctrine and in *Evil and the God of Love* he claims that the notion of evil as privation was not offered as a solution to T.P.E.,[249] but simply as an explanation of the nature of evil. We have treated the evil is illusion solution as a full-blooded possible solution to T. P . E. (and not as an outright contradiction of the evil thesis) and the reader need only recall our presentation of Augustine in Chapter I as ready proof that the good Saint and those mystics in the Plotinian tradition saw it precisely as a solution to T.P.E. (that depended, of course, on the explanation of evil as privation).

(1) But this solution has come in for some common sensical hard knocks, whether evil be seen in its metaphysical aspect as non-being, or as just an illusion because it is less than real. Thus Henry Aiken challenges it as a notion inimical to the whole Judeo Christian tradition :

> "No ordinary Jew or Christian, so far as I can see, could entertain it for more than a moment ("evil, that is to say, is merely apparent, and the common view that such things as earthquakes, insanity, and cancer are evils is illusory"), for it makes nonsense of the moral life. If nothing is evil, choice is pointless, and responsibility has no meaning."[250]

The suggestion that evil is non-existent is like the suggestion that evil is good as under the discipline solution above. And we've seen what non-sense the soul-making solution can lead to when carried out far enough.

(2) Another commentator echoes Aiken's remarks : Arthur O. Lovejoy, speaking of William James, says of the Idealist tradition following Hegel :

> "This is (James') conviction that the rather prevalent fashion of intellectually playing fast and loose with evil of calling in the religious consciousness to bless what the moral consciousness has pronounced accur-

> sed—is not, in the long run, compatible with either logical or moral integrity. Especially since the time of HEGEL....this sort of bookkeeping by double entry has become exceedingly common....evil is neither annulled nor absolutely compensated by being—as it happily may be—passed beyond or even utilized to further future good."[251]

Evil is real. To deny it is to violate one's logical and moral integrity, i.e., common sense. Whether or not it is ultimately real is another question that need not concern us. Neither should the fact that suffering is subjective and personal involve us in hedging on this issue. Suffering is subjectively real, and the cause of suffering is either subjectively real or objectively real.

(3) Finally, as J. M. E. MCTAGGART once remarked, even if it were only an illusion that evil existed, that illusion would itself be an evil.[252]

Conclusion

The evil is illusion solution violates common sense if it baldly holds that what is real is not real. In doing this it is also inconsistent. Further, whether or not anyone would actually hold this position in its baldest form, or whether it was only held in its metaphysical form, is beside the point as far as the rejection of the evil is illusion solution as an adequate solution to TPHE is concerned. If there is no evil, then surely millions of people have been deluded for thousands of years in the belief that there was evil; and that in itself would be an evil. Furthermore as has been often pointed out, if there is no evil in the world, but only good, we shall have turned the tables on ourselves by creating a problem for the good. We may well have, then, a theological problem of human, subhuman, and superhuman good. While interesting as a possible alternative to our present puzzle, we shall leave it to someone who can find more adequate reasons for defending the evil is illusion solution (cf. Part III).

The solution that follows directly denies one of the theological theses, the all-powerful thesis, and therefore cannot be called a *bona fide* solution to T.P.E. But it has a place in the history of theodicies that makes it worthy of consideration, nonetheless.

5. The Not All-powerful Solution : God is not all-powerful.

We have seen that this position is well represented by JOHN STUART MILL

> "Whatsoever, in nature, gives indication of beneficent design, proves this beneficence to be armed only with limited power ; and the duty of man is to co-operate with the beneficent powers, not by imitating but by perpetuallly striving to amend the course of nature..."[253]

Thus, MILL contends, the empirical evidence points to a deity with something less than omnipotence :

> "The evidences, therefore of Natural Theology distinctly imply that the author of the Kosmos worked under limitations..."[254]

To this extent, MILL is echoing DAVID HUME, who in the *Dialogues Concerning Natural Religion* had proposed in effect that God does not approve evils, but permits them because every possible alternative would involve even greater evils than those in the present scheme of things.[255] And previously, as we have also seen, LEIBNIZ had summarized formally his opponent's position along similar lines when he said :

> "Whoever does not choose the best course is lacking either in power, or knowledge, or goodness. God did not choose the best course in creating the world. Therefore God was lacking in power, or knowledge, or goodness."[256]

LEIBNIZ' own theodicy is, of course, contrary to MILL 's, for it is established on *a priori* grounds rather than on empirical grounds. Both may point to the same facts to support their conclusions, but those conclusions are established in entirely different ways. Nonetheless we can conclude from LEIBNIZ' defense of his best-of-possible-worlds argument, that God worked under the limitations of what possibles were available. The difficulty that leads finally to the not all-powerful solution in MILL and makes its *a priori* appearance in LEIBNIZ is summarized by John HICK:

> "Thus the two ultimate and co-ordinate realities that stand over against each other within the God-head

> are, on the one hand, the creative divine will, and, on the other hand, the eternal compossibilities, in conformity with which the divine will must operate. Given the limitation imposed by these compossibilities, God has made the best world that He could—indeed, within the given restrictions, the best possible world."[257]

(1) But if God produced under such limitations, and if God's power was thereby necessarily limited to such external, logical limitations, then the evil in the world is a necessary consequence of that creation. This latter position is of course the necessary solution; and the not all-powerful solution, under the interpretation here given of LEIBNIZ' argument, would seem to entail the necessary solution.

(2) But the not all-powerful solution cannot be a solution to TPHE. It violently attacks T.P.E. by radically denying one of the premises necessary to generate the problem. In place of attempting to solve T.P.E. by finding a way of making the premises of the problem live with each other, it attempts to obviate the practical inconsistency of those premises by categorically denying one of the premises. This is not a solution to T. P. E. but the destruction of T.P.E.

Conclusion

The not all-powerful solution does not solve T.P.E. and for the simple reason that it refuses to play the T.P.E. game according to the rules laid down for that game. It patently refuses to recognize the rules which establish the theological theses and the evil thesis, and which then direct the player to make these theses consistent. On these grounds alone the not all-powerful solution should be rejected. Thus our three criteria cannot even be applied to test out an attempted solution, for what we have before us is really a spurious solution to T.P.E. and not a *bona fide* solution.

The not all-powerful (pseudo) solution seems to lead naturally into a discussion of the nature of one of the limitations imposed upon the creator, the necessary solution, and we turn to it next.

6. The Necessary Solution: Evil is logically and metaphysically necessary for the existence of good.

This solution has obvious affinities with the man is free solution, for both are attempts to solve T.P.E. logically, i.e. through an understanding of what "creature","imperfection", "good" and "evil" mean. But once, both arguments state, one understands the logical nature of these words, one comes to see that evil is bound to creatures necessarily through their will, and good and evil are bound necessarily to each other as well as to the creation. St. AUGUSTINE states the notion first:

> "...there can be no evil where there is no good..... Nothing evil exists in itself, but only as an evil aspect of some actual entity...Evils, therefore, have their source in the good, and unless they are parasitic on something good, they are not anything at all."[258]

But while the necessary solution appeared most strenuously later in LEIBNIZ, it has various popular forms as well. FYODOR DOSTOIEVSKY uses a form of it to describe a view that he opposes. IVAN KARAMAZOV has just described an atrocity against a little girl of five, wherein she was beaten and mauled in a horrible way by her parents. Ivan asks his brother Alyosha, a religious novice :

> "Can you understand why a little creature who can't even understand what's done to her, should beat her little aching heart with her tiny fist in the dark and the cold, and weep her meek unresentful tears to dear, kind God to protect her? Do you understand that, friend and brother, you pious humble novice? Do you understand why this infamy must be and is permitted (by God)? Without it, I am told, man could not have existed on earth..."[259]

The evil is logically necessary because man, creation, exists. WILLIAM JAMES strikes a similar note when discussing 'obligation", "good" and "evil" :

> "First of all, it appears that such words can have no application or relevancy in a world in which no sentient life exists. Imagine an absolutely material world containing only physical and chemical facts, and existing from eternity without a God, without even an interested spectator: would there be any sense in

> saying of that world that one of its states is better than another ?"[260]

Pace G. E. MOORE, JAMES goes on to assert that such words can have no status or meaning in an insentient world but that,

> "The moment one sentient being, however, is made a part of the universe, there is a chance for goods and evils really to exist."[261]

WALTER STACE has summarized the view with the following argument :

> "...it is logically impossible that there could be a world with living beings in it but without evil and suffering...life entails evil."

Hence God could not have created life without evil. STACE concludes :

> "...life in a perfect world is a logical impossibility... God could not have created living beings who would never experience suffering and evil."[262]

(1) Again we ask, as we asked under the man is free solution, Who said so and when that created living beings are somehow logically bound with suffering and sin ? We attacked this position before by saying that metaphysical imperfection need not entail moral imperfection (see 3 below also), i.e., man is created hence he is metaphysically imperfect, that at least is what is claimed. But why may not a man learn to act and behave and do rightly all the time, even though he be a created being ? If our discussion regarding the paradox of perfections was at all meaningful, it would seem that man alone, and not God, is capable of moral perfection; but being capable of perfection surely does not entail total and absolute depravity and suffering in this life.

(2) STACE, a Christian, states that life in a perfect world is an impossibility. Now many Christians who believe in a life after death, and the resurrection of the body, and all that the recompense solution entailed consistent with this, believe strenuously that a perfect life *with the body* is indeed not only a possibility but an assured theological fact. If such a life is possible then surely it's possible now. And if it's possible now, why is it not actual now ? Thus the necessary solution loses its force and its principle support if perfection is possible whether now, as we are hoping, or later.

(3) It seems to me that a number of authors confuse metaphysical being with moral imperfection, e.g., P.M. FARRELL in his "Evil and Omnipotence" says :

> "Thus evil is involved in the very concept and definition of contingent being. Evil, i.e., is a necessary consequence of contingency."[263]

I think FARRELL like STACE plays fast and loose with "evil", and that he confuses "evil" as an ontological imperfection because it is created, with "evil" as immoral conduct or sin leading to suffering. Philosophers who defend this kind of thesis must show the connection between metaphysical imperfection and moral imperfection. Most seem to assume it exists, but never demonstrate in what manner. Since they don't, we must assume there is an illegitimate leap from ontology to ethics that underlies the faith in the necessary solution.

(4) In the literature, the positions have polarized around JOHN HICK and P.M. FARRELL who both favour the necessary solution (and also the man is free solution), and J. L. MACKIE and Antony FLEW, who attack it.[264] The principal view under discussion and attack is best represented by JOHN HICK and I will dwell on this in conclusion. First, there is what I call the metaphysical thesis that imperfection lies in man because man is a created being. Then the leap to the moral thesis :

> "The idea of a person who can be infallibly guaranteed always to act rightly is self-contradictory. There can be no guarantee in advance that a genuinely free moral agent will never choose amiss."[265]

HICK concludes rather mildly that the possibility of sin is logically bound up with man :

> "Consequently, the possibility of wrongdoing or sin is logically inseparable from the creation of finite persons, and to say that God should not have created beings who might sin amounts to saying that he should not have created people."[266]

But this is a far cry from saying that men must sin, as FARRELL and STACE would seem to have it. For if it is only possible that men might sin, then it is equally possible they might not. J. L. MACKIE seizes on a situation just like this when he says :

> "If there is no logical impossibility in a man's freely choosing the good on one, or on several occasions,

> there cannot be a logical impossibility in his freely choosing the good on every occasion."[267]

And there the matter would seem to rest. The point being, that man could be metaphysically imperfect but nonetheless morally perfect.

(5) If the retort is made as HICK might :

> "But He cannot without contradiction be conceived to have so constituted men that they could be guaranteed freely to respond to himself in authentic faith and love and worship."[268]

then, the metaphysical issue aside, one can say that since God gave man some nature why didn't He give man a better nature ? To assume, as HICK appears to do, that God had to go all or nothing in the nature He gave man, all evil or all good, is silly. God could have created man such that the moral responses he made would, while not perfect, have been better than the ones he now makes : A mouth needs teeth for chewing food, but those same teeth needn't chew up the lips, tongue, cheeks, etc. when they chew up the food.

Conclusion

The defenders of the necessary solution or necessary-like solutions are hard put to justify the leap from metaphysical imperfection in creatures to a guaranteed moral imperfection. And even if the possibility of moral imperfection can be shown there is no further guarantee that that possibility must be actualized. Thus the force of the logical and metaphysical necessity of evil for the existence of good is considerably blunted. But further, even if it is shown that there could not be good without something like evil, we may still ask "Why so much evil ?" Is it the case that so much evil is necessary because there is so much good ? This is not at all clear. And even if it were, we would have to say with DOSTOIEVSKY:

> "It's not worth the tears of that one tortured child who beat itself on the breast with its little fist and prayed in its stinking outhouse, with its unexpiated tears to 'dear, kind God' ! It's not worth it..."[269]

Even if good and evil are logically bound to each other, it would still seem to be false that the creator couldn't have made man capable of less evil. Hence the necessary solution in the form it is usually presented, i.e., as justifying the most outrageous acts of violence and suffering, fails to satisfy common sense.

7. The Metaphor Solution: The language describing God is merely metaphorical.

This solution represents a classic way of dissolving P. E. It implies that the ways of God are beyond human comprehension, and man had better leave well enough alone. It represents to this degree an anti-intellectual or irrational solution, like the mystery solution to P.E. JOHN STUART MILL who attacks the metaphor solution vigorously in his *An Examination of Sir William Hamilton's Philosophy*, quotes HENRY MANSEL 's *Limits of Religious Thought* as follows :

> "The infliction of physical suffering, the permission of moral evil, the adversity of the good, the prosperity of the wicked, the crimes of the guilty involving the misery of the innocent, the tardy appearance and partial distribution of moral and religious knowledge in the world—these are facts which no doubt are reconcilable, we know not how, with the Infinite Goodness of God, but which certainly are not to be explained on the supposition that its sole and sufficient type is to be found in the finite goodness of man."[270]

MANSEL , undoubtedly, most ably represented that view in the 19th century that we are calling the metaphor solution.

(1) MILL begins his attack by responding :

> "To say (as Mr. MANSEL does) that God's goodness may be different in kind from man's goodness, what is it but saying, with a slight change of phraseology, that God may possibly not be good.'[271]

What MANSEL is (unsuccessfully) trying to do is to call God "Good" and at the same time work his way around to meaning by "Good" what we ordinarily mean by "good", i.e., MANSEL is using metaphors or symbols to talk about God. Thus with respect to T.P.E., the metaphor solution is a solution precisely because one may say that God is Good, but evil may still exist and never shall the twain interfere with each other.

(2) MILL presses the point that to use language at all one must use the language we know,

"I know something of Man and Nature, not as they are

> in themselves, but as they are relatively to us; and it is relative to us, and not as he is in himself, that I suppose myself to know anything of God."[272]

And he continues,

> "When I reject a doctrine as inconsistent with God's nature it is not as being inconsistent with what God is in himself, but with what he is as manifested to us."[273]

MILL then leans on the attack and goes after those writers who would use a double standard of language. "Good" for God and "good" for man :

> "Here, then, I take my stand on the acknowledged principle of logic and of morality, that when we mean different things we have no right to call them by the same name, and to apply to them the same predicates, moral and intellectual."[274]

He continues,

> "Language has no meaning for the words Just, Merciful and Benevolent, save that in which we predicate them of our fellow-creatures; and unless that is what we intend to express by them, we have no business to employ the words."[275]

MILL, and I think justifiably, recognizes that language must be used literally, or if it is not, then the meaning of the non-literal expressions must themselves be capable of literal translation or interpretation. To do any other is to violate common sense, to retreat to mysticism, to the position we labelled the mystery solution', and from there into utter silence.

(3) Earlier in the same work, MILL has taken Sir William HAMILTON to task for playing the same hanky-panky game with God's attributes. HAMILTON had apparently argued that because the set of attributes contained in a general notion must be finite, anything infinite cannot be thought under it. Thus the comprehension (MILL's term for the set of attributes contained in a concept) of goodness must be finite, with the result that a being possessing in an infinite degree a given attribute cannot be thought, save finitely, under that attribute. HAMILTON's point is similar to MANSEL's : What man thinks he thinks with concepts that have finite comprehension. But concepts pertaining to God have infinite comprehension.

Thus man cannot think about God or know his nature, or else he can only know God inadequately. MILL concludes HAMILTON's argument and appraises it :

> "Infinite goodness cannot be thought as goodness, because that would be to think it as finite. Surely there must be some great confusion of ideas in the premises, when this comes out as the conclusion."[276]

The trouble MILL sees, I take it, is not that goodness is not goodness, for HAMILTON's and MANSEL's point is precisely that Goodness is not goodness. The point for MILL is not over confusion between upper and lower case G's leading to a contradiction, but rather that there is some concept which it is claimed is a genuine concept and yet it cannot be understood by man. MILL makes his point clear in a footnote farther on :

> "My argument is that we need not exhaust the infinite to be enabled to conceive it ; since, in point of fact, we do not exhaust the finite numbers which it is admitted we can and do conceive."[277]

Though his intent is clear, MILL is on shaky set-theoretic ground with his example, for "infinity" as applied to natural numbers is not the same infinity applied to God's concepts. The former can be understood in terms of a set placed into a 1-1 correspondence with a proper subset of itself, whereas theological infinity as often as not simply means whatever is ungraspable by the finite mind.

(4) MANSEL's metaphor solution as well as HAMILTON's, is that God-language is special and incomprehensible. Thus TPHE becomes dissolved since the theological theses of the puzzle are no longer open to attack or doubt—they aren't open to any rational approach whatsoever. MILL's response is one of put up or shut up. Since the metaphor solution cannot put up any literal concepts at all, its only alternative is to keep silent; this it does and thereby retreats into a form of the mystery solution.

Conclusion

The metaphor solution in refusing to use literalistic language would seem to offend common sense. It surely offends rational common sense with its anti-intellectual retreat into unanalyzable or inexplicable metaphor or simile. The upshot of the employment of this solution is surely a solution to TPHE but it purchases that conclusion, once again, at too high a price : Simple quietism.

The outcome for the metaphor solution is ultimately to give up all talk whatsoever and retreat irresolutely into mystery and silence. The metaphor solution when pushed to its logical conclusion then turns into a species of the mystery solution and it is to that solution that we turn next.

8. The Mystery Solution : Evil is a mystery.

This solution means to assert that T.P.E. must be seen as a mystery and challenge to man's faith. To this extent it would seem to flow out of the metaphor solution and into the discipline solution insofar as this inexplicability leads to soul-building.

The position is well represented in the modern literature. Bishop Joseph Butler provides a good bridge between the metaphor solution and the mystery solution, and comes down hard on the possibility of a rational solution to P. E. when he says :

> "Upon supposition that God exercises a moral government over the world, the analogy of His natural government suggests and makes it credible that this moral government must be a scheme quite beyond our comprehension; and this affords a general answer to all objections against the justice and goodness of it."[278]

David Hume in *Dialogues Concerning Natural Religion* has Demea, a religiously orthodox soul, state the position in the following way :

> "The question is not concerning the *being* but the *nature* of God. This, I affirm, from the infirmities of human understanding to be altogether incomprehensible and unknown to us. The essence of that supreme mind, his attributes, the manner of his existence... these...are mysterious to man."[279]

Paul Tillich in his *Systematic Theology* has argued like John Hick after him, that even the existence of what we have called extraordinary evil is an ultimate religious mystery for man.[280] He states that God's creativity in the universe"....is identical with the divine mystery and beyond calculation and description"[281]

(1) The problems that loom for the mystery solution are basically the same ones we found for the not all-powerful solution, the evil is illusion solution and the metaphor solution, viz., it violates common sense by removing T.P.E. from the arena where it can be talked about and discussed. John Hick argues in his *Philosophy of Religion* that moral evil "...lies forever concealed within the mystery of human freedom."[282] To say that human freedom is a mystery, and to say that God's nature is a mystery, as with the previous authors, and to say that evil is also a mystery, as Hick has in *Evil and the God of Love*, means that freedom, evil and God are not topics for human understanding, debate, or discussion. The mystery solution becomes an intellectual surrender *par excellance.*

(2) But the repercussions from the mystery solution for the moral life, and not just the intellectual life, are also difficult to bear. Henry Aiken in his *Reason and Conduct* has pointed to the secularization of the moral life and from this, consequently, to a limiting of the domain of the religious life : either consequence is apparently unhealthy for the life of soul-minded people :

> "....the holy personality of God is placed in jeopardy when his perfection as a moral person is impugned .... It is therefore entirely understandable that certain monotheistic theologians should have sought to treat the holiness of almighty God as something which absolutely transcends his moral personality. Yet a too emphatic emphasis upon the absolute transcendence of God's holy self is bound to result in a tendency toward the secularization of the moral and hence in a radical circumscription of the domain of the religious itself. Such tendencies are plainly discernible in Kierkegaard and even, at times in Martin Buber (and, we might add, certainly in Paul Tillich and probably in John Hick as well)."[283]

The mystery solution leads as an inevitable consequence to the withering away of the foundations of the moral life for the religious man ; and this jeopardizes the religious life itself as traditionally understood.

(3) H. J. Paton has a more compelling criticism to throw at those theologians who have so to speak left the moral field with a shrug of their mystical shoulders :

> "Plain and honest men cannot but have a proper feeling of repugnance when a theologian or philosopher ignores the horrors of the world—still more when he tries to have it both ways and tells us that the good in the world is a proof of God's goodness, while the evil shows that we cannot expect to understand the mystery of the divine will."[284]

It is indeed curious that these mystery mongers have a ready-to-hand explanation for good, but retire in a shroud of inexplicableness when it comes to evil. The plain and honest men that would reject the mystery solution, I would assume, must be inclined also to reject the evil is illusion solution and the metaphor solution as well. All three require man to sell his intellectual soul for a pot of solutions—and solutions at any price at that.

Conclusion

The principal objection to the mystery solution is then that it violates common sense by retreating into mystical silence. It is a solution to T.P.E. but as radical and unacceptable as the evil is illusion and the metaphor solutions with which it shares certain honest affinities.

Further, the fact that theologians would perform such an utter withdrawal in the face of extra-ordinary evil, must needs give heart to those persons in the West who feel that T.P.E. cannot indeed be solved. At the same time that God is removed to Aristophanes' cloud-cuckoo land, never to return, the religious plain man is abandoned; and the separation between morals and religion, as Aiken has pointed out, becomes a crevice and then a gulf; and presumably this bodes ill for the religious life as he is at some pains to expound. It might very well be that when a theologian says that a certain phenomenon is a mystery for building faith, this is theologian-ese for what others would translate in ordinary language as "there is no known solution to T.P.E." But if so, then it seems that the mystery solution cannot stand as a solution to T.P.E.

4. Conclusion to Chapter III

Very briefly put, we have seen that none of the eight proferred solutions to T.P.E. can survive the standard est set for an adequate solution. We must conclude then that of the solutions examined, the eight reduced solutions or the twenty-one original solutions, none will suffice to dissolve the problem we have examined. In the Conclusion to Part I which follows, I will try to say why I think this result must be inevitable for all such similar attempts undertaken within the context of the traditional Western approach to T.P.E.

CHAPTER IV

Conclusion to Part I

1) There is a kind of logical weirdness about T.P.E. Those who agonize through the puzzle must satisfy two seemingly connected but seemingly incompatible demands : That predicates describing the personality of God must always remain honorific and perfect in intent; That the predicates describing the character of the world and man must always remain less than honorific and imperfect in intent. The problems involved in wedding these demands break down into two types which I will call internal problems and external problems in relation to the personality of God.

1. *Internal problems*

a. The principal difficulty here, as we saw in Chapter II, 2a, is that when the specified properties of God are joined together they produce, not a logically contradictory set but a practically inconsistent set. God's unspeakable agony resulting from the Cassandra paradox[285] must needs give the theologian pause before joining total goodness with divine omniscience.

b. Further, the paradox of omnipotence[286] seems to lead to an apparently inconsistent set, when God's ommipotence leads God into making things He cannot control, or into declining to do things which He apparently cannot do.

c. Finally, there is the internal paradox resulting from God's omniscience joined with His omnipotence, that we called the paradox of divine fatalism.[287]

These internal troubles we called collectively the paradox of perfection, and we argued that it is guaranteed to show up whenever honorific perfections, such as those three items involved in the theological theses, congregate together. Anyone who would attempt a solution to the T.P.E. must be prepared to deal with the paradox of perfection, and as we have seen theologians from St. Thomas onwards have arguments to engage these various puzzles in that paradox.

2. *External problems*

When the predicates descriptive of the perfection of God are conjoined with predicates descriptive of the imperfection of man (TPHE) and the animal world (TPSbE) we generate external problems, such as those dealt with in Chapter II, 3. Our super, sweet sagacious Smith served as a model for the deity, and Smith in conjunction with evil in the neighborhood (a fire, you will recall), disposed us to call into question one or another of Smith's perfections. A practical inconsistency resulted, and the external problems involved with deity and evil are such as to be extremely troublesome but not as we noted, insuperable for anyone wishing to deal with T.P.E. from this direction.

Thus insofar as the internal problems led us into the paradox of perfection, and the external problems led us into a practical inconsistency between deity and evil, we have to all intents and purposes what I have called a logical weirdness or practical inconsistency about T.P.E. By this notion of practical inconsistency, I simply wish to assert that first the problems are connected with meanings, and second they are serious.

2) But practical inconsistency is not the only strange goings on with the attempts to solve T.P.E. There is a strangeness involved in flying in the face of the above two problems, internal and external, and bravely and fiercely trying to effect a solution, nonetheless. If one were aware of the logical weirdness involved to begin with perhaps one wouldn't be so foolhardy; but then as with all fools who dash off into the maw of the unknown and the perilous one can't help but admire their venture anyway, knowing *a priori* that somehow, somewhere, the brave fool is doomed to sorrow because of his (Western) presuppositions.

We cautiously dipped into Western philosophic lore for our list (in Chapter I) of twenty-one really used solutions to T.P.E. The caution was necessary, for the list did not pretend to be exhaustive, only representative. Perhaps knowing what we know now, that the T.P.E. is a true philosophical puzzle because it seems truly insoluble, we could have bravely agreed to take on all comers, knowing ahead of time that we had nothing to fear. But since hope does spring eternal, especially in the hearts of erstwhile theodicists, caution seemed and still seems the better part of philosophic valor for us.

The solutions attempted were *prima facie* solutions because, as we have seen, they met T.P.E. by various subterfuges and nefarious logical devices. They had to! Taking T.P.E. in its baldest, literal, straight-from-the-shoulder sense led to disaster: We showed this in Chapter II, 2a and II, 3. The defender of the solutions therefore, must needs resort to chicanery and pedantry and wiles. Thus he must reinterpret evil; wrench common sense out of its habitual, literal molds; deliteralize the language about God; offer candy sweets and honied words; prey upon our love and fears of the unknown; attack the ancient creeds about God's perfections; flatter and cajole, threaten and banter with talk of heaven and hell; and so on, and so on.

The solutions we examined in Chapter III, 3 have all failed somehow to measure up to the standard we set for philosophic solutions to philosophic problems in III, la. I have hinted rather strenuously that the reason for the failure can be found, not only in the inadequacies of the eight separate solutions we analyzed, but also in the foundations to the problem itself examined throughout Chapter II.

Having said all this, however, I want next to move on to a final attempted solution to P.E. It is a solution found in the Indian texts, and comes closest to the position we labeled the rebirth solution and rejected under the man is free solution in III, 3. The excursion promises to be interesting, and that in itself may be a justification for staying with the argument. For to make the rebirth solution, the view that man because of his previous births is responsible for evil, at all acceptable will involve some rather interesting reinterpretations of both T.P.E. and the presuppositions or assumptions out of which that problem arises. I think the Indians have done this and I want to show how it was done, and why some philosophers have thought that it does indeed solve T.P.E. We introduce a solution therefore, not traditionally open to Western philosophers and theologians, and by it we will attempt to show that T.P.E. can be solved.

PART II

THE INDIAN DOCTRINE OF REBIRTH

INTRODUCTORY

Contemporary Indian philosophers, generally, and a number of their apologists, as we shall see, believe that the doctrine of rebirth will solve T.P.E. The attempt in the two parts which follow will be to analyze this claim in order to discover what merit it has and what kinds of things must be accepted or rejected if the claim be true. The task presently before us will be to examine the notion of rebirth (*saṁsāra*) rather closely to find out first what it is for the Indian, second what it is as a doctrine of transmigration on an even wider non-Indian scale, and finally, what it can and cannot claim as a philosophic principle.

The Part II is divided into three Chapters viz. V, VI and VII. In Chapter V, I shall sketch out the doctrine of *saṁsāra* in the classical *śruti* and *smṛti* literature in order to get a rough but working definition of *saṁsāra*. In Chapter VI, I shall examine the four assumptions which appear to underlie not only this Indian doctrine of rebirth, but any doctrine of rebirth; also in Chapter VI, I shall illustrate this doctrine by demonstrating the assumptions *in situ* in a number of rebirth systems, one western (Plato's), two Indian *nāstika* and approximately four Indian *āstika* systems. These rebirth systems in Chapter VI will cover an historical period from about 500 B.C. until the present century, and the variations in the rebirth systems will be found to rest on minor variations in the accepted assumptions. We shall find two quite separate rebirth systems emerging, and in Chapter VII, the concluding portion of Part II, I shall set these two systems up in a rigorous way to prepare them for our discussion of rebirth and T.P.E. in Part III.

Chapter V

*The Historical Background of Saṁsāra**

In this Chapter, I want to trace quite rapidly the Indian doctrine of *saṁsāra* as that doctrine evolved and changed through four sets of texts and through four historical-philosophical periods. I will be examining the concept, but not the word, in the *Vedas*, the *Brāhmaṇas*, in the early *Upaniṣads*, and finally in the *Bhagavad Gītā*. I believe that two things can be concluded as a result of this study : First, that the concept of *saṁsāra* changed through the four periods, but that the change is not as startling as has been supposed; and second, one can conclude, contrary to current theories, that a doctrine of *saṁsāra* satisfying certain assumptions can be found in the later *Vedas*.

The present Chapter is divided into four parts: 1. deals with whatever *Vedic* and *Brāhmaṇic* sources are available for exploration; 2. will discuss the *Upaniṣadic* sources, which are indeed much more abundant: 3. will show the turn events have taken with respect to our subject in the *Bhagavad-Gītā*; and 4. finally, will attempt to summarize our investigations with respect to the two points mentioned in the preceding paragraph.

1. The Mobile Soul Doctrine in the Vedic Period

Saṁsāra has been variously translated from the Sanskrit as 'transmigration', 'reincarnation', 'metempsychosis', 'rebirth' and 'the round of birth and death.' It has be entraced to the Greek and, as a consequence, it has been attributed as a belief to Homer, the Orphics, the Pythagoreans, and Plato, from which sources it has travelled thither and yon to the Gnostics, the Manicheans, Bruno, Goethe, Lessing, Herder, and various contemporary apologists from Max Weber to Wilmon Sheldon.

Saṁsāra is a Sanskrit word from the root *sṛ* which means, variously, 'to flow', 'run swiftly', or 'glide'; conjoined with the prefix *saṁ*, meaning 'with' or 'together', the word has the

* Previously published in *The Journal of the Ganganatha Jha Research Institute*, April, 1971, as *Saṁsāra*.

original sense of 'a flowing with or together'. In the history of Indian thought where the most interesting evolution of the concept is detailed, the current scholarly belief is that the doctrine of rebirth, as I shall translate '*saṁsāra*', is a Dravidian and not an Aryan contribution to Hinduism.[288]

In the *Vedas* we first meet what might be called "the doctrine of the mobile soul". And since having a soul (a name for the travelling stuff) which can leave the body is, it would seem, necessary to any doctrine of *saṁsāra*, we can say that *saṁsāra*, however it may develop later, has its roots in the *Vedic* texts. In the early *Ṛgveda*, the dead go to the world of the Fathers; all the dead do this apparently, and no distinction is made between the souls of good men as opposed to wicked men. But in the later *Ṛgveda*, the distinction is made, and the principle governing what goes where would seem to be, "Heaven for the righteous and hell for the wicked."[289] Thus in *ṚV* I. 35, three heavens are indicated or three abodes for the dead,[290] and in *ṚV* X. 14.8, there is the following:

> "Unite Thou with the Fathers and with Yama.
> With thy good works reward in highest heaven.
> To home return, all imperfection leaving
> Unite with thine own body, full of vigour."[291]

The last verse not only points to a mobile soul but a mobile soul that is capable of going and then coming back—"returning" with good works. *ṚV* X. 15.14 makes a reference to the rejoining or uniting with a body—a body that now is able to move to heaven :

> "They who, consumed by fire or not cremated, joy in their offering in the midst of heaven.
> Grant them, O sovran lord, the world of spirits and their own body, as thy pleasure wills it."[292]

But while these later hymns are quite clear on the mobile soul's returning abilities, it is not clear that the earlier hymns are all in agreement on just what the status of the soul is once the body is dead. Thus while *ṚV* I. 154.5 and 68 make a plain reference to the soul's surviving the body's death: "May I attain to that his well-loved mansion where men devoted to the gods are happy. . . . Fain would we go to your dwelling place where there are many horned and nimble oxen",[293] another early hymn, the lovely song to *Uṣas*, makes no such reference to soul-survival in a poem where it would seem to be most pertinent; "Dawn, at her rising, urges forth the living: him who is dead she wakes not from his slumber...."[294]

But however these early passages may tend to cloud the mobile soul issue, I think we can conclude that the *ṚV* does hold to two essential elements present as necessary conditions for any *saṁsāra* doctrine. Let me denominate these as :

S1: There is a soul and it is not bound to or identified with the place where it resides, e.g., the gross human body.

S2: One's separable soul can leave the gross body and travel about to trees, sky, and sun (*ṚV* X.58) or to the abode of the fathers and/or Yama's world.

Ṛgvedic saṁsāra, such as it is, holds only to S1 and S2. There is no mention of the mobile soul coming back to earth, however, and to this extent *Ṛgvedic saṁsāra* differs from later developments to be described below.[295]

The *Atharvaveda* and the *Brāhmaṇas* are both much more explicit on the mobile soul doctrine. Edgerton in *The Beginnings of Indian Philosophy* translates *AV* VIII. 10. 19, 20. 21 as follows :

> "She (Virāj) ascended; she came to the Fathers (*Manes*, or departed spirits). The Fathers slew her. In a month she came into being (again)...She ascended; she came to the gods. The gods slew her. In a half month she came into being....She ascended; she came to men. Men slew her. She came into being (again) immediately."[296]

And in the *Brāhmaṇas*, we have a theory of rebirth that moves to yet a third stage of development. Thus, in *Śatapatha-Brāhmaṇa* I. 5.3.14 :

> "Now the spring, assuredly, comes into life again out of the winter, for out of the one the other is born again : therefore he who knows this is indeed born again in this world."[297]

From this we can conclude that by the time of the *Brāhmaṇas*, a third essential element is present for our doctrine of *saṁsāra* :

S3: The mobile soul (S1 and S2) is mobile with respect to the world, i.e., it is *punar ha va 'asmin loke bhavate*, "born again in this world".

The goal-determining actions of the soul are however absent here, and it will remain for the *Upaniṣads* to make them explicit.

2. *Upaniṣadic Saṁsāra*

The *Upaniṣads* abound in rebirth doctrine, and the necessary elements of *saṁsāra*, S1, S2, and S3, are found from the oldest to the latest texts.[298] In fact, though the word *saṁsāra* first appears in *Kaṭha Upaniṣad* III.7, the whole notion is already present in the earliest *Upaniṣad,* the *Bṛhadāraṇyaka*, e.g., IV.4.4:

> "As a goldsmith, taking a piece of gold, reduces it to another newer and more beautiful form, just so this soul, striking down this body and dispelling its ignorancc, makes for itself another newer and more beautiful form like that either of the fathers, or of the Gandharvas, or of the gods, or of Prajāpati, or of Brahmā, or of other beings."[299]

And in the later *Kaṭha Upaniṣad* we have,

> "He, however, who has not understanding,
> Who is unmindful and ever impure,
> Reaches not the goal,
> But goes on to *saṁsāra* (reincarnation)."[300]

But at least one element missing previously is that element which would explain to us the cause of rebirth, the rationale behind repeated birth. The *Upaniṣads* fill this *lacuna* very well, and I want to look briefly at two of the oldest *Upaniṣads*, since what they say regarding rebirth and its rationale would seem to be presupposed by those *Upaniṣads* that came later.

In the *Bṛhadāraṇyaka Upaniṣad* a curious question prefaces the discussion of rebirth, and the question is repeated again prior to a similar discussion in the *Chāndogya* (V. 3.3). In both *Upaniṣads*, a young disciple Śvetaketu, goes to a *Kṣatriya* teacher, Jaibali, and Jaibali asks the youth :

> 'Know you how people here, on deceasing, separate in different directions?'
> 'No', said he.
> 'Know you how they come back again to this world?'
> 'No', said he.
> 'Know you why yonder world is not filled up with the many who continually thus go hence?'

'No', said he."[301]

Why doesn't that yonder world fill up, indeed? Could this have been a problem for Vedic Brahmins? The question is not explicitly answered in the *Bṛhadāraṇyaka*. Instead, there follows a description of the souls' journey after the body's death that takes those souls who know and those who truly worship faith to the *Brahma*-worlds from which they never return. But of the souls who practise charity, austerity, and sacrifice, they are born again on the earth; and those who do not know these two ways are reborn as insects and biting animals. Yonder world, presumably, never fills up because of the fact of rebirth. Thus there is a mirror, certainly, of the Vedic doctrine, but only a mirror of it. The *Bṛhadāraṇyaka* looks to three ends of the soul's going, *Brahma* world, the returners (as men, supposedly), and the returners as lower animals, while the *Vedas* provided (at least) three similar abodes for the departed soul.[302]

The *Chāndogya* gives a more explicit answer to our strange question about the non-filling up of heaven. At the same time it repeats the reasons or ground for rebirth, but does it more explicitly. Thus, the question is asked again :

> " 'Do you know how (it is that) yonder world is not filled up?'
>
> 'No, sir'."[303]

And later after a discussion of rebirth, we have

> "Thereby (it comes about that) yonder world is not filled up."[304]

In between the question and this "conclusion" to it, there is the account of Śvetaketu's visit to Jaibali. And here the *Chāndogya* parallels but differs noticeably from the account in the *Bṛhadāraṇyaka*. First there is a virtual repetition of the description of the deaths of ascetics whose souls go to the gods. Then follows the account of the deaths of sacrificers whose souls go to the Fathers and are then reborn on earth as plants, trees, and beans, thus preventing, it would appear, a population explosion and ecological crisis in heaven. But following this, the *Chāndogya* provides a rationale for the mechanism and determination of rebirth by speaking of conduct, good and bad, as the determinator of how, when, and where rebirth shall occur. Thus it provides us with a *Upaniṣadic* criterion for *saṁsāra*; for, granted that the mobile soul must move and move into the world, we must have, to complete the picture, criteria regarding *who* goes *where* and why. If we did not, oddly enough, then conceivably all could be reborn at the same place, at the same time, though this might still happen, even with the criterion. In truth no overcrowding problem in general has been solved at all, therefore, but only an overcrowding problem in the other world. There is nothing to prevent souls from being models of Brahmanic virtue, thereby filling up the wombs of matrons in some of the few most righteous families in the world community. The *Chāndogya* says :

> "Accordingly, those who are of pleasant conduct here—the prospect is, indeed, that they will enter a pleasant womb....But those who are of stinking conduct here—the prospect is, indeed, that they will enter a stinking womb...."[305]

Accordingly as a necessary element in defining *saṁsāra* we would seem to have the following :

> S4: The determining conditions under which the mobile soul re-enters the world are conditions with respect to the conduct of the person in his previous life (Law of *Karma*).

That this conduct is moral conduct as opposed to intellectual, devotional or priestly-sacrificial conduct is borne out, I think by *Chāndogya Upaniṣad* V.10. 9, which follows hard upon the above verses and in which the conduct one should seek to guard ones self against is mentioned. Thus the sinful are :

> "The plunderer of gold, the liquor drinker
> The invader of a teacher's bed, the Brahman-killer—
> These four sink downward in the scale,
> And, fifth, he who consorts with them."

The *Upaniṣads* we have examined then, lend to the doctrine of *saṁsāra* a moral criterion in virtue of which the direction and end of rebirth may be gauged, described and, oddly, even predicted, i.e., good people get their good rewards, and the wicked get painful ones. This is not to gainsay other routes than moral conduct to a better birth, however, as will be explained next in 3.

3. *Saṁsāra* in the *Bhagavad-Gītā*

There is one final dimension that remains to be given to our notion of *saṁsāra*. This is a broadening of the notion of "conduct" to include, besides moral conduct, other intellectual (*jñāna*) and devotional (*bhakti*) paths which lead to the surcease of *saṁsāra*. The mechanism of rebirth graphically described below, will thus add to itself later conditions of release even broader than those laid out in our discussion of the early *Upaniṣads* (I am aware of the *jñāna* and even *bhakti* elements in the *Upaniṣads*, but insofar as our treatment of *saṁsāra* in 2 did not display them, I am letting them enter more naturally here in our discussion of the *Gītā*).

> "As leaving aside worn-out garments, a man takes other new ones, So leaving aside worn-out bodies to other new ones goes the embodied (soul)."[306]

With these picturesque words the doctrine of rebirth is introduced by Kṛṣṇa. From this point on, the *Gītā* will take at least three attitudes with regard to the determination of particular future embodiments. These attitudes are the three *mārgas* presented in the *Gītā*: *jñāna*, *bhakti*, and *karma mārga*. Since it is assumed, quite generally, that all three do have an effect on the mechanism of rebirth, determining souls upwards or downwards (and I don't know of any scholar who would deny this) we must assume that the kind of conduct specified in 2 above under S4 must now be broadened to include conduct specified by these three *mārgas*. Let me now move to the final essential element in *saṁsāra* and a summary of the preceding elements :

> S5 : The determining conditions under which the mobile soul re-enters the world are conditions relating to the conduct of the person in his previous life, and that conduct can include intellectual, devotional and/or moral elements.

A complete discussion of S5 will necessarily lead us into a discussion of the following: The law of *karma*; the rebirth doctrine with respect to *Kṛṣṇa*, who is also reborn but under conditions which might seem to violate S5; a discussion of the nature of the reincarnating soul or transmigrating stuff, its ontological nature, for instance; the order of importance of the three *mārgas*, i.e., which is paramount, and which might be said to include the other two, and so on; the three types of conduct as they specifically affect the soul; and, finally, how that soul is changed, if it is, by those types of conduct. We will take up some of these matters in the chapters that follow.

4. Conclusion

What I have tried to stress throughout this chapter is the evolution of a concept, rebirth or *saṁsāra*, as that concept grew and developed in the ancient texts of India. S5 thus represents the final summary stage in that evolution and includes within itself, obviously, those earlier stages, S1, through S4. I think it is the case that the rebirth doctrine in later Hinduism (though not Buddhism) can be said to be generally described by S5.

We found in the *Vedas*, a mobile soul doctrine, where the direction of the soul to "heaven" or "hell" was dependent in some sense on "works". In the *Vedas*, at least the later *Ṛgveda*, all the essential machinery for rebirth was apparently present, if by "rebirth" we mean what follows in S5. That is to say, S1 and S2 would appear to have all the rudiments of S5. Those rudiments certainly are there by implication, however unclearly and inexplicitly. Thus if one is rewarded in highest heaven for good works (*RV* X. 14.8), and if one's soul can return home after going out into a body, all that need be done is to further specify the nature of these works and identify the home as either heaven or earth, and then one has S5. Thus contrary to what many scholars (e.g., HUME, RADHAKRISHNAN, EDGERTON, and BASHAM) have tended to say about the absence of *saṁsāra* doctrine in the Vedas, I think a strong case for it, or something very close to it, can be made out, once one grants that S1 and S2 are *Vedic* in origin.

In Chapter VI, which follows, I want to analyze S_5 and its parts, S_1 through S_5, in greater detail in order to see what the nature of these necessary elements of S_5 are like. I shall be speaking of S_1 through S_4 as assumptions, and shall consequently be re-labelling them A_1, A_2, A_3, and A_4 to signal their assumptive nature. S_1 through S_4 are not equivalent to A_1 through A_4 (for one thing S_2 is more like A_3, and S_3 is more akin to A_2), but as sets each group more or less expresses the necessary conditions for S_5 or the doctrine of rebirth.

It might be noted in passing that since S_5 is found in both the *śruti* and the *smrti* literature, all of the socalled *āstika* systems are duty-bound to accept it as an orthodox truth. Further, we shall find that two of the most well known of the *nāstika* systems accept it as well. This is not to say anything terribly significant, however, for as we shall shortly discover, the universal acceptance of S_5 among the general Indian *darśanas* is hedged about with multiple *caveats* and exceptions.

Chapter VI

The Assumptions of the Rebirth Thesis

If *saṁsāra* is described, however roughly, by S_5, I think it can be shown that there are four assumptions or presuppositions that it rests on. These four theses are present in one form or another in Indian *āstika* and *nāstika* systems which hold to the doctrine of *saṁsāra*. The systems may disagree on the precise wording of the assumptions or theses, but once the quibbling about terminology is set at rest, what emerges is a grand acceptance of all four theses. The latter point remains to be demonstrated. In the present section I wish to set forth these assumptions, analyze them, show what puzzles they raise in themselves and among themselves, and demonstrate precisely wherein their necessity lies not only for the Indian doctrine of *saṁsāra* but for any rebirth system. At the same time I want to illustrate the four assumptions as they appear in the various Indian and one non-Indian rebirth systems.

Looking at S_5 once again, I think one can see quite intuitively that to have a rebirth doctrine one must have certain elements or conditions present, viz., a something-or-other to be born and reborn, a place or places where it comes from or goes to, and rules governing the movement of the something-or-other. Quite specifically one needs a soul or something like a soul which can move or change from one place or body to another according to some rule or rules; the latter is necessary so that things won't get all botched up.

Intuitively, once again, the four assumptions which S_5 seems to support are the following (and here A_1 through A_4 repeat, but in greater depth, S_1 through S_4 of A above).

A_1. There is something-or-other in a certain place, and it is either what goes on to a new place or directly causes a new place's being constructed when the old place disintegrates or passes away. Call this assumption 'the soul thesis'.

A_2. Further, a residence or place for the soul is necessary. Call this assumption, 'the soul-locus thesis'.

A_3. We have seen that S_5 further provides for the transfer of souls, whatever they are, from some loci to others, hence it is assumed that the soul moves. Call this assumption 'the mobile-soul thesis'.

A_4. In addition, S_5 holds that there are conditions under which the mobile soul does its moving among or between various loci. These determining conditions I want to call collectively by their Indian name, though we shall see that all four of these assumptions in one form or another find their way into such a non-Indian rebirth system as Plato's (illustrated below). Call this assumption 'the Karma thesis'.

In summary then we would seem to have the following four assumptions necessary for the doctrine of rebirth as described in S_5 :

A_1 The Soul Thesis
A_2 The Soul-Locus Thesis
A_3 The Mobile-Soul Thesis
A_4 The Karma Thesis

To illustrate their relation to S_5, let me requote S_5, putting in the signs for the assumptions where they appear in that description of *saṁsāra* :

S_5: The determining conditions (A_4) under which the mobile (A_3) soul (A_1) re-enters the world (A_2) are conditions relating to the conduct of the person in his previous life....

It remains now to speak to each of these four assumptions, and attempt to analyze the essential characteristics of each one. In what follows, I shall take each of them and try to locate the concept within the Indian tradition in general, and within rebirth systems (Plato's, for example) in particular. At the same time I will try to give an elucidation of the assumptions in some representative rebirth system. I call them "assumptions" for the simple reason that they are not proved or argued for herein. Indeed, as one commentator, NINIAN SMART, has put it, *saṁsāra*, itself, historically, was more or less accepted, and without proofs (though there are some):

> "While there was considerable debate, in the Indian tradition, about the existence of God, since atheistic viewpoints were well represented, there is surprisingly little argument which seeks to establish the truth of the doctrine of rebirth."[307]

As assumptions, they are neither proved nor disproved in what follows, but accepted on grounds of sheer usefulness alone.

A1. *The Soul Thesis*

The Indians have a number of different names for what we loosely call "soul", e.g., *jīva*, *pudgala*, *Ātman* and *Puruṣa*, and generally they have a single name, *sūkṣma-śarīra*, "subtle body", for what moves from body to body, or locus to locus. For the European, in general, 'soul' means 'person', the ego-entity that thinks, wills and feels through the mechanism of the body. But the European tradition recognizes two distinct sorts of centers for such consciousness. I think one can get at the historical difference best by looking at the etymology of "person" The word refers to the *personae* or masks worn in the Greek theatre, and in virtue of wearing which, the actor was distinguished from the parts, masks, or *personae*, that he played or wore. Thus behind the mask, as it were, the actor remained separated from his roles. The Latin word *persona* then came to be identified apparently, with the roles one played and from thence to mean the off-stage parts one played in life. The Stoics who loved to see the world as a stage and all men as actors on it, were probably the first to systematically realize and accept as doctrine that behind the masks we wore there was another 'person', an abiding, unchanging, central self or 'fire', which could not be identified with the masky roles that fate had assigned the actor or witness within. Some commentators have made a great deal of this distinction going to the Latin again to pluck out "individual" as descriptive of that other, abiding, and unchanging, and hence 'undivided' self, which wears the masks and stands behind the romps upon the stage. Speaking of *persona*, HEINRICH ZIMMER says:

> "It is not a manifestation of his (the actor's) true nature but a veil. And yet the Western outlook—which originated with the Greeks themselves and was then developed in Christian philosophy—has annulled the distinction, implied in the term, between the mask and the actor whose face it hides."[308]

The distinction is present in early Christian history, wherein the Roman Paul of Tarsus, perhaps with a Stoic-like distinction in mind, separates soul or ego from spirit which latter item he identifies with Light and the Christ. Paul says that a man must hate or deny his self (ego) if he would save his Self (spirit), and thus the bifurcation of the 'self' comes into European thought from another direction.

Without stretching truth beyond reasonable bounds, I think the same kind of distinction is being made in Indian thought, though the terminology is a bit more perplexing. SURENDRANATH DASGUPTA says of the soul in Indian intellectual history :

> "All the Indian systems except Buddhism admit the existence of a permanent entity variously called *ātman*, *puruṣa* or *jīva*. As to the exact nature of this soul there are indeed divergences of view. Thus while the *Nyāya* calls it absolutely qualityless and characterless, indeterminate unconscious entity, *Sāṁkhya* describes it as being of the nature of pure consciousness, the *Vedānta* says that it is that fundamental point of unity implied in pure consciousness (*cit*), pure bliss (*ānanda*) and pure being (*sat*)".[309]

But all these systems agree, according to DASGUPTA, that this permanent entity is pure and unsullied in its nature and further that "all impurities of action or passion do not form a real part of it".[310]

1. *Theravāda* Buddhism

The Buddhists in turn would seem to constitute an exception to the above for the simple reason that they, the early Buddhists are meant, deny that any permanent entity including therefore soul has reality. Karl POTTER has summarized this early Buddhist attitude very well when he asks :

> "....what is a human being? The Buddhist answer to this is unequivocal: there is no Self in the sense of an enduring substance underlying change; what we ordinarily call the "Self" is a group of events.. The author of the *Abhidharmakośa* admits (that) the flux of momentary forces is arranged in patterns (*saṁtāna*). He holds that there is a ubiquitous sort of

force called assimilation (*prāpti*) which holds events past, present, and future together in a single series."[310a]

It is, of course, the fact of these *patterns* that allows us to say that the Buddhists do have a "soul" theory, however odd that soul may indeed be. But the Buddhists of the sort under discussion here do present one special sort of problem since they hold to rebirth doctrines but deny the permanence and hence the reality of a self. A more complete discussion of this concept of soul in Buddhism must await our analysis a few paragraphs below. For the time being I think we can distinguish the Buddhist patterned phenomena mentioned above from the Hindu permanent or substantial entity mentioned by DASGUPTA. Call these two "souls", SoulB and SoulH, respectively, though shortly we shall have to expand SoulH into two quite separate types.

Problems arise in trying to explain the functions of each of these stuffs in rebirth systems, for obviously if the basic "soul"-stuff differs from one system to another, then the rebirth mechanism is also going to be different. And this is precisely the case for the two systems holding SoulB and SoulH. At this point two rebirth doctrines emerge that we shall call respectively 'reincarnation' and 'transmigration'. According to reincarnation there is no soul substance that moves from one body to another retaining its self identity in the moving. That is to say, according to the Theravāda Buddhists, for example, who maintain a doctrine of rebirth with respect to SoulB, there is no enduring (*piṇḍa*) substance which moves across space and time from body to body. The self is impermanent for there is no enduring being, presumably, that moves from one body into another. SoulB doctrine is well represented in a 1st century A.D. Theravāda text, *The Questions of King Milinda*. A Buddhist monk, Nāgasena, is attempting to explain Buddhism to the great Greek King Milinda (Menandar) with the intention of converting him to Buddhism :

"The King said: 'Is there such a thing, Nāgasena, as the soul?' 'In the highest sense, O King, there is no such thing'."[311]

The King then poses the next most obvious question regarding rebirth :

The King said : 'Is there any being Nāgasena, who trans-

> migrates from this body to another?' 'No, there is not. ....this name-and-form commits deeds either pure or impure, and by that Karma another name-and-form is reborn'.[312]

This follows from SoulB theory. There is a continuity maintained however even though identity is lost. To explain this Nāgasena had earlier used the analogy of a burning lamp. The flame of the lamp is ever changing from moment to moment, yet, after the fashion of Heraclitus, there is a continuity through time of the various fire-moments even though the flame proper is never the same. Nāgasena comments :

> "Just so, 'O King, is the continuity of a person or thing maintained. One comes into being, another passes away; and the rebirth is, as it were, simultaneous. Thus neither as the same nor as another does a man go on to the last phase of his self-consciousness."[313]

The passage is worth one comment. If rebirth is indeed simultaneous with the death of the old body, then the last soul-moment of $body_1$ must be identical, on any ordinary understanding of 'simultaneous', with the first soul moment of $body_2$, where $body_1$ is earlier than $body_2$. But then there is a sense and a very real sense in which to the question, does the same SoulB move from one body to another or, can the same SoulB that is found in one body also be found in another and later body, one must answer, yes.

The reincarnational sense of Theravāda SoulB doctrine is underscored at length in the *Visuddhi-Magga* where it is said:

> "It is only elements of being possessing a dependence that arrive at a new existence: none transmigrated from the last existence, nor are they in the new existence, without causes contained in the old. By this is said that it is only elements of being, with form or without, but possessing a dependence that arrive at a new existence. There is no entity, no living principle, no elements of being transmigrated...nor, on the other hand, do they appear in the present existence without causes in that one."[314]

The *Visuddhi-Magga* continues, stating that desire and ignorance which cause consciousness continue over into a new life with the passing away of the old, and they in turn cause a new consciousness to arise.

> "But it is to be understood that this latter consciousness did not come to the present existence from the previous one, and also that it is only to causes contained in the old existence,—namely, to karma called the predispositions...—that its present, appearance is due."[314]a

Sir Charles ELIOT has stated regarding this doctrine :

> "One we must not suppose that the man's self is continued or transferred in this operation. There is no entity that can be called soul and strictly speaking no entity that can be called body, only a variable aggregation of skandhas, constantly changing. At death this collocation disperses but a new one reassembles under the influence of taṇhā, the desire of life, and by the law of karma which prescribes that every act must have its result."[315]

The insubstantial SoulB theory is quite distinguishable, consequently, from its substantial conterpart SoulH.

Problems of interpretation arise, however, to plague the Buddhist. In discarding the Hindu SoulH theory and in holding to the doctrine of momentary *dharmas* underlying the world of mind and matter, the Buddhists might seem to have gone too far. For if there is no self, but only heaps (*skandhas*) or clusters of momentary impulses, desires, or impressions, then how can there be any identity of a self, an enduring something-or-other through time? And if there is no such identifiable self through time, what becomes of the religious and moral life? And in the case of rebirth it would seem at first glance that "I" can be unjustly reborn and punished for deeds that "I" didn't even commit. The Buddhists themselves, according to EDWARD CONZE, were concerned about their *anātman* doctrine, and part of the history of Buddhism can be seen to be an attempt by the Buddhists, themselves, to smuggle a self or personality back into the mainstream of their basically non-self philosophy :

> "All these theoretical constructions (by the *Sautrāntikas* with their *āśraya*, substratum; by the *Mahāsaṅghikas* with their *mūla* or basic consciousness; by the *Saṁkrāntikas* with their transmigrating *skandhas*; by the

> *Sarvāstivādins* with their *prāpti* and *Saṁtāna*; and by the *Sammitīyas* and *Pudgalavādins* with their *pudgala*: all are rather suble concepts for a 'self') are attempts to combine the doctrine of 'not-self' with the almost instinctive belief in a 'self', empirical or true. The climax of this combination of the uncombinable is reached in such conceptual monstrosities as the 'store-consciousness' (*ālayavijñāna*) of Asaṅga and a minority of *Yogācārins*, which performs all the functions of a 'self' in a theory which almost vociferously proclaims the non-existence of such a 'self'".[315a]

But while the Buddhists may have had a problem squaring their intuitive beliefs with their doctrinal theories, the fact remains that with their theory of the self as a pattern (*saṁtāna*) of psychophysical forces (*saṁskāras*), they were able to establish a "soul" theory quite contrary to the Hindu substantial soul theory. *Theravāda* Buddhism emerges as a refined nominalism when it comes to treating soul. Thus "ego", "self", 'individual", or "person" are simply names for a multitude of interconnected facts. These causally interconnected facts are held together in a single stream, as we have seen in POTTER, by *prāpti*, and it forms thereby, a continuous series, divided off into arbitrary *saṁtānas* demarking individual existences.

> "This stream of elements kept together, and not limited to present life, but having its roots in past existences and its continuation in future ones—is the Buddhist counterpart of the Soul or Self of other systems."[316]

ome critics, like Sir Arthur B. KEITH, are quite wrong, consequently, when they argue that the two conceptions of soul the Hindu SoulH and the Buddhist SoulB, must in the end come to the same thing :

> "(Buddhism) abolishes....the principle of an absolute, with which the individual souls are identified, and it goes further than that system in seeking to deny the existence of soul. The latter aberration need not, however, be taken very seriously: the Buddhists, being determined believers in transmigration, had to produce an entity which would transmigrate; the entity provided does not differ in any very essential way, from the ordinary view in India of a transmigrat-

> ing soul, and certainly is philosophically inferior to the ordinary conception, unsatisfactory as that in itself is."[317]

The two soul theories are quite distinct, ontologically and historically. Further, $Soul_B$ does not support a solution to T.P.E. since the Southern Buddhists traditionally are atheists.[317a]

2. Plato (427-347 B.C.)

If $Soul_B$ and reincarnation represent one extreme of a rebirth continuum, the other extreme is represented by transmigration and a soul theory we have not yet considered. I refer to the rebirth and soul philosophy of Plato. Call what we are about to develop '$Soul_P$ theory'; while it is like the Hindu system of transmigration in some respects, the doctrine of $Soul_P$ is, I think, clearer and easier to identify. Thus, as we shall see shortly, while Hindus haggle over who or what transmigrates, a self or a Self, a subtle body or the Lord or *Ātman*, Plato is remarkably clear and consistent in maintaining that it is the psyche or self that moves about. This *psyche*, furthermore, remembers past deeds and desires future states of itself, and would seem to carry a certain positive identity in virtue of those memories and desires that distinguish it from other selves. In the *Republic* the story is told about a youth named Er, who was for ten days thought to be dead but who after the tenth day returned from the world of the dead and told of his wanderings:

> He said that when his soul went forth from his body... to a mysterious region···two openings side by side in the earth (appeared), and above...in the heaven two others and judges between these...righteoust o the right and upward through the heaven (travelled) ..., unjust...to the left and downward... (From the other hole) there came up from the one in the earth souls full of squalor and dust, and from the second there came down from heaven...souls clean and pure...they had paid their penalty...the punishment ten times the crime.'[318]

Finally, after resting seven days in an underworld meadow, Er is witness to the souls' choices of their future bodies. Lachesis, one of the Fates, those daughters of Necessity, and she who sings of the things that were, says that each soul must choose for itself how it will live in its next life :

> "Souls that live for a day, now is the beginning of another cycle of mortal generation where birth is the beacon of death. No divinity shall cast lots for you, but you shall choose your own deity. Let him to whom falls the first lot select a life to which he shall cleave of necessity. ....The blame is his who chooses. God is blameless."[319]

The mechanism of rebirth relates more to assumption A_4 to be covered below. The fact that it is the soul which does the choosing makes the outcome entirely the result of free choice, or as free as one of Plato's souls, bound up as they are with passion as well as with wisdom, can be. More from Plato will follow shortly.

What we have now are three soul theories relative to three types of souls, SoulH, SoulP, and SoulB; and these relate to two distinct kinds of rebirth theories, SoulH and SoulP to transmigration, where a real stuff, capable of memories, desires, interests and choices passes from one place to another, intact and maintaining personal self-identity somehow; and reincarnation, where no stuff is passed on but where one *saṁtāna* or continuity of desires and momentary impressions gives rise to a totally distinct and different continuity.

We have now to contend with transmigrating SoulH which seems to lie somewhere between the two extremes noted above. The controversy that surrounds SoulH is essentially this : How much personal essence does the soul contain ? Is it more like SoulP, which is as personal as the soul continuum could possibly conceive it ? or is it more like the ceasely changing and impersonal SoulB. Characteristically the controversy seems to have polarized around two interpretations : First, that the "soul" is impersonal and absolute *Brahman*, and hence *Brahman* is the transmigrant; the second is that the "soul" is more personal than this and capable of individuality, personality, memory, craving and all the rest. The first view is well represented by ANANDA K. COOMARASWAMY and AUROBINDO GHOSE is one famous exponent of the second point of view. Both men claim to be giving "correct" interpretations of the Hindu tradition, and one might well speculate on how it is that such divergent views are possible within contemporary Hinduism regarding the nature of the transmigrating soul. But the same or a similar divergence can also be found in the medieval controversy between Śaṁkara (780-820 A.D.) and Rāmānuja (1175-1250 A.D.) over the transmigrating soul, so it is perhaps not surprising that the impersonalists and the personalists should be fighting out an issue in the 20th century that itself may go back at least one thousand years.

3. A. K. Coomaraswamy and Śaṁkara

A. K. Coomaraswamy sets forth his interpretation of the transmigrating soul in his paper "On the One and Only Transmigrant". He quotes Śaṁkara and thereby states his own case :

> "Saṁkarācārya's dictum, 'Verily, there is no other transmigrant but the Lord' (Br. S. Bhāṣya 1.1.5) ..., startling as it may appear to be at first sight, for it denies the reincarnation of individual essences, (is) amply supported by the older, and even the oldest texts, and is by no means an exclusively Indian doctrine."[320]

For evidence to support this thesis that Soulh is the Ātman, Coomaraswamy turns to the *śruti* and *smṛti*, arguing,

> "....it is the undivided and never individualised Self that having now re-collected itself (ātmānam upasaṁharati, cf. *B. G.* 2.58), and free from the 'ignorance' of the body (with which it no longer identifies itself) transmigrates...."[321]

Coomaraswamy explains the fact of bondage of *Brahma*, God or the Lord by a curious, and some might argue heterodox twist, viz., the Self becomes attached to the world :

> "....this re-collected Self is the Brahma that takes on every form and quality of existence, both good and evil, according to its desires and activities; if it is still attached, still desirous, this Self returns from that world to this world, but if without desire, it loves only itself (*ātmakāmaḥ*, cf. *BU.* 4.3.21), then 'the mortal becomes the immortal (*BU.* 4.3.6, 7)".[322]

But many commentators, among them people that COOMARASWAMY would like to count as allies, e.g., Śaṁkara, himself, would quite rightly balk at the ascription of desire and attachment to the *Ātman*. Thus in his own commentary on *B.U.* IV. 3.6, 7 Śaṁkara makes it quite plain that he can't mean what COOMARASWAMY means by "attached self", for it is our own failure to discriminate, not *Ātman's*, that leads to rebirth :

> "...the self is so called ["vijñāna māyā," i.e., identified with intellect] because of our failure to discriminate its association with its limiting adjunct, the intellect, for it is perceived as associated with the intellect...."[323]

Further, the *Bṛhadāraṇyaka* at IV. 3.6 and 7 makes no mention of *Brahma* whatsoever. One wonders which *Upaniṣad* COOMARASWAMY has read. I dwell on this point for COOMARASWAMY has a large following, still, throughout the world, and he has always, while presenting a polar view of the self and the soul, been the subject of heated defense and attack on this issue. I am suggesting that caution is needed here when reading COOMY.

COOMARASWAMY continues with his transmigration doctrine involving a kind of $Soul_H$:

> "If we were in any doubt on this point, it is made very clear by the words of *B. U.* 4.3. 35-8, 'Here comes Brahma!' that it is not an individual, but God himself that comes and goes when 'we' are born or die."[324]

But reading Śaṁkara on these *ślokas* makes it not at all clear that he and COOMARASWAMY are again in any sort of agreement. Śaṁkara states that the Self or *Ātman* does not transmigrate in its pure and unsullied state alone, but goes with its subtle body. Śaṁkara comments on this same *śloka*:

> "...this infinite being, completely detaching himself from the parts of the body, again [does] go, in the same way that he came, to particular bodies, for the unfoldment of his vital force".[325] Śaṁkara says:

> "As the fruit is detached from the sap or the stalk by the wind and many other causes, so *does this infinite being*, the self that is identified with the subtle body i.e., has this as its limiting adjunct, *completely detaching itself from the parts of the body* such as the eye... withdrawing the organs together with the vital force-

> *again goes* etc. The word 'again' suggests that he has before this also gone many a time from one body to another."[326]

We really have then two soul-versions going here. First Śaṁkara's, and then COOMARASWAMY's. Let us call COOMARASWAMY's version of $Soul_H$, "$Soul_{HI}$". We will return to Śaṁkara's, with its subtle body in tow, later. $Soul_{HI}$ refers to the *impersonal* soul in Hinduism which carries with it none of the elements of individuality or personality characteristic of the human self. COOMARASWAMY summarizes his interpretation by saying:

> "The thesis of the present article is that the omnipresent omniscient is 'the only transmigrant'; and that in the last analysis this 'transmigration' is nothing but his knowledge of himself expressed in terms of duration."[327]

A few comments are certainly in order regarding this view and $Soul_{HI}$ theory.

1. Elements of person surely do accrue to COOMARASWAMY's "lord", *Brahma*, as opposed to *Brahman*. In the history of Indian thought whether thought of as Lord or as God, *Brahmā* is a deity with personality. Though the Sanskrit plainly mentions *Brahma*, few translators render it that way but more often, *Brahman* ; for example, Śaṁkara says "Here comes Brahman". So if COOMARASWAMY really wishes to juxtapose the personal $Soul_P$ to his own theory of $Soul_{HI}$, he could have chosen *Brahman* at least in place of *Brahma*, as a translation for the Sanskrit.

2. COOMARASWAMY, despite his disclaimers, ends with a personalized entity which seems suspiciously close to $Soul_P$, for he charges this Lord with curiously anthropomorphic attributes such as desires, activities, attachment, loving and so on. Thus while his intentions are clear, i.e., to argue that not an individual but only an impersonal God transmigrates, his expression of this intention is far from clear.

But while COOMARASWAMY does have certain problems with the presentation of the theory we are labelling $Soul_{HI}$, for our present purposes it is sufficient to represent it as a possible soul theory and let the matter go at that. We are seeking ideal limits or extremes for our soul theories, and will come to closer grips with actualities below.

Thus far we have four soul theories and two rebirth systems. Soul$_{B}$ a Buddhist theory of the insubstantial and momentary soul in a reincarnation system; Soul$_{P}$, Plato's soul theory with a psyche complete with memories and will in a transmigration system; Soul and in particular Soul$_{HI}$, an impersonal soul theory, wherein the soul is not a person but the Lord in His impersonal aspect, in a transmigration system; and finally an unlabelled theory of soul, put forward by Śaṁkara, that seems to lie somewhere between these other extremes since Śaṁkara opts for a soul as *Ātman* (the particularized, impersonal *Brahman*) together with certain of its limiting adjuncts. We shall refer to this latter theory as Soul$_{HP}$, and take it up below. Our concern with T.P.E. in part III will be with Soul$_{HP}$ alone. For Soul$_{HI}$ in a transmigration system would be unable to solve T.P.E. since Soul$_{HI}$ lacks, ideally anyway, the personal characteristics that would make a rebirth solution meaningful and satisfying as a solution. Soul$_{HI}$ in other words, does not have the characteristics needed to explain personal suffering, hence it cannot be used to justify for example my own suffering now. Only Soul$_{P}$ and Soul$_{HP}$ theories can be used to justify suffering and hopefully solve T.P.E. It is to that part of soul continuum or scale that we must now turn. Śaṁkara's *Ātman* with its subtle-body, so called, would be a place to start; hence we turn to that philosophical system which originated the subtle-body theory in Hinduism, *Sāṁkhya*.

4. *Sāṁkhya*

One of the Indian *darśanas* that we will be following rather closely in our discussion of A_1 to A_4 is the *Sāṁkhya* system and its principal textual source, the *Sāṁkhya Kārikā*. Our other assumptions, in addition to A_1, will be amply illustrated by this text.

The Sāṁkhya kārikā of Iśvara Kṛṣṇa is one of the oldest systematic texts in Indian thought, dating from about the 4th century A.D. *Sāṁkhya* is typical of the orthodox systems, systems relying on the authority of the *śruti* and certain *smṛti*, in its expression of *saṁsāra*, S_5, and the assumptions underlying that doctrine, A_1 to A_4. *Sāṁkhya* is a key philosophical doctrine, for as cosmology it finds expression in the *Gītā* and in the Vedānta philosophies of Śaṁkara and Rāmānuja; its microcosmic-macrocosmic metaphysical approach to bondage and release is unique in Indian literature, though on both levels it reflects *Upaniṣadic* doctrines enunciated separately in those earlier documents. *Sāṁkhya* thus synthesizes an earlier metaphysical tradition and passes this on to the later philosophical tradition.

The text to be examined is important for our purposes, further, because the text's commentator, Vācaspati Miśra, seems actually conscious at one point of T.P.E.[327a] But our primary purpose for introducing the text is its importance and significance in the Indian tradition, its paradigmatic nature with respect to assumptions A_1 to A_4, and the fact that it is typical of later Indian philosophy.

The *Sāṁkhya* system of philosophy is a metaphysical dualism holding that there are two kinds of basically ultimate stuffs, *puruṣa* and *prakṛti*. The former is referred to as "spirit",

> XIX. "... the spirit is 'witness', and has 'isolation', 'neutrality', and is the "seer" and inactive."[328]

and the latter is referred to as "Primal Nature" or "matter"; from it there evolves the entire universe or nature:

> III. "Primal Nature (*prakṛti*) is not an evolute [has not evolved]; the Seven [intellect, individuation, and the five subtle elements which I will describe below], beginning with the Great One [*mahat*, the intellect] are both evolvents [giving rise to other things out of itself] and evolutes; the sixteen [five sense organs, five action organs, mind, and five gross elements] are only evolutes".[329]

In contrast, the spirit is neither evolvent nor evolute.

By a curious process that need not concern us, the *prakṛti* is induced to go from an unmanifest state into manifestation or evolution, wherein the worlds are brought forth.

As far as A_1 is concerned the *kārikā* speaks of a plurality of spirits, obviously related to the *puruṣa*, which are capable of being deceived by the evolutionary elements in such a way that they, these spirits, come to identify themselves with the manifested creation. This deception is bondage :

> XX. "Thus from this union [the juxtaposition of the spirit with the evolved *prakṛti*], insentient evolute [*prakṛti*] appears as if "sentient"; and similarly, from the activity really belonging to the attributes [the *guṇas* of the evolutes], the spirit, which is neutral, appears as if it were active".[330]

In his commentary accompanying these passages in the *Kārikā*, Vācaspati Miśra (975 A.D.) says of this bondage, i.e., he says of our assumption A_2 :

> "The spirit, while in union with the "enjoyable" Nature, believes the three kinds of pain [internal, external, and divine sources of pain]-the constituents of Nature-to be his own; and from this [self-imposed bond] he seeks liberation, isolation . . .".[331]

Vācaspati then describes the route to liberation :

> " . . . this isolation is dependent upon due discrimination between the spirit and the three attributes; this discrimination is not possible without the Nature . . . thus it is that for his own isolation the spirit needs Nature".[332]

Thus, curiously enough, bondage is due to the spirit's being entranced with nature, and yet it is only through the source of its entrapment that release can be found. From this initial union of *puruṣa* and *prakṛti*, the two metaphysically ultimate stuffs of the universe, comes the evolution or manifestation of the rest of the elements. I want to focus on a few of these evolved elements, because they will help to explain further the notion of the ego, that counter-Self or counter-Spirit, that we mentioned earlier, and they will help us to focus on the mechanism of transmigration in *Sāṁkhya*:

> XXII. "From *prakṛti* [primordial matter, Nature] issues *mahat* [*buddhi*, the Great Principle]; from this issues *ahaṁkāra* [I-principle]; from which proceed the "set of sixteen"; from five of this "set of sixteen" proceed the five elementary substances".[333]

Two things are to be noted here, first the *ahaṁkāra*, and second the five of the sixteen, which are the five primary or subtle elements which produce the five elementary substances. The *ahaṁkāra* is the principle by which the ego or self is individuated. Notice that the self is not *puruṣa* (Self). Further the subtle elements or rudimentary elements form one of the limiting ends of entities which make up the transmigrating or subtle body:

> XL. "The "mergent" [subtle] body formed primevally, unconfined, lasting, composed of will [*Mahat* or Intellect] and the rest down to rudimentary elements [subtle elements], migrates, is devoid of experiences, and is invested with dispositions".[334]

Thus the subtle body is composed of will, ego, and the subtle elements. Vācaspati, commenting on this *Kārikā*, informs us that the subtle body was the first body to evolve from Nature, and that for each spirit there is one subtle body, showing again, as with Śaṁkara later, that spirit and subtle body are taken to be different entities. Further this subtle body is so constituted that it could enter into a piece of stone; and finally, it continues to exist from first evolution to the final dissolution, thus displaying its permanence. Vācaspati continues, speaking to the assumptions we labelled A_2 and A_3:

> "It migrates" [means] the subtle body goes on deserting and occupying one six-sheathed physical body after the other".[335]

And why does it thus migrate ? Because it is devoid of experience and can only have experience when it is connected with a body. And why does it want experience? Because it is connected with the will, and the will has certain dispositions for experience that drive it; and these dispositions, virtue, vice, wisdom, ignorance, passion, dispassion and power and weakness, invest the subtle body and hence drive it too. Two things to note so far here with regard to A_1 :

1. The subtle body which migrates includes intellect, ego, mind, and the five subtle elements. Hence while devoid of experiences it has "personality".

2. The subtle body does include the ego, the I-principle, which is not Spirit. A critique of these notes will appear below.

What transmigrates is a set of individual dispositions which are nonetheless non-Spirit, but personal in some sense. Thus the concept of the soul, in the *Kārikās* at any rate, would seem to lie somewhere away from Soul_{HI} (for it is not Spirit,

Lord or *puruṣa*), and yet close to $Soul_P$ (for it contains dispositions of ego, memory and mind). Call this version of the soul again, "$Soul_{HP}$"; $Soul_{HP}$ is a substantially real transmigratory entity within the Hindu context that retains elements of personality, will, ego, and mind and various subtle elements.

A comment is in order before we proceed, for we have a certain oddity in the combination of the subtle body, composed as it is of intellect, ego, mind and various subtle essences, while at the same time it is devoid of experiences and enjoyment. Can such a set of characteristics really constitute a "person"? Further, how can you have ego and mind without having experiences? In Gauḍapāda's (Ca. 7th century A.D.) commentary on the *Māṇḍūkya Kārikas*, there is an answer to these questions based on what Vācaspati will later call 'dispositions'. Commenting on *Kārikā* XL, Gauḍapāda says in his *bhāṣya* regarding "What the subtle body is, and how it migrates" :

> "This [subtle] body is composed of *Mahat* and the rest down to subtle elements . . . . i. e., intellect, ego, mind, and the five subtle elements; down to the subtle i. e., subtle elements, it migrates; it traverses the three worlds like an ant on the body of Śiva. Incapable of enjoyment [Gauḍapāda is quoting from the *Kārikā*, of course], i. e., devoid of any enjoyment".[336]

That is, devoid, now, of any actual enjoyment, actual experience, and actual memory, or any of the other elements usually associated with personality. So how can this be $Soul_{HP}$? Gauḍapāda continues:

> "This means that the subtle body becomes capable of enjoyment, because it assumes activity through the aggregation of the external body born of parents".[337]

The dispositions inherent in the subtle body become activated when that migrant soul enters a suitable body. The point being, of course, that while personality is not actual in the subtle soul, it is there dispositionally. Hence $Soul_{HP}$ is indeed a soul with personalized (I-ness, me-ness identity) attributes such as consciousness, memory, will, and the like, though they stand as possibilities rather than actualities as $Soul_{HP}$ migrates.

This list of elements in the subtle body, together with

the subtle body as the migratory agent will remain fairly standard throughout the history of Indian thought. Thus T.M.P. MAHADEVAN traces the origin of the subtle body to the *Upaniṣads* from which he rightly claims the concept receives its orthodoxy and acceptance in the Indian systems:

> "In the *Taittirīya* doctrine of *Kośas*, five sheaths of the soul are mentioned: *annarasamaya*, which is the outermost sheath made of food, viz. the physical body; *prāṇamaya*, the sheath of vital airs; *manomaya*, the sheath of mind; *vijñānamaya*, the sheath of intellect; and *ānandamaya*, the sheath of bliss. In later Vedānta, the first is also known as the gross body (*sthūla-śarīra*), the next three constitute the subtle body (*sūkṣma-śarīra*), and the last is called the causal body (*Kāraṇa-śarīra*), viz. ignorance or nescience (*avidyā*). These constitute the empirical home of the soul. Being conditioned by these, the soul becomes the subject of experience and enjoyment.[338]

In that history, the one significant change will be from that of viewing the mind, intellect, and ego as elements of *prakṛti* as in *Sāṁkhya*, to that of seeing them as reflections of the self (*Ātman*) or *puruṣa*-like Soul as in *Vedānta* and *Vaiśeṣika*. The important point is that however much the terminology may change, Soul_{HP} in some form or other, i.e., with a capacity for personal identity, forms the basis for future transmigration systems.

5. *Nyāya*

Thus in the *Nyāya Sūtras* of about the 3rd century A.D., it would seem that the soul constitutes one of the objects of right knowledge and possesses what would be distinctly "mental" elements:

> "Soul (Self), body, senses, objects of sense, intellect, mind, activity, fault, transmigration [rebirth], fruit, pain, and release—are the objects of right knowledge".[339]

And the marks of the soul are also catalogued:

> "Desire, aversion, volition, pleasure, pain and intelligence are the marks of the soul".[340]

When the body dies, and the self moves on, we can then assume that these soul characteristics move with it. Transmigration, therefore, would seem to involve Soul_{HP} insofar as desire, aversion, volition, and the rest are made specific, and individualized sufficiently to make personality (personal identity) possible. Vātsyāyana (ca. 400 A.D.) comments as follows on *Nyāya Sūtra* 19 which reads, "Transmigration means rebirths":

> "Having died, when [the self] is born again in an animate body, this being born again constitutes the rebirth of that [self] which is born . . . . The recurrence of this process of birth and death should be regarded as without beginning, and ending only with final release".[341]

We will have more to say about the beginninglessness of *saṁsāra* in Part III of this book where it will loom large in the response to Western criticisms of the rebirth solution as a solution to T.P.E. For the time being it is enough to note here the fact that the *Naiyāyikas*, at least in this very early work, are in the historical mainstream of Indian Soul_{HP} theory.

6. *Śaṁkara*

Again, Śaṁkarācārya, the great *advaitin* of the 8th century A.D., takes up the nature of the soul in his *bhāṣya* on the *Vedānta-Sūtras*. He holds once more, that the transmigratory soul or *Ātman* carries with it elements we've already seen in the *Sāṁkhya* theory of Soul_{HP}, but some additional elements to boot :

> "The soul accompanied by the chief vital air, the sense organs and the mind, and taking with itself nescience (*avidyā*), moral good or ill-desert (*karman*), and the impressions left by its previous existences, leaves its former body and obtains a new body.[342]

In just what manner all these items, particularly sense organs, are carried along with the soul and exactly what the nature of that soul is that does the carrying need not concern us. What does concern us is the problem of personal identity, and the maintenance of that identity in Soul_{HP}, if, indeed, Soul_{HP} is to be attributed to Śaṁkara. Śaṁkara continues :

> " . . . we must understand that the soul when passing from one body to another is enveloped by the subtle

> parts of the elements which are the seeds of the new body.'[343]

These seeds are karma determined and they form the continuity between the present and the past. Presumably, though Śaṁkara doesn't explicitly say so in these passages, the subtle parts or seeds retain elements of personality and thereby maintain the continuity of the self with the past. It is these seeds, produced by past acts and carried along as *karma* in the soul, that determine the future place of the soul. Śaṁkara uses the familiar simile of the caterpiller :

> "[This is] compared to the (action of the) caterpillar (*Bṛ. Up.* IV. 4,3) [and] is (not the abandonment of the old body but) merely the lengthening out of the creative effort whose object is the new body to be obtained which (new body) is presented by the *karman* of the soul."[344]

The *Bṛhadāraṇyaka Upaniṣad* that Śaṁkara quotes from, is the source, of course, for all the things that he finds carried along by the soul (Śaṁkara goes on to add water, fire, earth and life as further elements surrounding the soul). This *Upaniṣad* offers an interesting aside to the problem of personal identity, and an answer of sorts to the question What is my self composed of? and Who am I?, questions not lost on Śaṁkara. We might look briefly at this passage in the *Bṛhadāraṇyaka* before resuming our search for Soul_{HP} in Śaṁkara.

King Janaka is being instructed by the great sage Yājña-valkya, and the discussion is about the soul at death. Yājñavalkya enters on a description of the nature of the soul and begins with what we previously described in COOMARASWAMY as Soul_{HI} :

> "Verily, this soul is Brahma."[345]

but then goes on to show of what the *Brahma* of the soul is composed :

> "Verily, this soul is *Brahma*, made of knowledge, of mind, of breath, of seeing, of hearing, of earth, of water, of wind, of space, of energy and of non-energy, of desire and of non-desire, of anger and of non-anger, of virtuousness and of non-virtuousness. It is made of everything."[346]

There follows the famous *karma* dictum that as one conducts himself so does he become, bad by bad action, good by good action. Now if one were to ask the question 'Who am I' or 'What defines me' at this point, two answers or perhaps three are possible. First, I am *Brahma*, hence everything; this is the answer that the Vedāntists, of course, are ultimately aiming at. For our purposes it is the least interesting answer philosophically, since it stands at the end of a long train of other questions, and represents the end, the utimate end, of all questioning. If there are ultimate questions in Stephen TOULMIN's sense mentioned above in Part I, there could possibly be ultimate answers like *ahaṁ Brahma* in that same sense, i.e., questions and answers that represent philosophical limits, ideal or logical limits, beyond investigation and consideration. However that may be, this answer is not the answer that will help us to analyze Soul_{HP} since it is a species of Soul_{HI} which we have already looked into. Second, I may be, not *Brahman*, but in some penultimate sense, *whatever I do*. My acts define me : "According as one acts, according as one conducts himself, so does he become".[347] Suppose that we were faced (as we shortly shall be) with the problem of personal identity as understood by LOCKE, BERKELEY, REID, BUTLER, RYLE, and the other Western thinkers who have put their heads against this particular conundrum. We might ask, How am I defined as a person ? What gives my self continuity through time ? How do I know I am the same person today that I was yesterday ? Wherein does that identity lie ? LOCKE, one recalls, turned to life and consciousness, settling finally on the latter together with memory ; and in varying degrees what one has thought defines what and who one is. Despite criticisms by LOCKE's successors, this solution to the problem of personal identity still attracts support to this day. The *Bṛhadāraṇyaka* offers a second suggestion by stating that a man is what he has *done*. I am defined not by what I remember but by what I *do*. But then what I do depends in turn on what I *want*. My desires determine my actions ; they, as precedents to my acts, as causes of my acts, therefore take precedence over my acts. Hence we have a third suggestion for identifying the self : Not as *Brahman*, not as a set of acts, but as desires, i.e., a set of desires defines and identifies me :

> "But people say : "A person is made (not of acts, but) of desires only." (In reply to this I say :) As is his

> desire, such is his resolve ; as is his resolve, such the action he performs ; what action (*karma*) he performs, [into that does he become changed].[348]

The $Soul_{HP}$ is defined from its personal side, not by mind or intellect, not by consciousness or body, but by what it desires.

Thus it is that Śaṁkara in his *Bhāṣya* on the *Vedānta Sūtras* explains that it is *karma* from a previous life that determines the nature of existence in this life. It is this *karma*, interpreted now as desire or attachment, that defines the person and identifies him in this life as well as in his last life. It is this bundle of desires as karma, set into the subtle body of $Soul_{HP}$ that makes the rounds as a limiting adjunct with the *Ātman*, from births to deaths. By this means original human differences (involving eventually T.P.E.) can be explained. Śaṁkara states :

> "Moreover, the different degrees of enjoyment which are implied in the difference of birth on the part of the living beings point, as they cannot be accidental, to the existence of such a remainder of works."[349]

The Law of *karma*, A_4, assures us that there can be no accidents of birth, and Śaṁkara cites *śruti* and *smṛti* to make this point. We will return to Śaṁkara for a completer analysis in Part III, below.

The conclusion which we wish to draw from this discussion is of course that $Soul_{HP}$ is indeed found in Śaṁkara and *advaita* and possibly in *Vedānta* in general. But this will need some discussion and I propose to do that now before turning to Aurobindo Ghose and his doctrine of the soul. Let me rather briefly take up what is known in the West as the problem of self identity, and after stating it more clearly than was done above, show what the problem has meant to a few Western critics. Following this I will try to restate the problem in Indian terms, making use of our distinctions between $Soul_B$, $Soul_P$, $Soul_{HI}$ and $Soul_{HP}$.

7. The Problem of Personal Identity : West and East

The problem of self identity in the West is no doubt as old as Heraclitus and Parmenides: For if all is ceaselessly in flux, how can anything remain constant enough for me to *know* or *be* anything; and if everything is forever unchanging, then how can I *come to know* or *become* anything. Thus knowledge or being as something constant, and coming-to-know or growing as a kind of change or becoming would all be impossible where all is flux or all is static. Plato takes up the challenge in the *Sophist* and treats there the epistemological problems of knowledge as a kind of being, and coming-to-know as a kind of becoming. He meets the dilemma with the doctrine of the forms. But while this might lead to a self which was identical through time and able to be known, the problems of individuation, particularity, and difference raised by Plato in the *Dialogues* were notorious by Aristotle's time.

Aristotle rejects the doctrine of forms which couldn't solve the question of individuation, and places his hope and trust in the doctrine of substance as formed matter. Individuation came to depend, then, on the matter that was informed. Thus while you and I may share the same form, man-ness, let's assume, we are to be differentiated on the basis of our matter which is space-time-and-accident distinct. All well and good as far as distinguishing you from me is concerned, but how do I tell me from me, i.e., how do I tell or distinguish me today from me yesterday, or more to the present point; Granted that matter distinguishes me today from me yesterday, how do I know I am the same person today that I was yesterday? This is the problem of personal identity as developed in the West.

It was not until the 17th century that the problem of the person and his self identity through time received any memorable and lengthy treatment. I want to look briefly at that treatment in John Locke, then follow it up with some very brief foot-noted comments on the solution he offered, from Joseph Butler, Alexander Pope, Thomas Reid, and Antony Flew, together with some longer remarks by George Berkeley and David Hume. These remarks must be brief but they will, I hope, set the stage for a just comparison between the Western approach to the problem and the Indian approach *via* the *Upaniṣads*.

a. John Locke (1632-1704)

1) *Four Types of Identity*

John Locke's treatment of *personal identity* and identity

in general is found in his *Essay Concerning Human Understanding* Book II, Chapter XXVII.[350] For LOCKE, "identity" is an idea attributed to other ideas which "vary not at all from what they were that moment wherein we consider their former existence, and to which we compare the present".[351] Thus, the objects to which the idea corresponds may be considered identical if they are invariant, in some sense, through time; in just what sense of invariant, we shall see. We can distinguish four major types of "identity" in this chapter, since LOCKE holds that each kind or type of identity, whatever else it may be, differs from the others according to the nature of the ideas being related; that is to say, the different notions of identity are different because the ideas they relate are different. LOCKE says of three of these notions of identity, viz., sameness with respect to *substance*, *man* and *person*, that these identities differ because the names for the ideas they relate differ, and ". . . such as is the idea belonging to that name, such must be the identity."[352]

Type one: We might call this type "mathematical or logical identity." It is the least clearly presented and actually involves the principle of self-identity, i.e., everything is identical to itself and to no other.[353]

> "For we never finding, nor conceiving it possible, that two things of the same kind should exist in the same place at the same time, we rightly conclude, that, whatever exists anywhere at anytime, excludes all of the same kind, and is there itself alone."[354]

The principle is that 'a is a' that '5 is 5', ". . . it being a contradiction that two or more should be one . . ."[355] That this atom is this atom for any instant of its existence and "it is in that instant the same with itself"[356]

Type two: We might call this type "physical object identity." Where *Type one* identity is concerned with entities of universal time and space, i.e., at any time and at any place, *Type two* is concerned with identity between objects in particular time and space, i.e., time and space are necessary factors in determining the identity of *Type two*. Here we want to say that physical object P_1 at time T_1, in space S_1 is the same as P_2 at T_2 in S_2, provided that the atoms making up those objects remain the same throughout that time and that space.

> "But if one of these atoms be taken away, or one added, it is no longer the same mass or the same body."[357]

Type three : We might call this type "animate object identity." The identity of a living body existing through time and space is dependent on that object's possessing the same "life":

> "... partaking of one common life, it continues to be the same plant as long as it partakes of the same life ..."[358]

Type four : We might call this type "personal identity." The identity of a living, physical object endowed with reason (i.e., a man) existing through change in space and time, is dependent upon, chiefly, the consciousness of that man remaining unaltered:

> "For it being the same consciousness that makes a man be himself to himself, personal identity depends on that only."[359]
>
> "... and as far as this consciousness can be extended backwards to any past action or thought, so far reaches the identity of that person."[360]

It can be seen, consequently, that personal identity is associated with memory, and that insofar as I remember doing certain past actions or having certain ideas, it can be said that I am the same person now that existed then. More of this shortly.

This ends our discussion of the four *Types* of identity. In the next part I am going to attempt to piece together a discussion of personal identity in order to answer the "problem of personal identity." This will involve making a number of distinction and attempting a reinterpretation of LOCKE's own view as traditionally understood by his critics, in order to make sense of what seems to be a perfectly ordinary question: Who am I and how do I know this ?

2) *Personal Identity*

A. LOCKE's discussion of personal identity forms the second part of what we might call a two-part discussion of the identity of man. The first part may be considered to be a presentation of identity *Types two* and *three* as an answer to the problem of man's identity; the second part is a presentation of personal identity *per se* (*Type four* identity). In this part I shall want to argue contrary to LOCKE, that all three types are necessary to man's identity, and that all three as a unity of *Types two*, *three*, and *four*, play an important part in answering the various puzzles regarding his identity. In order to show the importance of *Types two* and *three* to our discussion, we turn first to the problem of personal identity.

A further division of personal identity will greatly facilitate our argument. If the problem of personal identity[361] is the problem of how a person knows that he is the same person at T_2 that he was at T_1, we can see that the problem can be stated in such a way that "person" might mean:

1. one's self or
2. another man

Restated as two questions using this distinction, we have:

1. How do I know that I am the same person today that I was yesterday? or
2. How do I know that he is the same person today that he was yesterday?

A still further distinction must be made in the notion of "person", and here we go beyond LOCKE's own rather narrow use of "person", if we understand that use at all correctly.[362] For LOCKE, a person is *in the strict sense*, "a thinking intelligent being".[363] Thus, since I cannot get inside the mind of such a being to see if his consciousness today is the same as his consciousness yesterday, it would follow that 2 is apparently unanswerable. But if "person" is interpreted in a wider sense (*less strict sense*), as "living, physical body," (*Types three* and *two*) the question becomes answerable to some degree. Now in ordinary discourse, 2 sounds like a perfectly meaningful question; consequently if "person" is interpreted in the *less strict sense*, it can be answered by reference to *Type two* ("Have your body atoms changed over the last 24 hours?"), and *Type three* ("Do you possess the same life today that you possessed yesterday?"). According to our account of LOCKE, both questions could therefore be answered, and 2 would be a meaningful question with a meaningful answer. It would not be meaningful on the other (*strict sense*) interpretation of a "person." But whether LOCKE would accept this *less strict* interpretation is doubtful :

> "...it being one thing to be the same *substance*, another the same *man*, and a third the same *person*, if *person*, *man*, and *substance*, are three names standing for three different ideas..."[364]

He is then hung on this dilemma: If he rejects 2 with the *less strict* interpretation of person, he rejects a common, sense, rather ordinary question about personal identity as unanswerable. If he accepts 2 with the *strict* interpretation then he cannot get inside the other person to check the data, and the question is unanswerable. If he accepts 2 and the *less strict* interpretation, he contradicts what he says on fn. 364 about the separateness of "person" from "man" and "substance".

But despite the exigencies of 2, and LOCKE's dilemma, it would seem that 2 can be answered, and answered by what we have referred to in the opening paragraph of as a unity of the three *Types* of identity.

B. For example, take what we might call "the problem of the transmigrating Pythagorean," and now we approach the problem as it relates to Indian thought:

> "Whether Euphorbus and Pythagoras, having had the same soul, were the same men, though they live several ages asunder."[365]

As the problem is stated here, we have to give answers to three different questions, depending on whether "men" refers to (cf LOCKE's quotation above from fn. 364) *substance*, *man*, or *person*, i.e., whetl ’ refers to physical object (*Type two*), life (*Type three*), or person (*Type four*) (we take the rather questionable liberty of identifying *man* with *life*). Following our discussion of 2 in Chapter V, above, we must assume that this problem asks only that Euphorbus be able to tell whether he is the same as Pythagoras: The answers must be: (1) in physical body, i.e., as physical object, -"no" and (2) in living body, - "no" and (3) in self or person, - "perhaps." At least 2 seems meaningfully answerable by the divisions mentioned in A.

If the problem of the transmigrating Pythagorean can be handled in this manner, it may well be that other similar problems of personal identity of the form presented in question

2 could be similarly treated.[366] We have yet to deal with 1 of A (cf. C below).

In B, we are presupposing that the puzzle of the transmigrating Pythagorean can be treated in the third person singular (2 of A), but it could also be stated in the first person where I am Euphorbus and I ask whether or not I am Pythagoras (again cf. C below).

But notice that insofar as B has a solution, it depends on answers to all three aspects, of that unity of the three *Types, two, three* and *four* in (1), (2), *and* (3) above. But (3) is in turn dependent on consciousness or memory, and an observer cannot check directly on Euphorbus' memory. An observer is held to whatever Euphorbus cares to tell about his memory experiences as evidence for Euphorbus and Pythagoras being the same person. But this in turn makes the question of answerability of (3) depend on the answerability of 1 in A, i.e., "How do I (Euphorbus) know that I am the same person today (Euphorbus) that I was yesterday (Pythagoras) ?" Despite the fact that an answer to (3) in B seems to run into difficulties on this point, we still have to our credit answers to human identity on (1) and (2). The *less strict* interpretation of "person" on this score, then, still makes sense.

C. We will now attempt to show that LOCKE's notion of personal identity involves an inconsistency that renders it useless as a concept for philosophical problem solving.

In his discussion of personal identity, LOCKE admits to, what we might call, three premises

(1) *Self consists of consciousness*, i.e. *self is consciousness*. ("For, since consciousness always accompanies thinking, and it is that which makes every-one to be what he calls self . . .").[367]

(2) *Self identity depends on memory of the self in the past* (". . . and as far as this consciousness can be extended backwards to any past action or thought, so far reaches the identity of that person").[368]

(3) *That which reflects on that past self is the present self; and they are identical* (". . . and it is by the same self with this present one that now reflects on it, that that action was done", i.e,, the remembered action). Two comments :

I. Let $Self_1$ be the present self which consists of consciousness. Let $consciousness_1$ be composed of memories M_1', M_1'', M_1'''

etc. (from (1) and (2), this is allowable). Now $Self_1$ will reflect on a past consciousness (3) which it is supposed contains M'_1 M''_1, M'''_1 etc. But this means that $Self_1$ in the past had memories which belonged to $Self_1$ in the future, i.e., this presupposes that, if the two selves are identical (3), then their memory content is identical, which means ; (a) I can know events before they happen to me and, (b) I could have *future* memories now, both of which seem odd, and (b) is probably self contradictory.

II. Another difficulty is plainly evident : At time T_1 suppose Self S_1 knows S_0 (and S_0 is a past consciousness). Suppose the memory content of S_1 and S_0 is the same so that the problem of "I" above does not spring up. What happens at time T_2 to Self S_2? (Again, the problem in "I" can be avoided only if S_2 and S_1 have the same memory content). What kind of being, it might be asked, can exist through time without acquiring new memories?[369] For if the memory content alters, then the Self with the new memories cannot be the same Self numerically as the Self without the new memories. Again "same" cannot mean, then, in *Type four* what it meant in *Types one and two*.

By arguments I and II, then, LOCKE's thesis of personal identity must be rejected.[370]

ANTONY FLEW has contended that LOCKE's mistake in regard to personal identity was in searching for the "real essence" of personal identity, a search which, incidentally, was not only a contradiction of the original intention of the *Essay*, but futile in addition.[371] If our discussion is correct, then, it must show that we don't have a static single Self, but rather a multitude of Selves, bound together (if we must talk of a Self) by a sort of continuity." "This kind of answer to the problem of personal identity would lead one to talk about Selves within Selves, where earlier-in-time Selves are "contained-in" later-in-time Selves, and all together as a sum or collection, or as a continuous series of memories, constitute a single continuative Self. Thus, one could say that at T_1, S_1 has M_1* (where M_1* contains $M_1'+M_1''+M_1'''$ . . . a sum of previous individual memories) and at T_2, S_2 has M_2* (where M_2* contains $M_1*+M_2'+M_2''$. . .) and so on for progressively later-in-time Selves. On this sort of approach S_1 is not the same as S_2 in any numerically identical manner (neither *Type one*, nor *Type two*, nor perhaps *Type three*, if we knew more what we were about with *Type* three), but rather they are the same in some "continuative" sense. Space does not permit us to carry further this conclusion. The continuative sense of *identity* needs analysis and extension; we note it here merely as the beginning of a possible alternative to LOCKE's attempted solution.

We have been some time with LOCKE for he sets the stage for the later drama on the problem; we shall be referring back to comments made in this excursis into LOCKE in the sections of this Chapter which remain. In particular we will attempt to show that for the Indians M_1, M_2,. . . and so on, when seen as elements of desire, can be used to define and identify a continuative self through time, from birth to birth.

b. GEORGE BERKELEY (1685-1753)

GEORGE BERKELEY in his *Common Place Book*, written between 1705 and 1708 while he was a student at Trinity College, Dublin, criticizes the doctrine that personal identity is connected with consciousness. It is a single statement that he makes but it is aimed, without doubt, at LOCKE ;

> "Wherein consists identity of person? Not in actual consciousness; for then I'm not the same person I was this day twelvemonth but while I think of what I then did. Not in potential; for then all persons may be the same, for ought we know".[372]

Earlier BERKELEY had queried,

> "Whether identity of person consists not in the will"?[373]

and, indeed, one of BERKELEY's editors, G. A. JOHNSTON, concludes regarding this problem :

> "It is willing, then, rather than knowing that constitutes personal identity".[374]

This willing furthermore is simply the active aspect of experience and, JOHNSTON states,

> ". . . as activity is the most fundamental characteristic of spirit, the will is the most fundamental aspect of the unity of mind".[375]

Thus for BERKELEY personal identity is connected more directly with what the mind does through willed activity than with cognition, mere thinking, or what LOCKE called "consciousness."

This bears a striking resemblance to the Indian theory as we shall note.

In *Alciphron* BERKELEY brings in his famous criticism of LOCKE's notion that self is consciousness wherein the latter is in some fashion identified with memory. Euphranor, the protagonist of the dialogue, is out to show Alciphron that personal identity does not consist in consciousness. Suppose you divide a time into three different periods. A person then has a number of ideas in each of these periods, call them A, B, and C. Now half the ideas in A, let's suppose, are retained in B, and half the ideas in B are retained in C, such that the half retained in B from A are lost in the half retained from B in C. In other words, A and B are the "same", and B and C are the "same" with respect to their half-retained identity of ideas. But A and C are not the same, i.e., they share no common core of ideas :

> "Euphranor . . . . The persons in A and B are the same, being conscious of common ideas by supposition. The person in B is (for the same reason) one and the same with the person in C. . . . But the person in C hath no idea in common with the person in A. Therefore personal identity doth not consist in consciousness".[376]

BERKELEY's conclusions are wholly negative here. But earlier in the *Principles* he had made a mighty but rather insignificant stab at the problem, identifying the self with the various operations of the mind, e.g., the understanding and the will. The reason for giving-up on the puzzle undoubtedly stems from the fact that the self for the good Bishop cannot be known through the mechanism of ideas, for we have only a mere "notion" of it. That is to say, we never perceive the self so we can have no idea of it. The alternative to unbridled skepticism is to resort to the questionable concept of a "notion". Therefore since we can have no idea of the self, the whole question of personal identity becomes theoretically unanswerable in BERKELEY. But the self as willed activity and willing, gleaned from both the *Principles* and the *Common Place Book*, will offer us an interesting parallel to the notion of self in the *Upaniṣads*.

c. DAVID HUME (1711-1776)

The skepticism that lurks in the dark dreams of "notions"

for BERKELEY comes out forcefully in David HUME's treatment of the self in the *Treatise.* The mind for HUME is simply a heap of particular perceptions. The "I" or "self", consequently, must be a convenient fiction as a name for this heap, or some particular members of the heap. Like BERKELEY and the Buddhists as well, HUME has no perception of a self, but unlike BERKELEY he has no notion of it, either. The mind as with the Buddhists again is a pure phenomenalism and contains merely happenings and occurrences. The fiction of the self arises when memory raises up past images in the mind, and imagination conveys itself along these arranged particulars, connecting them together. This whole connection, the product of memory and imagination, we denominate "mind", a fantasy, if you will. HUME concludes his section on Personal Identity in the *Treatise* by stating :

> "The whole of this doctrine leads us to a conclusion, which is of great importance in the present affair, viz. that all the nice and subtle questions concerning personal identity can never possibly be decided, and are to be regarded rather as grammatical than as philosophical difficulties. . . . All the disputes concerning the identity of connected objects are merely verbal, except so far as the relation of parts gives rise to some fiction or imaginary principle of union, as we have already observed."[377]

In swift summary then, the self for LOCKE consists problematically in consciousness and that in memories through time; for BERKELEY the self is tied obscurely to mental operations of understanding, but particularly to will or willings, i.e., things done by the mind as expressed in various actions of the body ; and finally for HUME the self is a fiction made by the imagination and memory out of a number of separate particular ideas or impressions. As far as the latter two philosophers are concerned, the problem of self identity through time is, for BERKELEY, soluble by resort to notions, obscure in themselves, or for HUME, it is merely verbal and consequently insoluble. My purpose here, save for a note on a *continuative self* in the discussion of LOCKE, is not to come up with a solution to the problem of personal identity, but simply to note certain classical attempts and their conclusions regarding its solution in the West. Whether the Indians fared any better remains to be seen.

d. *Some Distinctions Regarding Personal identity*

The problem of personal identity can take at least four forms. We have seen three of these at work in the West, and a fourth remains to be stated. These problems can be put forward as four questions, and it might be well to set them down now so that we know exactly what it is that we are looking for :

$P.I._1$ Who am I ?

This attempt at identifying the self goes back to ancient Greece, and relates not only to the question raised by the Oracle at Delphi, but relates as well to the attempt to discover the true nature of the self in Greek thought, as well as Indian and later Western thought. Colloquially the question is simply, what is the nature of the self? We have seen the answers given to this question by LOCKE, BERKELEY, and HUME. Actually, $P.I._1$ has two kinds of answers at two quite distinct ontological levels for those metaphysical "dualisms" that argue for a noumenal Self as well as a phenomenal Self, an *Ātman* as opposed to a *jīva*, a *pneuma* as opposed to a *psyche*. Thus we can distinguish $P.I._{1n}$ (noumenal Self problem of identity) from the $P.I._{1p}$ (phenomenal self problem of identity).

$P.I._2$ Am I the same person today that I was yesterday, the day before?, etc.

Again, this question is the principal 18th century British empiricist puzzle, banged about in the previous section. We have seen that if an answer is lacking to $P.I._{1p}$, then no answer can be given to $P.I._2$. The question remains open whether a failure to answer $P.I._{1n}$ leads *apriori*, though, to a failure to answer $P.I._2$. We must distinguish therefore two $P.I._2$ questions as well, where the subscripts n and p will relate back once again to the two quite distinct ontological entities, the noumenal Self or Person, and the phenomenal self or person. Once more it is obvious that the Western treatment of the problem of personal identity in the previous section was concerned primarily with $P.I._{1p}$ and $P.I._{2p}$.

$P.I._3$: Are you the same person today that you were yesterday?

We have seen this question in our treatment of LOCKE's *Essay* and it does not concern us in our attempts to discover whether the self retains identity through time. If we can answer the latter question, perhaps by generalization, $P.I._3$ could also be answered. For the time being however it is not of interest to us.

$P.I._4$ Is the self that I have or am today the same self that I had or was in a previous birth?

$P.I._4$ represents the distinctly Indian problem of personal identity, and its relation to $P.I._1$ and $P.I._2$ is obvious. Consequently, as with those previous questions, we will have two parts to the present question, for as we have seen in our discussion of the previous Indian systems, there seems to be an ontological "dualism", real or unreal, lurking about in the various soul theories we have examined; an *Ātman* or *Brahman* (or *Brahma* in COOMARASWAMY's sense), and a subtle body or *jīva*. Thus, in line with our previous distinctions we can distinguish $P.I._{4n}$ and $P.I._{4p}$. Our concern in the section that follows is to examine principally $P.I._{4p}$ and for reasons to be explained below.

e. *The Indian Problems of Personal Identity*

The latest literature in the West has, of recent years, grown to immense proportions on the subject of personal identity. LOCKE's original concern for the problem probably grew from two principal sources, as mentioned previously, a jurisprudential one and a theological one. Thus, unless somehow, somewhere, someone knows that I am the same man today that I was yesterday, it is terribly difficult to charge me with criminal or immoral acts on earth, in this life, or in Heaven, in the next. Thus $P.I._3$ and its variant $P.I._2$ become of tremendous concern to good, Christian, English philosophers once they begin to doubt whether or not they really are the same good, Christian, English philosophers from day to day; and more to the point, they both become of tremendous concern once one begins to search for reasons to stop the irritation of doubt about that identity.

This same background of concern, jurisprudential and theological, combine together to give the Indian exponent of rebirth a similar irritation of doubt. There must be some mechanism or a vehicle whereby identity, individuality or personality is maintained from life to life, or else there is no rationale behind the justness with which the law of karma, A_4, is going to work. We have seen already that those philosophers who hold to a Ṣoul_{HI} theory have refused to accept this conclusion, for they have opted for a soul-theory which does not involve them in the problems attendent upon $P.I._4$. But for those who maintain Soul_B, Soul_{HP}, or Soul_P theories together with reincarnation and transmigration doctrines, $P.I._{4P}$ looms large amongst things to worry about.

H. D. BHATTACHARYYA in an article, "Personal and Impersonal Persistence" has put the rather common Indian position for Soul_{HP} (and $P.I._{4P}$) as follows :

> "It has been felt by moralists and theologians alike that unless the individual consciousness is retained, reward and punishment lose all meaning. We do not know what transformation the psychic constellation undergoes as it crosses over . . . but we believe that it does not change so radically as to lose all sense of continuity with its earthly past."[378]

BHATTACHARYYA examines the problem of personal survival from the standpoint of one interested in heavenly self-survival—his immediate concern is with the soul in heaven rather than the soul as reborn on earth into another body. But the problems for a soul like Soul_{HP} whether reborn into some heavenly or hellish afterlife or into an earthly-bodily after life are pretty much the same. One such problem, then, shared by both is that of personal identity:

> "[Souls in heaven] are supposed to maintain in some form their personal identity or at least to develop a distinctive personality of their own."[379]

The form , that this common problem takes is familiar to us from LOCKE, and concerns itself with the principal vehicle of personality: memory. BHATTACHARYYA says:

> "If only the substance of the soul persists but not the memory of its earthly life, then the individuals of

> heaven would be quantitatively distinct but not qualitatively so we could count their number but not differentiate their psychic contents."[380]

The classical Indian texts are remarkably silent on the nature of personality as memory. Later Indians, like BHATTACHARYYA, show no such reluctance to identify the distinctness of Soul$_{HP}$ with memory, or with consciousness and memory. That the transmigrating body can be excessively complex we have seen in both *Sāṁkhya* and Śaṁkara, where variously *buddhi*, *manas*, *ahaṁkāra*, and even the sense organs are included among the items to make the trip from body to body. But which of all of these, if any, is the vehicle of personality, and what the nature of that person is, is not easily identified in the *darśana* texts, again, as we have already seen.

I think a clue to this puzzle as to what maintains the identity of the continuative self or person or individual, and hence a possible answer to P.I.$_4$, can be found as shown before in the *Upaniṣads*. Oddly enough, the answer that stands there will satisfy soul theorists who maintain either Soul$_B$ or Soul$_{HP}$ doctrines, i.e. , as we will show below, both reincarnationist as well as transmigrationist theorists can claim this notion of "personality" as their own. Very simply, the notion I propose is that the continuative self or personality is not identified with consciousness or life, or body, or memory, but, as the *Upaniṣads* are at some pains to point out, with desire. (Recall our discussion of Śaṁkara.)

The *Upaniṣads* are in general agreement, as we noted in chapter V, that it is as a consequence of certain kinds of acts that one is reborn into the world. They would also seem to be in general agreement with the *Muṇḍaka Upaniṣad*'s doctrine that it is the desire lying behind the action that is the cause of that action, and thus responsible ultimately for rebirth:

> "He who in fancy forms desires, because of his desires is born (again) here and there,"[381]

This is a thought that is found in the oldest of the *Upaniṣads*, the *Bṛhadāranyaka*, viz., that it is as one desires that one acts and that one becomes. I am going to contend therefore that one way of identifying a person is in terms solely of that set of potential and actual desires one possesses at any particular time. It would seem that this is the interpretation put upon the "person" by the *Bṛhadāraṇyaka*, (as we have noted previously in our discussion of Śaṁkara):

> "But people say; "A person is made of desires only."
> As is his desire, such is his resolve; as is his resolve, such the action he performs; what action (karma) he performs, that he procures for himself.[382]

Thus as a tentative answer to $P.I._{1p}$, one could simply say, I am a certain set of wants, interests, and needs, all of which I collectively call "desires". Further, I differ from you because my set of desires differs from yours. If they were the same we'd be the same person. This answer to $P.I._{1P}$ must now show precisely how two sets of desires do indeed or can indeed differ in order to avoid a criticism like BERKELEY's with respect to actual and potential desire. As a clue, and a very obvious one, I think that we have simply to show among other things that needs are always specific, i.e., my body's needs are not your body's needs because our bodies are quite spatially-temporally different. Hence my needs, since they differ from yours, will guarantee that my desires will also differ from yours. Thus the chance of two spatially distinct bodies possessing the same desires and being therefore the same person is neatly avoided.

Next, $P.I._2$ can similarly be answered by saying, No, I am not the same continuative self or person today that I was yesterday, since my desires have changed in that my *wants* in the world today, or my bodily *needs* experienced today (through growth and alteration of body cells if nothing else), or my *interests* in what I value today as compared to yesterday, may all be quite different. Thus suppose desire, d_1 be composed at any one time of wants w_1, needs n_1, and interests, i_1, i.e., $d_1 = (w_1 + n_1 + i_1)$. But d_1 is space-time specific, and applies to a particular period in my life—or desire-history. It will change for the simple reason, as with $P.I._1$ above, that the cells in my body are different from day to day, moment to moment. Hence I, as a set of desires, am not the same person today as I was yesterday.

Now $P.I._2$ is a big hang-up for Western philosophers as we have seen. For consciousness and memory are always fluctuating and changing, hence there seems to be no abiding person through time, hence, no identifiable man to reward or punish in some after-life, if we stay with LOCKE's and BHATTACHARYYA's concern for the moment. Thus if God wants to punish you for the pears you stole from the garden in Hippo as a child, you might well argue that you are not that same child, for you've forgotten the incident completely, and if you, or your self, is simply identical with its memories, how can God punish (or reward) you for something you had nothing to do with? Recall THOMAS REID and what we called the problem of the brave officer, above, in our discussion in LOCKE (Cf. note 366).

But the Indian unlike the Lockean need have no such trouble. Desires are not like memories. Desires are potencies and I can be identified with the latent *karma*-compelled desires which may surface or not at any specific time. Thus my self is composed of actual as well as *karma*-made possible desires. Memories, on the other hand, have been treated in the above cases like actualities : you either have them or you don't ; recall again our discussion on LOCKE and BERKELEY's criticism from the *Alciphron* which were both predicated on memories as explicit or actual entities. But ultimately, the Indian is not bothered by questions like $P.I._2$ or $P.I._3$, at least not for the discussion of rebirth : His puzzle is over $P.I._4$. Let me turn finally to that very, very Indian problem of personal identity.

$P.I._4$ is ambiguous as stated previously. It had asked, is the self that I have or am today the same self that I had or was in a previous birth. Now for $Soul_{HP}$ and $Soul_B$ theories the only question we really need to ask is a variant of $P.I._4$; call it, again, identifying the self or person with a set of actual or potential desires, $P.I_{4P}$: Is the set of desires which is transported into the new life of the soul (in a body, a heaven, a hell, a tree, an animal or what-have-you) the same set of desires that left the old life (a body, a heaven, a hell, a tree, an animal or what-have-you)? The answer must be, Yes. The set of desires, encased or existing in whatever kind of vehicle (*sūkṣma śarīra*) or pattern (*saṁtāna*) for transport, are not lost in the transport: they are neither added to nor lost from in the process of changing to a new life form (recall Nāgasena's simultaneous rebirth doctrine), and we shall see a contemporary expression of this when we turn to examine our final soul theorist, AUROBINDO GHOSE. For now, however, it is important to see that $P.I._{4}p$ is a considerably simplified version of the problem of personal identity with which this discussion began. As far as the problem of rebirth for $Soul_{HP}$ and $Soul_{B}$ is concerned, $P.I._{4p}$ is the only problem of personal identity they face.

On this interpretation of self as a set of desires, $Soul_{B}$ theories and $Soul_{HP}$ theories become practically indistinguishable, the only difference being whether to interpret desires, as substances, as $Soul_{HP}$ seems to do, or as merely immaterial patterns, as $Soul_{B}$ seems to do. The common point between both of these seemingly opposed soul theories is, however, that there is no self beyond the set of desires themselves, no self in addition to those desires. Further, I think this interpretation is consistent with the interpretation given in the *Bṛhadāraṇyaka*, and for that reason it is an interpretation that would be quite acceptable within the various *darśanas*.

Indian philosophers may be interested in $P.I._{1}$, $P.I._{2}$, and $P.I._{3}$ as philosophers. But as far as the question of the soul, its identity over one rebirth to another is concerned, the big puzzle is indeed $P.I._{4p}$. If it is answered in the manner proposed above, then one can move on to treat those other various problems of personal identity. I don't propose to do that here, since our interest is solely defined within the confines of $P.I_{4p}$.

What we have shown then is that the soul or self, interpreted as a set of desires, (needs, wants, and interests) can maintain its identity from one place or body to another, and that it does make perfectly good metaphysical sense to say: This is the same self in this life that existed in a previous life. It is curious that on this view, both $Soul_{B}$ and $Soul_{HP}$ theorists can reach agreement on the maintenance of the identity of the pattern ($Soul_{B}$) or stuff ($Soul_{HP}$) through change of places or bodies. Again this is a conclusion which follows given the nature of $P.I._{4}$ and the two soul theories that it comes up against. The position depends on Nāgasena's simultaneous rebirth theory mentioned previously, only now the rebirth is not necessarily into a body, but only a place (AUROBINDO will provide us with a catalogue of places or planes for the soul to migrate to).

Again, the claim made in answering $P.I._{4P}$ is a very simple one: Since once the body is left behind the intact soul (desire-set) can acquire no new *karma*, the desires it has *in potentia* must remain constant. And they will remain constant on $Soul_{HP}$ theory (or $Soul_B$ theory, as well) either until a new gross body is inherited and new desires are gained through new *karma*, or until $Soul_{HP}$ moves to a new plane where it can gain or lose the desires it already has. Our point is simply that there is no reason to believe that desire is lost either in the transport to a new body, instantaneously, or to a new plane of being, the smoke of the fire, the moon, the sun, higher psychic planes as with AUROBINDO, or what have you. And if no desire is lost in the transport from one place to another, body to body, or body to smoke, or smoke to moon, or what have you, then self-identity is maintained, and $P.I._{4P}$ can be solved.

But just how immediate this transfer from place to place is remains problematic. It is to this problem of the $Soul_{HP}$ that we turn next.

8. AUROBINDO GHOSE (1872-1950)

A contemporary Bengali brahmin, AUROBINDO GHOSE, wrote *The Life Divine* in which he set forth his own monumental thesis regarding life, man, God, and the world. It is a huge book, and this is practically the only point about the work on which his contemporaries would agree. He has, however, several interesting things to say about the soul, A_1, bondage, A_2, *karma*, A_4, and our other assumption for *saṁsāra* that make him worth considering.

AUROBINDO's chief concern with regard to rebirth is to solve a particular problem involved in the popular mind regarding that doctrine ; an inconsistency, he holds, obtains in the doctrine of rebirth which follows from the belief in a static, unchanging soul. This soul is caught eternally in *saṁsāra* with no chance of escape save temporary surcease in heaven or hell. There is no chance for release on this popular view of the soul and AUROBINDO attacks the whole notion :

> "In the popular ideas which derive from the religions that admit reincarnation, there is an inconsistency

> which after the manner of popular beliefs, they have been at no pains to reconcile. On the one hand, there is the belief, vague enough but fairly general, that death is followed immediately or with something like immediateness by the assumption of another body. On the other hand, there is the old religious dogma of a life after death in hells and heavens or, it may be, in other worlds or degrees of being which the soul has acquired or incurred by its merits or demerits in this physical existence. . . ."[383]

AUROBINDO resolves this antinomy between instantaneous body-rebirth, and the soul's sojourn in another place like heaven or hell, by his doctrine of the evolution of the soul. In resolving the antinomy of popular belief in rebirth, he has occasion to combine the above two beliefs into one grand one of his own :

> "Our belief in the birth of an ascending soul into the human form and its repeated rebirth in that form, without which it cannot complete its human evolution, rests, from the point of view of the reasoning intelligence, on the basis that the progressive transit of the soul into higher and higher grades of the earthly existence and, once it has reached the human level, its repeated human birth compose a sequence necessary for the growth of the nature ; one brief human life upon earth is evidently insufficient for the evolutionary purpose."[384]

From this discussion there emerges AUROBINDO's vision of the soul as an entity, mental and vital, which stands in need of growth and perfection, and apparently gets them :

> "It is the soul-person, the psychic being, that survives and carries mind and life with it on its journey, and it is in the subtle body ["the characteristic case or sheath"] that it passes out of its material lodging. . . ."[385]

The heaven and hell of popular belief are transformed for AUROBINDO into higher or lower levels or planes on which the soul can move toward perfection and eventual union with the Divine.

AUROBINDO resorts to talk reminiscent of the *Taittirīya Upaniṣad* in discussing the various sheaths which the soul must slough off as it passes from one existence to another (cf. T.M.P. MAHADEVAN, note 338) :

> "At each stage [of this after-life passage] he would exhaust and get rid of the fractions of formed personality structure, temporary and superficial, that belonged to the past life; he would cast off his mind sheath and life sheath as he had already cast off his body sheath : but the essence of the personality and its mental, vital and physical experiences would remain in latent memory or as a dynamic potency for the future".[386]

While AUROBINDO describes this progress of the soul as a matter of "dynamic probability", a number of truths about his beliefs regarding the extra-bodied and evolving soul tend to emerge. First, the sòul does undergo change during the between-life period. This would seem to violate the answer we gave to $P.I._{4p}$ above wherein we assumed that the soul *qua* a set of desires passed untouched and unchanged from one place to another, and without interruption. And now AUROBINDO's dynamically probable theory of the evolving soul seems to threaten that answer. But wait. Second, the changes that occur during this body period are changes that get rid of personality, but the personality that is thereby changed is simply "temporary and superficial" personality structure. Third, what remains after the sheaths have been shed and as the soul rises to still higher planes of perfection is the essence of personality, an element of self-identity, which is, fourth and finally, identified with memory on the one hand and "dynamic potency" on the other. I would contend that AUROBINDO is in the *Upaniṣadic* tradition that identifies personality or the self with desire, and that "dynamic potency" is precisely what is called "desire", as we explained that concept previously.

If all this does indeed follow, then AUROBINDO's concept of a soul challenges those doctrines that see the soul as a limited personality which survives unchanged from earthly birth to earthly birth. To see the soul in that static manner is, in AUROBINDO's words, to deprive rebirth of both spiritual utility and meaning :

> "But if that were so, there would be no spiritual utility or meaning at all in rebirth; for there would be the

> repetition of the same little personality, the same mental and vital formation to the end of Time".[387]

The view of the soul which emerges from this brief survey of AUROBINDO's philosophy is what we called previously $Soul_{HP}$. But the personality that is put forward, while on one level real enough in itself, is only a temporary fixture. It is not the abiding reality that stands behind that personality. To this extent AUROBINDO stands squarely with Śaṁkara and the *advaita* tradition in *Vedānta*. AUROBINDO says, restating what he had previously remarked :

> "In each return to earth the Person, the Puruṣa, makes a new formation, builds a new personal quantum suitable for a new experience, for a new growth of its being".[388]

But the same vital and mental forms are kept by this soul moving to another body, as the soul mentioned above kept certain traces of the personality in dynamic potency as it moved beyond the body, beyond all bodies to perfections on higher planes. Of this inter-body moving soul he says :

> ". . . but the forms or sheaths dissolve and what is kept is only the essential elements of the past quantum, of which some will but some may not be used in the next incarnation"[389]

These essential elements, what he has called above "dynamic potencies" can surface or stay submerged in subsequent embodiments. Then they may unpredictably surface, forming what he calls a "new personality". But that person is hardly new, for identity is maintained through the potencies, those dynamic forces of desire which may lie dormant or spring forth, seemingly unaccountably. Hence the answer given previously to P.I. $_{4P}$ stands intact.

This surfacing of past *karmic* potentials into present actualized desires, will prove troublesome for the holders of the assumption of the law of karma, below, in A_4. The sheer unpredictability, and oftentimes inexplicability of these actualized traces of personality will, I hope to show, prove to be a stumbling block to the moral life. For the present, it is sufficient that we have shown that AUROBINDO represents A_1, the soul thesis, with a theory of $Soul_{HP}$. We shall return to him again in the discussion of the other assumptions.

9. *Conclusions to A_1*

We have been a long time with the soul thesis, since getting straight on it is essential to understanding our other three assumptions, as well as in defining the notion of *saṁsāra*. We have seen that Indians by and large cling to a kind of $Soul_{HP}$ theory, though the other soul theories, $Soul_B$, $Soul_P$ and $Soul_{HI}$, can all stand as assumptions in various rebirth theories, whether transmigration or reincarnation types.

We have tried to hint and not too subtly that $Soul_{HI}$ theory connot be used in rebirth theories which hope to solve T.P.E. It may be used to *explain* evil, i.e., it may answer the question, why is there evil in the world?, or Why am I suffering so?, but it cannot be used to justify my suffering, i.e., show that suffering is deserved, or to justify the inequitous suffering and the seemingly gratuitous suffering in the world. In short, if rebirth is to solve T.P.E. it must involve a $Soul_{HP}$ theory.

Finally, we have tried to show that $Soul_B$ and $Soul_{HP}$ theories can solve the problem of personal identity seen as $P.I._{4P}$, i.e., as a problem about the continuative self's identity from life to life, or birth to birth, where actual and potential desire, rather than consciousness, body, or memory, carries the burden of that identity. This is a particularly big puzzle for rebirth theorists who have set out to solve T.P.E., since unless continuity is maintained within the soul, we end with merely an explanation of evil, if that, and no justification of evil, i.e., we end up with no rebirth solution to T.P.E.

A_2 *The Soul-Locus Thesis*

Any rebirth doctrine, whether transmigrationist or reincarnationist must hold that there is a place or places where the soul, whether $Soul_B$, $Soul_P$, $Soul_{HP}$, $Soul_{HI}$, can take up residence. This place or locus need not be in time and space, as it surely isn't for certain Buddhists, nor in the world, as it is for certain Vedāntins, nor need the place be "real" in an ontological sense as with those doctrines which hold that only *Brahman* or the Absolute is or can be wholly real.

The classical soul-locus theories, certainly the ones that spring to mind most easily when discussing the place of the soul, are those represented by PLATO and Jainism.

1. Plato

In the *Phaedo*, Socrates tells Cebes that "the souls of the dead must exist in some place from which they are reborn",[390] and this conclusion follows hard upon the famous myth in the *Phaedo* which Socrates has already recounted :

"There is an old legend, which we still remember, to the effect that they [souls] *do* exist there [in another world], after leaving here, and that they return again to this world and come into being from the dead"[391]

The good and bad souls, as we have seen previously in the myth of Er in the *Republic*, receive various fitting rewards or punishments. In the *Phaedo*, this is elaborated further with respect to the souls of the wicked :

> "Of course these are not the souls of the good, but of the wicked, and they are compelled to wander about these places [tombs and graveyards] as a punishment for their bad conduct in the past. They continue wandering until at last, through craving for the corporeal . . . they are imprisoned once more in a body. And as you might expect, they are attached to the same sort of character or nature which they have developed during life".[392]

In the *Phaedo* then, souls can find abodes in places like other worlds and graveyards, and places like bodies of living creatures.

In the *Phaedrus* the nature of these bodies is more finely spelled out. At 248d and e, nine separate human loci for the returning soul are detailed from that of a human babe, "that shall grow into a seeker after wisdom or beauty, a follower of the Muses, and a lover",[393] to a King, a statesman or business man, an athlete, a priest, poet or imitative artist, farmer, sophist and finally, the lowest birth of all, a tyrant. Further, for those souls who choose badly,

> ". . . then does the soul of a man enter into the life of a beast, and the beast's soul that was aforetime in a man goes back to a man again".[394]

The entombment theory of the soul (as I shall call this notion) in the West probably goes back to the Pythagoreans and is found throughout those enthusiastic religions of the Mediterranean basin from the 6th to the 4th centuries B.C. One thing to note about the theory is that while Pythagoras could hold that a human soul of a friend inhabited the body of a dog, the picture of the entombed soul is not so clear in PLATO. Thus three interpretations in general are possible with respect to the entombment theory :

1. There are human souls and they are imprisoned in various bodies.

2. There are neutral (neither human nor animal, let's say) souls and they are imprisoned in various bodies.

3. PLATO's theory.

1. On the first interpretation, the humanness of the soul, its rationality, let's assume, is maintained in whatever body the soul happens to find itself. Thus PYTHAGORAS could recognize the soul of a former friend in the body of that dog simply because the former friend's rational or human soul was entombed intact. On this view, it would be the body of the creature, the locus of the soul, that would determine the various manifestations of the soul, i.e., what the soul could or could not do. One is reminded of the *Jātaka* stories about the Buddha's former lives as elephant, jackal, tiger, and so on. But while the soul must act through the mechanism of the body, it nonetheless retains its identity as a human soul—supposedly one knows one is entombed, and one feels human anguish at being in the dog's body. Further, on this view, perhaps good dog souls could inhabit human bodies, though I'm not sure what that would be like. The important point, though, is that souls are value-specific, they are not neutral or value-free entities.

2. On the second interpretation souls are not inherently one kind of thing, human, or another, beast. What they become in their body-or-place-tomb, depends more on the tomb than on what they, the souls, are in themselves. These neutral souls, it must seem, receive what characteristics they do have from their surroundings, their loci, since in themselves they are indistinguishable one from another. The static soul doctrine attacked previously by AUROBINDO surely arises for this view. For once the soul is entombed and once it becomes body specific or body dependent, what is to prevent it from going one dreary, unchanging round after another, in wearisome succession. To say, Well, good dogs will be reborn as men, is opaque and silly

unless one has a ready answer to, What makes a dog good?, and even more bothersome, What is a bad dog? I take it, then, that this is the view that AUROBINDO is challenging in his attack on the static soul theories. I don't know of any soul theorist who has or could honestly hold such a view as this, for it would mean that the round of birth and death could go on incessantly and without end. But possibly the Stoics and perhaps FRIEDERICH NIETZCHE, in his more dionysiac moments, held to a doctrine of eternal recurrence, in which case this second view would be aptly represented.

3. On the third interpretation, which I shall dub "PLATO's view," the soul is able to slip between the above two extremes of the entombment theory in which the soul is either wholly human or wholly nothing. Thus PLATO can introduce a tripartite theory of the soul, speak about the human element in it being overcome by the appetitive beastly element, and thereby retain its human-rational part *in potentia* (thus saving the first interpretation) while at the same time steering clear of the totally neutral view of the soul (thus avoiding the second interpretation). The machanism by which this is accomplished is the mechanism of soul besmirchment, the ability of the soul to become smudged, dirty, or covered over with some sort of contamination in virtue of which its rational portion is temporarily prevented from exerting itself:

> "But... if at the time of its release the soul is tainted and impure, because it has always associated with the body and cared for it and loved it... beguiled by the body... its passions and pleasure... [loving that] which can be touched and seen and drunk and used for sexual enjoyment... [then it will not] escape independent and uncontaminated."[395]

I have spent not a little time on this third entombment theory for it is not unlike an entombment theory in Indian thought, the Jain. Again the soul carries certain capacities for the higher as well as the lower forms of existence, but the higher capacities are in temporary abeyance due to soul-smudging and contamination. The second of our realistic soul-loci theories now follows.

2. *Jainism*

In the *Tattvārthādhigama Sūtra* of about the 3rd century A.D., *Jainism* sets forth its theories about soul, the places of souls, and the other assumptions necessary to a theory of rebirth. *Jainism* in its metaphysics is a substantial dualism, like *Sāṁkhya*, and like the latter doctrine it holds to the belief in the bewitchment of Soul by matter; but in *Jainism* the bewitchment is one of direct material contact between the two. Simply put, there are selves (*jīva*) and non-selves (*ajīva*). The latter flows into the former and bondage occurs. The problem of liberation for the *Jain* then becomes one of stopping the flow, and getting rid of the matter already in the soul:

> "The categories (*tattvas*) are souls [or selves] (*jīva*), non-souls, inflow (*āsrava*) of karmic matter into the self, bondage (*bandha*) of self by karmic matter, stoppage (*saṁvara*) of inflow of karmic matter into the self, shedding (*nirjarā*) of karmic matter by the self, and liberation (*mokṣa*) of the self from matter."[396]

This entombment theory in order to account for the soul's rebirth is elaborated upon at some length, and the types of souls as well as their loci are further spelled out:

> "Selves are [of two kinds] : worldly and liberated. Worldly souls are [of two kinds] : with mind and without mind. Worldly selves are again [of two kinds] : mobile and immobile. Immobile selves are earth-bodied, water-bodied, fire-bodied, air-bodied, and vegetable-bodied. Mobile selves are with two senses, [three senses ... five senses]".[397]

Thus mobile souls with two senses or three senses or, as with humans, five senses, would inhabit various kinds of living creatures, while worldly immobile souls would inhabit various earth or vegetable bodied loci. But the *jīva*, while it may have these various accidental capacities, or inhabit these very accidental loci, has in itself an essential nature that demands to be freed of karmic matter and worldly habitation, i.e., its essence is liberation:

> "The self's (*jīva*) essence is life, the capacity of being liberated [for some souls]; and the incapacity of becoming liberated [for others]".[398]

Thus the soul's eventual locus is beyond the world. To get there rebirth and the inflow of karmic matter into the soul which causes that rebirth must cease. This is accomplished by various *yogas* or methods of release:

> "*Yoga* is the activity of body, speech, and mind. *Yoga* is the inflow of karmic matter into the soul. Inflow [is of two kinds]: good, of virtue or meritorious karmas; bad, of vice or demeritorious *karmas*. [Souls] affected with the passions have mundane [in ow, leading to the cycles of birth and rebirth]. [Those] without the passions have only transient [inflow, leading to fewer rebirths]".[399]

The world then, on the *Jaina* interpretation, is full of struggling souls imprisoned in matter and with matter. To this extent the entombment theory holds for the Jainas in a fashion similar to PLATO's theory. Unlike PLATO, the Jainas follow the old Vedic belief that souls can also be entombed in inorganic as well as in all organic substances. To this extent they differ from PLATO who doesn't seem to believe that carrot and rutabaga souls are capable of liberation. But like PLATO, the worldly souls possess minds, and presumably this establishes their identity through time, though again, the point is not terribly clear in the previous text.

Other Indian philosophic systems hold to the body, the human body, as the chief locus of the transmigrating soul.[400] But the nature of the connection between self and body is more *Sāṁkhya* and less Jaina-Platonic entombment theory.[401] Thus the *Vaiśeṣika Padārthadharmasaṁgraha* of *Praśastapada* of the 6th century A.D., argues that the self when connected with a body comes to be deluded, hence it seems to follow an bewitchment theory not unlike the delusion theory of the *Sāṁkhyas*:

> "In reality the self is neither the doer nor the enjoyer; it is wholly indifferent. And it is only when it becomes connected with such limitations as those of the body and the sense-organs, that it comes to

have such notions, as "I" and "mine", of its being the doer and the enjoyer; and such notions cannot but be regarded as false . . . . From these notions of "I" and "mine" follow an affection for the pleasant, and aversion to the unpleasant thing; these affections and aversions give rise to activity and cessation from activity; thence follow *dharma* and the self into the cycle of birth and rebirth . . . .".[402]

There is a difference however, depending on the nature of the connection between self and body. It is one thing to be entombed, and another to be bewitched. At any rate the *Vaiśeṣika* would seem to hold that the connection between the abode and the self is one of bewitchment and not simply one of being in *mere* contact with human bodies with sense organs. Further, the soul or self is capable of being in or near or in contact with more desirable bodies, including human ones:

"When the man does not attain true knowledge, . . . the doing of excellent virtuous deeds . . . leads him to contact with desirable bodies . . . in such regions as those of Brahmā, of Indra, of Prajāpati, of *pitṛ* [ancestors], or of men."[403]

Further, the self can be reborn in lower forms even than this:

"Similarly the performance of bad, sinful acts, . . . brings about his contact with bodies and sense organs and consequent experience of pain etc., in such regions as those of ghosts and of the lower animals. And thus by the performance of such virtuous deeds as are in the form of outgoing activity (of the self) .... the man passes through the various divine, human and animal regions again and again; and this is what constitutes his "wheel of bondage."[404]

The contact, *saṁyoga*, between the soul and the various bodies will eventually be realized and rebirth will cease:

"... the *dharma* and *adharma* of his previous lives being exhausted .... all his actions henceforth are only such as are of the nature of pure *dharma* tending towards "cessation" or "peace"... And thus there being complete cessation, the self becomes "seedless" and the present body falling off, it takes no other bodies, and this cessation of equipment with bodies and organs, being like the extinguishing of fire on all its fuel being burnt up, constitutes what is called *mokṣa* (final deliverance")".[405]

SATISCHANDRA CHATTERJEE in his paper "Early Nyāya-Vaiśeṣika" summarizes the view of the soul in this combined *darśana*:

> "The soul (*ātman*) is an eternal and all-pervading substance. The qualities of the soul are cognition, desire, aversion, pleasure, pain, merit, demerit, etc. These can't belong to any physical substance. So there must be an immaterial substance called soul, of which they are qualities"[406]

He continues, stating that knowledge and consciousness belong to the soul as separable attributes, i.e., as accidents. But these elements are sufficient, accidental though they may be, for the personalization of the soul. Thus the early *Vaiśeṣika*, like the Jain and PLATO, assumes that the soul is held to the body by the deeds or, as we argued in A_I above, by desires, engendered by the previous births. Like them it also assumes that the places of the soul are manifold, and not merely human-body oriented. Though all three differ from one another in just how many loci are available to the transmigrating soul, all are agreed that there are multiple loci graded according to some standard with (and this is the least we can say) the human at or near the top of the scale and animals at or near the bottom. All agree that the abode taken up by the soul is a function of the soul's desires or spiritual stage or evolutionary state on the trek to eventual release (save for PLATO, who seems loathe to speak about "release"). Some later philosophers, like AUROBINDO will even add extra stages:

> "A survival of the material body by the personality implies a supraphysical existence, and this can only be in some plane of being proper to the evolutionary stage of the consciousness or, if there is no

> evolution, in a temporary second home of the spirit which would be its natural place of sojourn between life and life . . ."[407]

AUROBINDO has simply extended the possible loci of the soul beyond this world, to a series of psychic planes or levels that are akin to the psychic or mental nature of man. On these extra-terrestrial planes the evolution of the soul can proceed unimpeded, until it is called down once again to a physical abode on earth.

3. *Buddhism*

But while $Soul_P$ and $Soul_{HP}$ and even $Soul_{HI}$ theories have no doubt committed themselves to A_2, the case is not so clear with $Soul_B$ theory. For if, as the *Theravādins* seem to say, all the world is in a state of constant flux, it becomes pretty hard to identify anything, much less a locus, for the non-existent soul. But the *Theravādins* are notorious, as is DAVID HUME, for stating officially the most outrageous philosophic doctrines, and then taking it all back by what they must unofficially and commonsensically believe (cf, fn. 315a). A case in point are the *Śūnyavādins* who spend volumes talking about why one should be silent.

It is obvious that there is a locus for those patterns of desire we called $Soul_B$, just as it was obvious that $Soul_B$, while not a soul in the ordinary sense of $Soul_P$ or $Soul_{HP}$ was still a soul, despite official pronouncements, i.e., it is a $Soul_B$ (and that is all we need).

Go back to the *Milindapañha* and that mysterious lamplight analogy:

> "Said the king: "Bhante Nāgasena, does rebirth take place without anything transmigrating [passing over]" "Yes, your majesty. Rebirth takes place without anything transmigrating. . . . Suppose, your majesty, a man were to light a light from another light; pray, would the one light have passed over [transmigrated] to the other light?" "No".[408]

The important point, here, is that while the flame alters and changes, the places of the flames, the two lamps, remain relatively constant. If one is going to have a flame, one needs a lamp; if one is going to have a pattern of desires, one needs a place for the pattern. Hence, the body is an abode, and there is at least one abode for $Soul_B$.

> "Bhante Nāgasena", said the king, "what is it that is born into the next existence?" "Your majesty", said the elder, "it is name and form . . . " "Is it this same name and form that is born into the next existence?" "Your majesty, it is not this same name and form that is born into the next existence; but with this name and form, your majesty, one does a deed—it may be good, or it may be wicked—and by reason of this deed another name and form is born into the next existence".[409]

Thus *Theravāda* Buddhism, at least, does hold to A_1 as an assumption, it would seem, for its rebirth system. And having admitted to the soul thesis as $Soul_B$ it needs and receives a place for $Soul_B$ just as the flame has a lamp for its place.

4. *Conclusion to A_2*

Thus all the rebirth systems we have examined would seem to hold to places for souls to be. Those places are very varied depending on what the ontology will or will not support human, subhuman, superhuman places, in space and time, or without space and time. But nonetheless the loci are there as they apparently must be for any full-fledged rebirth system, for the simple reason that wherever a soul is, that place is its locus. It is simply an accident, but a rather important one, that bodies are the most frequently talked about loci of souls, and we understand "body" in its ordinary sense as a container or receptacle capable of "holding" souls, or being in some kind of contact with them.

A 3. *The Mobile-Soul Thesis*

1. *General Conditions*

Not only then are there souls, however defined, and places for souls, but further souls are capable of moving from one of these places to another. I think this mobilesoul thesis is much in evidence in the texts we have been examining, from the *Vedas* and *Brāhmaṇas*, to PLATO, and to AUROBINDO. There are three things that can happen to souls relative to bodies, it would seem:

1. A soul can stay in a body and never leave it, such that it dies with the body (e.g., in materialistic systems like *Cārvāka*).

2. A soul can never enter a body, but moves instead thither and yon without ever touching base (a body). This does not violate our conclusion from A_2, viz., that wherever a soul is it must be in some locus or other. All we claim now is either that it is possible for souls never to have bodies to enter, or that if there are such loci as bodies (as ordinarily understood), souls need never enter them.

3. A soul can enter a body and leave a body; and it can do so either erratically and unpredictively, or it can do so in some regular fashion, according to rules.

Neither 1 nor 2 will lead to a rebirth theory. Both locus and soul, and habitation of the former by the latter, are necessary for the kinds of rebirth systems we have been examining; but further rebirth would seem to imply being born again, hence movement again would be necessary. Thus 1 and 2 are out. But 3 will give us a rebirth system, either with rules or without rules for the soul's rebirth. Because the systems we are examining would all seem to be systems with rules, we move to those systems and that assumption in A_4.

2. *The Mobile Soul System*

It is interesting to note in passing, and in connection with 3, that certain theological systems which are not ordinarily thought of as containing rebirth systems, espouse such a system in holding, as certain sects of Christianity do, to the belief in the resurrection of the body. Thus 3 is the claim that the soul leaves one body and enters another (not necessarily different from the one it left). I suspect that on this interpretation of 3 as espousing a once-returned-soul doctrine that of the *New Testament's* Lazarus risen from the dead, similar in all respects to the *Republic's* Er, might be accounted a rebirth story. Further, those religions which hold to savior and *avatāra theses* wherein a God or hero is reborn on earth to save the suffering world from sin and damnation must also be accounted as rebirth religions. Those deities who are reborn as *avatāras*, if the assumptions for rebirth are not to be held in temporary abeyance for them, must be reborn under the same rules as other beings: Thus they must have souls, these souls must be *Karma* laden with desire in some sense, e.g., the desire to save the suffering world, the desire of love for creatures, as with Lord Kṛṣṇa and the various Bodhisattvas of the Hindu and Buddhist tradition. This, of course, implies that the God who incarnates is not perfect because he still possesses a trace of desire which must be worked out in an earthly locus and in a human form. Thus the peculiarity that since savior or *avatāra* religions worship their incarnated God, and since this God is not perfect (free from desire) else he would never have incarnated, one ends by supplicating oneself to an imperfect God.

Finally, one who holds the mobile soul thesis with rules must be able to specify, seemingly, what those rules would be like. A rebirth system, consequently, would be made truly systematic only when the rules regarding the relationship between souls and bodies (or places), had been carefully laid out. For example, the system would have to specify, I would think, some of the following things :

1. The conditions under which a soul could leave a body. Only when the body dies ? in sleep ? at any other time? How does it leave ? What makes it leave ? Does it know when to leave ?

2. The conditions under which a soul could enter a body. Living bodies only ? or bodies capable of living ? stones ? tables ? plants ?

3. The conditions regarding how many souls may occupy one body at any one time. Do cases of possession count as two souls in one body ? Can multiple souls be in one place at any one time ? How many ?

4. The conditions regarding a body occupying a soul. Does this constitute contamination as with PLATO and the Jainas ?

5. The conditions regarding a soul occupying or moving into another soul. Does, e.g., the tripartite soul theory of PLATO or ARISTOTLE, constitute souls within souls as the *Taittirīya*

Upaniṣad sheath-doctrine seems to do? Hence are there souls within souls?

6. The conditions regarding the "choice" of body by a soul or vice versa. These are partly spelled out in PLATO as we have seen, and we shall come more fully into it in the discussion of assumption A_4 which now follows. The question raised with respect to it is. What are the conditions governing which mobile soul goes where?

3. *Conclusion To A_3*

Whatever problems might be met in specifying such a mobile soul system, it follows from our discussion here and above that any rebirth system must assume that its souls can move, however that is specified, from one locus, place or body to another, however they in turn are specified.

A_4 The Karma Thesis

1. *The Indian Context*

Karma or the law of karma is an essential element to the Indian's concept of rebirth. We have seen references to it in our discussion of *saṁsāra* in A_1 above, but I want now to speak about it more explicitly. The doctrine is as old as the *Bṛhadāraṇyaka Upaniṣad* where at 3.2.14 it is regarded as a great secret not to be spoken of in public, and later in 4.4.6 it is stated :

> "Now whenever it [the self] is composed of this thing or of that thing,—however it acts, however it operates, so it becomes [in the next life]. Acting well it becomes good; acting ill it becomes evil. As a result of right action it becomes what is good; as a result of evil action it becomes what is evil".[410]

In the *Chāndogya Upaniṣad* (as we have seen) the same theme appears :

> "Accordingly, those who are of pleasant conduct here—the prospect is, indeed, that they will enter a pleasant womb, either the womb of a Brāhmaṇa or the womb of a Kṣatriya, or the womb of a Vaiśya. But

> those who are of stinking conduct here—the prospect is, indeed, that they will enter a stinking womb, either the womb of a dog, or the womb of a swine, or the womb of an outcast".[411]

The doctrine of karma then becomes a device for linking up conduct and consequences, in this life, perhaps, or in the next. More on this in a moment. Finally, in a later *Upaniṣad*, the *Śvetāśvatara* the doctrine of karma is enunciated in a typical fashion :

> "According unto his deeds (karman) the embodied one successively
> Assumes forms in various conditions.
> Coarse and fine, many in number.
> The embodied one chooses forms according to his own qualities.
> (Each) subsequent cause of his union with them is seen to be
> Because of the quality of his acts and of himself".[412]

FRANKLIN EDGERTON has said of this so-called "law" in his *The Beginnings of Indian Philosophy* :

> "The relative excellence of any new birth is rigidly determined by the net balance of good and bad actions in previous births. This is the famous law of 'karma' (Sanskrit *karman*, 'action, deed'). It is a law of nature and works automatically; it is not administered by any God or superhuman agent".[413]

Two comments before we continue : First, we will have to ask what kind of law this law of karma is, for getting straight on this is essential to being precise with respect to the doctrine of rebirth; second, since God according to the above account is not responsible for the meting out of punishment and discipline under this law, plainly no T.P.E. can be associated through it to God. We will return to this shortly, however, for there are some confusions present. EDGERTON continues :

> "It is man's relation to propriety or morality, *dharma*, which alone determines. For more than two thousand years, it appears that almost all Hindus have regarded transmigration, determined by 'karma', as

> an axiomatic fact. 'By good deed one becomes what is good; by evil deed, evil''.[414]

The reasons for regarding transmigration as determined by karma as an "axiomatic fact" is, as I pointed out in the conclusion to the *Sāṁkhya* discussion above, that both rebirth and karma are enjoined by the *Upaniṣads*, hence orthodoxy compels assent on this matter.

2. *Right and Wrong under the Law of karma*

What is going on with this law of karma ? The doctrine seems to be saying that for some kinds of behavior b, there will be a result r, such that if b is good or bad then r will be good or bad. But this needs further examination. Suppose that we have three kinds of behavior, good, bad, and indifferent, i.e., bg, bb and bi, respectively. Then there will be three types of responses to these three behaviors, rg, rb and ri, respectively. If the law works, it would be impossible supposedly to have rb or ri associated with or follow from bg, and the same could be said for the other behaviors and results. Further, if the law of karma is just, and that seems to be what the above texts imply, then each man would have to get exactly what's coming to him, his due, no more and no less. Could there be any overcompensation or under-compensation ? Suppose I kick a dog who is bothering me and shortly after a semi-trailer truck comes roaring into Ames Library loaded with concrete culverts and squashes me such that I die horribly and hideously. Haven't I been overpaid—a harsh result for such a trivial thing ? There are two ways to deal with such apparently hard or extraordinary evils, as we called these cases in Part I, within the karma system, i.e., within the province of A_4 :

1. A mistake really was made for there are chance events, fortuitous clashings of bodies.

2. Getting squashed was a just compensation but one must distinguish short term justice from long term justice : thus the squashing was my just payment for a long line of unpaid-for and nasty acts done previously by me.

Let me speak briefly to each of these alternatives :

1. To say that I was squashed when I should only have been bruised is to admit overcompensation, and to admit that an injustice, consequently, was done. But, an apologist might respond, the injustice can be made up by a karma reward, as he might call it, in your next life. It's the law's way of apologizing for accidents. But I don't think this will work. The law of karma, according to the consensus of the above sources, operates with respect to my behavior, joining that behavior to certain results. Strictly speaking, in the situation previously reported there are only two kinds of behavior exhibited : First, my hitting the dog, and second, my being hit in Ames Library. The first is a species of bb, but the second was merely a species of bi. The truck's hitting me was, to speak lightly, the truck's deed, and not mine. The truck, if there were a law of karma for trucks, ought to be punished (or rewarded !), not me. Thus while overcompensation may occur, this was not an instance of it—for getting hit was not something I did, but something done to me, hence the law of karma is not involved in this sense at all, hence there is nothing to be compensated for, since my behavior at that time was not the cause of the truck's hitting me. Thus extraordinary or hard evil within the karma system seems to be permitted where seeming accidents occur. One will be reborn, but there is no ground for assuming that one will be rewarded for being squashed by a truck. Thus, unlike the recompense solution to T.P.E. in Part I, where I could be compensated in Heaven for my squashing experience here on earth, the karma theory, and the rebirth solution in general, cannot compensate for accidental acts or indifferent-behavior acts, i.e., acts done to me but which I did not do, hence it cannot justify such acts by proffering future better rebirths.

However the law of karma can justify them in terms of past karmic acts, by explaining the squashing in terms of my being in Ames Library because of those past acts. Hence my being in a place where cement trucks might come, was brought about by my past lives. Hence the law of karma can explain and justify my squashing in Ames Library, though it cannot, as a result of that alone, give me a better birth next time around. This brings us now to our second explanation of seemingly unjust compensation for seemingly trivial acts.

2. Suppose it was no "accident". Suppose I am being "paid off" We are of course put in the position of asking "Why wasn't I paid off before now?" Since "before now" can refer to any time in the past, presumably we are speaking about a past in this life or in some previous life. The law of karma, in any event, is not like a natural law to this extent, since natural laws (inertia, gravity, chemical and physiological statements summarizing relations between events) "pay off" immediately. To defer payment is curious to say the least, and unlawlike at the most. More on this shortly. With respect to 2, we are requested to take the long view. It may well be that such an apparent overreaction on the part of the world to me does indeed appear to be a case of extraordinary evil, hence unjust. But this is to leave out the fact that the law of karma operates with respect to a whole host of past deeds, in this life and conceivably in others, too. Justice will be served in the long run ; if short run injustices are noted, one must remember that they are short run. The truck squashing me was rb, not to the dog incident but to a whole host of other bb's that suddenly and unforeseeably surfaced—like bubbles clinging to the side of a glass that grow and grow, and then suddenly burst to the surface.

The problem is, of course, that we can explain bubbles in water through hydro-dynamical laws, and predict rather accurately what amount of gas in the bubble will cause it to surface, when, and with what results. No such prediction is possible with the law of karma, apparently, nor should we seek any. We will return to the law-like nature of karma shortly.

While every bg and bb behavior will eventually produce an rg and rb response, and while it will do it without remainder, i.e., it will do it justly in the long-run, there are certain kinds of behavior, bi, that are karma-indifferent ; common sense with a little help from ethical theory tells us that many things that we do, do not have apparent moral (karmic) effects : automatic responses like blinking the eyes, yawning, sneezing, actions wherein no "moral" activity is involved at all such as walking on the sidewalk, stretching the arms, talking to people, etc., etc. There are a whole host of *prima facie* activities that are karma neutral.[415] That is to say, there are morally neutral or value neutral acts, and we know this from the experienced results of these acts in the past. But this reliance on experience can be easily challenged now under the reign of the law of karma. For if we are *a fortiori* to believe that rg or rb can result for bg or bb performed in a past we know not when, then an element of uncertainty and unpredictability is suddenly thrown over the entire moral venture : For if one can't explain the rg and rb happening now in terms of known, identifiable, and isolatable bg and bb in the past, then how can one be sure that the act one is performing now, which might *seem* to be bi, is not really bg or bb ? Perhaps one guide might be a list of prohibited or enjoined acts from the *śruti* or *smṛti.* But what about proposed actions not even mentioned there? Like drinking coca cola or buying foreign cloth? Surely one knows they are right or wrong only by noting their immediate effects.[416] And the law of karma, with its unpredictable and unforeseeable habit of suddenly paying off, would obviate such experimental tests for right and wrong. My point is this. One of the best guides we have for acceptable and unacceptable behavior is the fact of the immediate results, pleasurable or painful results, connected somehow to that behavior. The law of karma, with its possible delayed results, unrequited consequences, and odd overcompensations for past deeds, throws this entire right-pleasure, wrong-pain machinery out of theoretical alignment. I can't trust the present consequences I get from present actions as a guide for future moral behavior because, pow! I may suddenly get paid back for what I thought was right by a semi-trailer truck hauling concrete culverts.

Finally, under this doctrine, of course, there may be no bi's at all : If experienced past consequences can no longer guarantee a sharp separation between present bg and bb, neither can consequences guarantee which acts are bi, if there are indeed any at all. Today's sneeze, yesterday's stretch, tomorrow's laugh, may lead to a sudden meeting with a cement truck, thereby causing my friends to avoid sneezing, stretching, and laughing, at least in Ames Library.

But while living under the umbrella of the law of karma may prove to be morally unsettling, isn't it the case that it's nice to know everyone is going to get, or has gotten, what's coming to him sometime, somewhere? Perhaps this feeling for justice will outweigh the insecurity in action that the law produces. But to believe that one may be every moment of every day gathering karma with every snort, blink, and scratch, is somewhat exhausting. And this latter surely follows from the fact that we can no longer be certain, because of delayed rb's and rg's, which behaviours are after all really right and which are really wrong and which are really neutral. We will return to this problem of moral uncertainty engendered by the law of karmic justice shortly.

3. *The Law in the Law of Karma*

The law of karma is a curious blend of both descriptive and metaphysical elements. For on the one hand it states predictively that if you do so-and-so (and we've seen now that this might mean anything and everything that you do) you can expect, you know not when, but you can expect certain moral results. It says that whenever bg or bb, then absolutely, not merely probably, rg or rb. There is no question of statistics or empirical test runs to establish this relationship ; it is an *apriori* metaphysical law, with an empirical content and empirical consequences. It's a curious "law" to say the least.

It shows the same sort of relationship to the cosmos as OCKHAM's law of parsimony. OCKHAM has said, or so many philosophers believe, that one ought not to multiply entities beyond necessity. OCKHAM's law can be interpreted prescriptively, i.e., for best results, keep things simple ; or descriptively i.e., Nature herself is simple, i.e., this law reflects nature's simplicity. In a similar way, the law of karma is descriptive of the world, and yet with prescriptive force it commends itself to the disciple : the law of karma is universally operative ; watch out lest ye fall into sin.

As with most full-blooded empirical laws one can *explain* past events and *predict* future events given the law of karma. Why did the cement truck crush me? Well, sometime in the past you exhibited bb_1, bb_2 ... bbn, and there is a law that says, whenever bb_1, bb_2 . . . bbn occurs, then rb_1, rb_2 . . . rbn must occur. We have seen rb_1, the cement truck crushing you, so there must have been a bb sometime in your past life or lives. Or, What will happen if I slap this dog? Well, sometime in the future you can expect rb. Why? Because, Whenever bb_1, bb_2 . . . bbn . . . and so on.

But a most disturbing thing about the law of karma as a descriptive or, as EDGERTON calls it, a natural law, is that it is not grounded empirically, or justified empirically, itself. We cannot be sure that we have seen real cases of bb followed by real cases of rb for reasons of moral uncertainty pointed out previously. The law of karma is not meant to be empirically law-like in the sense that it comes from repeated observations of past empirical associations of bb's and rb's. It is not empirically justified, and consequently it cannot be compared to a natural law at all. To this extent, the law of karma is like the principle of causation, that every event must have a cause. KARL POTTER in a paper "The Naturalistic Principle of Karma" has summarized their similarity very well when he says, first of the "law of causation:"

> "Thus the "Law of Causation" is not a law at all, but a principle. As such it serves an extremely important function : it formulates a basic presupposition of scientific inquiry . . .".[417]

and then of the "law of karma" :

> "If the Law of karma" is to be thought of as parallel in function to the "Law of Causation", it, too, must be viewed as a principle, a principle which formulates a certain program for moral inquiry."[418]

Both the causal principle and the karma principle then have exhortative functions ; the former urges us to keep looking for explanations of physical phenomena, the latter urges us on to seek explanations for moral occurrences, i.e., it "commits us to seeking a deterministic order beneath the quantum order or whatever other incompletely determined order science may arrive at through further investigation."[419] More particularly, it urges us to seek out the cause of habituation or bondage in our own lives, and to seek release from such binding habituation. The upshot of the discussion for our purposes is simply that karma as a principle is assumed for heuristic or practical reasons, and that these reasons justify its acceptance. Similar reasons underlay our other assumptions, A_1 A_2 and A_3, as we have argued above.

The point that karma must be an assumption and cannot be proved by any of the valid means of knowledge has been pointed out by ELIOT DEUTSCH in his book, *Advaita Vedānta, A Philosophical Reconstruction.* DEUTSCH refers to the law of karma as a "convenient fiction", for it enables the Indian to solve a number of rather baffling problems that would otherwise be insoluble without it. Among the four or so problems it solves according to DEUTSCH is the general problem of evil :

> "The last problem for which karma offers a solution is the one most frequently pointed to : the problem of inequality and evil, of why there are such great differences among men in spiritual and mental capacity or why men occupy such different places within the socio-economic order".[420]

To such puzzles the law of karma has an answer :

> "The spiritual and intellectual differences between *jīvas* are the result of their conduct. The place in society that they occupy at any one time is the result of their past action".[421]

And because the law of karma itself cannot be established through any of the *pramāṇas*, (we shouldn't expect that it could be so established, POTTER might say, for it is a principle and not a law) we can call it a fiction, but a convenient or useful one. Thus whether one dubs it a fiction, a principle, a heuristic device, or an assumption, the point is that is not capable of proof in the ordinary sense, but that it is accepted none-theless as an essential element in rebirth theories. The latter point remains now to be demonstrated and to that end we now bend our efforts.

4. PLATO

Rebirth systems, as we noted in A_3 above, are dependent on some mechanism of rules whereby souls and bodies are brought into regular, systematic, and lawful relations of immersion, contact, or conjunction. The principle of karma, or a principle very much like it, simply governs the movements (A_3) between loci (A_2) and souls (A_1). Without such a principle or convenient fiction or assumption operating, i.e., without there being a mechanism described by such a principle, convenient fiction or assumption, i.e., without such governance, the rebirth system could not be operative, or if it were it would be erratic and irrational. The rebirth systems we have been examining may be a lot of things but they are not, their proponents claim, irrational.

PLATO does not mention by name the mechanism by which rebirth gets done, but it is patently there, unnamed but obvious. The myth of the *Phaedo* plainly describes the mechanism of fixed or stable periods of waiting for purification and rebirth :

> ". . . the Acherusian Lake, where the souls of the dead for the most part come, and after staying there for certain fixed periods, longer or shorter, are sent forth again to the births of living creatures".[422]

No God or demons would seem to determine what and who goes to which place, the ultimate decision being left up to the individual's own destiny :

> "And when the newly dead reach the place to which each is conducted by his guardian spirit, first they submit to judgment, both those who have lived well and holily, and those who have not. Those who are judged to have lived a neutral life set out for Acheron . . . [after] undergoing purification are both absolved by punishment from any sins that they have committed and rewarded for their good deeds, according to each man's deserts. Those who on account of the greatness of their sins are judged to be incurable . . . these are hurled by their appropriate destiny into Tartarus, from whence they emerge no more".[423]

This is the first mention we have had in PLATO of the round of rebirth coming to an end. But it is well-documented that such a release can be had at both ends of the continuum, one in Tartarus, the other supposedly in the realm of the blessed. Neo-Platonists were to make much of the way out of the cycle of birth and rebirth; PLATO's concern seems mainly to be with the stages within the continuum rather than with its extremes of absolute damnation or absolute salvation, to use some borrowed epithets. Of the latter, there is a passage in the *Phaedo* describing those lucky few who will live apparently body-less, free from rebirth, on the surface of the earth (the eternal gods ?):

> "But those who are judged to have lived a life of surpassing holiness—these are they who are released and set free from confinement in those regions of the earth... [and] make their dwelling ("without bodies") upon the earth's surface".[424]

Though these points do not relate directly to A_4, they are worth noting here; the implications to be made from all this with respect to A_4 is that the judgment regarding the future embodied disposition of the soul is decided justly, but mechanically and impersonally, by a judgment based upon one's own past deeds. One's appropriate destiny hurls one into this place or that.

In the *Phaedrus* this impersonal nature of the judging mechanism is made even more apparent :

> "Hear now the ordinance of Necessity. Whatsoever soul has followed in the train of a god, and discerned something of truth, shall be kept from sorrow until a new revolution shall begin, and if she can do this always, she shall remain always free from hurt. But when she is not able so to follow . . . but meeting with some mischance comes to be burdened with a load of forgetfulness and wrongdoing, and because of that burden sheds her wings and falls to the earth, then thus runs the law".[425]

This "law" also receives mention in the *Gorgias* where SOCRATES tells Callicles about an ancient universal *nomos* :

> "Now in the days of Cronus there was this law about mankind, which from then till now has prevailed among the gods, that the man who has led a godly and righteous life departs after death to the Isles of the Blessed and there lives in all happiness exempt from ill, but the godless and unrighteous man departs to the prison of vengeance and punishment which they call Tartarus".[426]

Once again we have a mention of the two absolute eternal ends or releases of the soul and a mention of a law that, consistent with the previous passages, prevailed among the gods but was not instituted by the gods. In other words, the Platonic principle of karma would seem to be an eternal principle, not a convenient fiction. We shall find a similar principle at work, of course, in our Indian systems as well, and to those we turn next.

5. *Buddhism*

In Buddhism with $Soul_B$ theory, some curious puzzles develop around A_4. That Buddhists generally accept the doctrine of karma has been pointed out by many scholars :

> "In Buddhism the objects of faith are essentially four, viz. (1) the belief in karma and rebirth, (2) the acceptance of the basic teachings about the nature of reality, such as conditioned co-production, 'not-self', 'emptiness', the assertion that this world is the result of the ignorance of non-existent individuals with regard to non-existent objects, etc.; (3) . . . the three refuges . . . (4) . . . Nirvāṇa . . .".[427]

Further the principle of karma for the Buddhists is taken as an assumption generally, i.e., as an article of faith; since the empirical evidence for it is negligible. Thus EDWARD CONZE says of the first pair of objects of faith above :

> "The first of the four 'articles of faith' may illustrate the situation. The factual evidence for karma and rebirth appears imposing to some, and quite negligible to others. In any case it is scientifically inconclusive. The doctrine contains two fairly unverifiable statements; it claims (1) that behind natural causality... there are other, invisible chains of a moral causality which ensures that all good acts are rewarded, all bad actions punished; and (2) that this chain of moral sequences is not interrupted by death, but continues from one life to another".[428]

Thus the pattern of desire goes on out of one body-locus where it was caused and into another where it causes. Return to Nāgasena and his proselyte :

> "The King said : 'What is it, Nāgasena that is reborn?' 'Name-and-Form is reborn.' 'What, is it this same name-and-form that is reborn?' 'No : but by this

> name-and-form deeds are done, good or evil, and by these deeds (this karma) another name-and-form is reborn".[429]

The King then asks Nāgasena: Can I be responsible for another's deeds and another's suffering resulting from those deeds? Nāgasena answers, Suppose a man builds a fire in the cold season : He warms himself and then goes away. Subsequently that fire starts another fire in a farmer's field and the latter is burned up. Is the first man guilty of the second fire? The King answers, Yes :

> "Because in spite of whatever he might say, he would be guilty in respect of the subsequent fire that resulted from the previous one".[430]

And Nāgasena responds :

> "Just so, great King, deeds good or evil are done by this name-and-form and another is reborn. But that other is not thereby released from its deeds (its karma)".[431]

But since the continuity of desires is maintained in a continuous causal series, the chain of desires can be identified with a continuative self ($Soul_B$) through time, marked off by separate *saṁtāna's* of desires arbitrarily labelled as "me-now", "me-in-another-life", and so on. Thus it follows from this that I have inherited the "fires" of my previous *saṁtānas*. Hence the fires I received are really mine, and not someone else's. I am made to pay the piper for a tune which I heard as another name and form (to mix the metaphor a bit), but a name and form that was part of my whole continuative self. Thus the principle of karma operates in Buddhism to maintain the justness of reward and punishment along the continuous causal series identified as a self.

Recall for a moment what we are about in all these examinations of assumptions of the principle of rebirth or *saṁsāra*. We are attempting to answer the question as to whether the doctrine of rebirth, whether reincarnationist or transmigrationist, will solve T.P.E. in some one or another of its forms. The principle of karma, being one of the assumptions standing behind any rebirth doctrine, if it is to solve T.P.E. must in itself explain certain sorts of phenomena that it has been claimed it can explain. Can it do this? A typical expression affirming this claim is made by SATISCHANDRA CHATTERJEE and DHIRENDRAMOHAN DATTA:

> "This law helps us to explain the differences in the lot of individual beings, which are so striking and unexpected under the common circumstances of their lives . . . Some men are happy and some miserable . . . some virtuous men suffer and many wicked people prosper in this world. How are we to explain these variations and anomalies in our worldly life? Some . . . [are] due to different actions performed by us in this present life. But many of them cannot be explained by reference to the deeds of this life".[432]

But karma not only explains one's present lot but it justifies it too, as we have seen repeatedly from the *Upaniṣads* on:

> ". . . there is no happening of events to a person except as the result of his own work".[433]

The point is that in some sense it must be my action's consequences that I suffer for in my next existence, not yours. And as we have seen above the Buddhists can *explain* and *justify* individual differences among men, that "some are long-lived others short-lived, some healthy and some sickly"[434] by reference to the principle of karma. Thus Nāgasena quotes the Buddha:

> "All beings, O youth, have karma as their portion; they are heirs of their karma; they are sprung from their karma; their karma is their kinsman; their karma is their refuge; karma allots beings to meanness or greatness".[435]

The upshot is, of course, that Theravāda Buddhism, or any other Buddhism with a Soul$_B$ theory (one must distinguish this, of course, from certain forms of Mahāyāna Buddhism, Mahāsaṅghika, and Sammitīya Buddhism with its *pudgala* soul theory, and other similar Soul$_P$ or Soul$_{HP}$ theories) can explain differences among individuals with A_4, and it can justify those differences, hence it can be used to explain individual suffering due to inherited evils, but not to explain T.P.E. We have been at pains to repeat this conclusion throughout Part II, for much misunderstanding comes about as a result of overlooking it. The reason for the misunderstanding is not hard to find. The

Buddhists have held to the *anātman* theory strenuously. Hence it is philosophically natural to assume that since there is no self in any sense, there can be no justification for a self's being born the way it is. We have attacked this notion in Chapter V above, and throughout Part II. Here is STCHERBATSKY again:

> "The term *anātman* is usually translated as "non-soul", but in reality *ātman* is here synonymous with a personality, an ego, a self, an individual, a living being, a conscious agent, etc. The underlying idea is that, whatsoever be designated by all these names, it is not a real and ultimate fact, it is a mere name for a multitude of interconnected facts, which Buddhist philosophy is attempting to analyse by reducing them to real elements (*dharma*)".[436]

Those real elements (*dharmatā*) we have identified in part as a chain of interconnected desires composing the continuative self ($Soul_B$). Hence the names "self" or "soul" are simply convenient nouns standing for that chain of real events.

The conclusion to be drawn from all this for the Buddhists is simply that karma operates in Buddhism as in Hinduism; that Buddhist $Soul_B$ theory together with the principle of karma allows the Buddhists to explain certain types of evil as the result of previous births, though, because the Buddhists are atheists, it does not engage the Buddhists with T.P.E. proper.

6. *Other Indian Systems*

The principle of karma is recognized by the other systems of Indian thought though the principle's autonomy is disputed by some. Thus the *Jaina*, Buddhist, *Sāṁkhya* and *Mīmāṁsā* systems hold that the principle is autonomous and works independently of the will of God. But the *Nyāyavaiśeṣika* hold that the principle is under the guidance and administration of God:

> "It is God who controls our adṛṣṭa ["stock of merits and demerits of karmas of the individual souls"] and dispenses all the joys and sorrows of our life in accordance with our karma".[437]

The argument that they give that leads to this conclusion is simply that *adṛṣṭa* by itself is unintelligent and cannot lead to the proper, i.e., just effects that the principle is supposed to bring about. Thus an intelligence is needed that justice might be done. Hence God emerges to guide and control the whole process. This conclusion regarding *Nyāya* and *Vaiśeṣika* will have significant results in our discussion of rebirth and T.P.E. in Part III below.

The impersonal and mechanistic operation of the principle of karma is held then by nearly all the Indian schools of thought, as is the doctrine of rebirth itself.[438]

7. AUROBINDO GHOSE

Finally, AUROBINDO GHOSE representing a latter-day *Vedāntic* position holds also to the automatic operation of the principles of karma and rebirth:

> "Our first conclusion on the subject of reincarnation has been that the rebirth of the soul in successive terrestrial bodies is an inevitable consequence of the original significance and process of the manifestation in earth-nature . . . ."[439]

But we must remember that AUROBINDO does not want to accept the simple and what he regards as traditional treadmill theory of rebirth and karma as his norm :

> "Reincarnation is commonly supposed to have two aspects, metaphysical and moral, an aspect of spiritual necessity, an aspect of cosmic justice and ethical discipline".[440]

He then offers his famous critique of this notion of rebirth, and at the same time criticizes the law of karma:

> "These are very summary popular notions and offer no foothold to the philosophic reason and no answer to a search for the true significance of life. A vast world-system which exists only as a convenience for turning endlessly on a wheel of Ignorance with no issue except a final chance of stepping out of it, is not a world with any real reason for existence. A world which serves only as a school of sin and virtue and consists of a system of rewards and whippings, does not make any better appeal to our intelligence. The soul or spirit within us, if it is divine, immortal or celestial, cannot be sent here solely to be put to

> school for this kind of crude and primitive moral education . . ." .[441]

Aurobindo's principle criticism is that man has taken a rather crude human rule of justice and has then erected that "puny standard into the law and aim of the cosmos". However that may be, each being nonetheless reaps the harvest of his own works and deeds, and present karma (action) determines future birth. But now Aurobindo balks. He seems to want to argue that the law of karma cannot have full sway over the Spirit that resides within man :

> "But if the fundamental truth of our being is spiritual and not mechanical, it must be our self, our soul that fundamentally determines its own evolution, and the law of karma can only be one of the processes it uses for that purpose : Our Spirit, our Self must be greater than its karma" [442]

For, he contends, if the principle of karma controls the Spirit, the *Ātman,* then the Self would be simply a slave or automaton in the hands of karma. Thus, he concludes, seemingly like the *Nyāya-Vaiśeṣikas* before him, that another being, God, controls karma, and the latter is not purely automatic in its operations His reasons to this conclusion differ from theirs but the result is the same : God has some sort of control over the principle of karma :

> "If a certain amount of results of past karma is formulated in the present life, it must be with the consent of the psychic being [God] which presides over the new formation of its earth-experience and assents not merely to an outward compulsory process, but to a secret Will and Guidance. . . . an Intelligence which may use mechanical processes but is not their subject".[443]

Thus for one contemporary Indian at least, the more or less traditional doctrine of the mechanical and impersonal doctrine of karma would be obviated. What repercussions this will have for T.P.E., we shall note below.

8. *Conclusion*

For any rebirth system we must conclude, on *apriori* grounds alone, that if it is to be a rational system and not an erratic ruled-by-chance affair, it must have certain rules governing the relation of souls to bodies or places. On historical grounds we have noted such a law that explains, that in some cases justifies, the kinds of rebirths that take place in that particular rebirth system. The Indians call it the law of karma; PLATO assumes it but gives no name to it.

We have seen that to avoid confusing the law of karma with descriptive scientific empirical laws, or legal moral prescriptive laws, it is best to treat it as an assumptive principal, justified by its sheer utility alone. This has been our claim, further, with the other theses, A_1, A_2, and A_3, as well, viz., that they are simply assumptions that must be made by any rebirth system that would have the kinds of properties of regularity and orderliness, that the systems we have examined, Buddhist, Platonic, Jaina, and Hindu, seem to have.

CHAPTER VII

Conclusion to Part II

What we have described in Part II comes down to four major points :

1. Rebirth systems in general, must possess the four necessary characteristics described in our analysis of S_5, the doctrine of *saṁsāra*. Those characteristics were treated as assumptions and were described as :

A_1 The Soul Thesis

A_2 The Soul-Locus Thesis

A_3 The Mobile-Soul Thesis

A_4 The Karma Thesis

2. Two separate rebirth systems have been noted and analyzed with respect to the four assumptions mentioned above. Of the two systems, transmigration and reincarnation, only the former, transmigration, will be used to solve T.P.E.

3. Within transmigrationist (substantial soul) doctrine, only $Soul_P$ and $Soul_{HP}$ theories can solve or attempt to solve T.P.E., for the remaining $Soul_{HI}$ theory is impersonal in character, and while it may explain rebirth, it cannot justify it.

4. Transmigrationist systems with $Soul_{HP}$ which hold to the impersonal operation of the principal of karma may solve T.P.E. more readily than those systems like AUROBINDO's which hold that God controls and administers the principle of karma. For such control directly implicates God in punishment and pain, and this leads directly to T.P.E.

This concludes our discussion of rebirth. We now push on in our final effort to join the problem of evil of Part I, with the conclusions regarding rebirth here in Part II.

PART III

REBIRTH AND THE PROBLEM OF EVIL

This final part of the book is divided into the following chapters.

Ch. VIII. *The Indian Assumptions for T.P.E.*

I want to look at Indian attitudes towards the premises necessary to generate T.P.E. We shall find that the four theses necessary to develop T.P.E. are all present, with some interesting variations, in the Indian tradition. Thus we shall be examining the omnipotence thesis, the omniscience thesis, the ethical thesis, and the evil thesis in the Indian literature. I shall conclude that since all these theses or assumptions are present, the ground is laid for the existence of T.P.E. in that tradition.

Ch. IX. *Two Indian Solutions to T.P.E.*

Next I turn to two solutions that can be found within the Indian context, the necessary solution, which is given relatively short shrift, and the rebirth solution which will occupy us for the remainder of the book.

Ch. X. *Conclusion to Part III*

I conclude with some general remarks, critical and otherwise, on our metaphysical pilgrimage into the theological problem of evil by way of the rebirth solution.

In dwelling on the rebirth solution in Ch. IX, I shall of necessity be leaving out other more contemporary Indian attempts at solving T.P.E.[444] I want to spend my time primarily on the rebirth solution and for two reasons: First, it has received the most attention from critics and supporters alike, and it involves more tangles and confusions that need clearing up before anyone can either attack it or defend it; and second, it seems *prima facie* to be the most promising of all the solutions dealt with in Part I for solving P.E. in its theological form.

In examining the rebirth thesis as an attempted solution to T.P.E. I want to briefly look at what its supporters have had to say in its defense. Some of the claims are gross exaggerations of the potentialities of the rebirth solution based on what seems to me to be a misunderstanding of rebirth itself, as well as a failure to distinguish transmigration from reincarnation together with a consequent failure to differentiate Soul_{B} from Soul_{HP} and Soul_{HI} in the Indian tradition. These confusions I will attempt to clear by dealing with the attacks, real and unreal, justifiable and unjustifiable, against the rebirth solution. Penultimately in Ch. IX, I deal with a Vedāntist's attempt (by Śaṁkara and Rāmānuja) to defend the rebirth solution against the attacks presented previously. I close this chapter with a summary of our investigations.

In Ch. X I shall conclude with some remarks in summary of what we have been about in this entire book, and make some statements regarding what the defender of the rebirth solution must be willing to put up with if he is going to cling to that doctrine as a solution to P.E.

One point stands out that should be treated separately, here, however. From our discussion in Part I we had settled on dealing primarily with T.P.E., hence dealing with God as opposed to the Godhead in our discussion of that problem. Now insofar as the Indians are disposed to look upon *Brahman* as *nirguṇa Brahman*, they are dealing with the Godhead, about whom human language becomes inapplicable. Thus insofar as *nirguṇa Brahman* is the "God" being related to the world's evil, no T.P.E. can arise. Consequently, in what follows, the nature of the deity always under discussion, unless otherwise specified, will be a personal God, Īśvara, or the like, i.e. *saguṇa Brahman*. This is obvious since the theological theses, necessary to generate T.P.E., could only be presented where the deity had the characteristics which the theological theses describe.

CHAPTER VIII

The Indian Assumptions to T.P.E.

Classical and medieval Indian philosophy has not shown any great concern for P.E. in any of its theological forms (as TPS_p E, TPS_b E or TPHE). The overwhelming problem for the Hindu, Buddhist and Jain has been evil, certainly, but an evil connected with existence or birth in general which he could not lay to any God or Gods. When a problem about evil appears, consequently, it appears as a practical problem about evil, i.e., one states that all is suffering, *saṁsāra* is itself evil, the world is a domain of travail and bondage; and then one asks, not a theoretical question like Who caused It ? or Who made me bound ? but rather, one asks the more practical question, How can I escape this round of birth and death? When T.P.E., itself, is discussed in the older texts it is almost as an aside, or it appears secondarily in the context of Who made the world ? as we shall see in our discussion of rebirth below.

One way, and perhaps a novel way, of approaching the assumptions necessary to generate T.P.E., is to investigate and analyze the various kinds of attacks made against these assumptions in the Indian literature. The Indian theists, like theists elsewhere, have concertedly held that Iśvara possesses all the characteristics usually attributed to a deity by Western theists, viz., omnipotence, omniscience, and all-goodness. In addition, as we have noted in part II, the Indians quite generally will argue that there is evil in the world, for *saṁsāra* is one very powerful indicator of that evil. To establish the reality of these theses, therefore, we might very well profit by analyzing the attempts in the literature to deny these respective theses, and thereby through this kind of approach, examine the results for our set of four theses. Let us begin then by noting what these attempted denials of the four theses have been like, or might be like, and how the theses have fared as a result.

1. Indian Analysis of the Theological Theses

From our discussion in Part I we can recall that the theological theses relative to P.E. were necessary in order to generate P.E. Thus without the omnipotence thesis, the omniscience thesis and the ethical thesis (that God is all powerful, all knowing, and all good) as those premises were analyzed in Part I, T.P.E. could not be produced. In the Indian tradition there is ample evidence that all three theological theses have been both accepted and questioned, defended and attacked. I want to display very quickly what some of these attacks might look like given the Indian context, and then equally quickly offer a comment or two on each of the theses.

a. The Omnipotence Thesis

From our discussion in Part II regarding the principle of karma and its relation to God, we saw that God seems as much under the sway of karma as are other creatures. Two apparent exceptions, the *Nyāya-Vaiśeṣika* and Śrī AUROBINDO argued, contrary to the Vedic tradition, it would seem, that God controls the principle of karma, but for two quite different reasons. However, with the former, it is not clear that God does anything more than simply act as an intelligent intermediary between souls and the principle of karma. Thus God dispenses rewards and punishments but always with an eye on the individual's former deeds. One is reminded of Śaṁkara and Rāmānuja in their various discussions of God's causing the soul to act. God may force me, they both say, to act in a certain way but always He acts with regard to my former efforts in a previous life, i.e., the condition of my soul as determined by my former efforts leads God, e.g., to arrange favorable or unfavorable circumstances for me now. It may very well be that this is all that the Naiyāyikas have in mind when they say that God controls and directs the principle of karma, in which case He too is more controlled than controlling, more limited than limiting.[445]

The situation with AUROBINDO is certainly clearer. Aurobindo comes closer to the views of, say, the Vedāntic *dvaitist* Madhva, whose doctrine of divine grace seems plainly to stand outside both the principle of karma and the Vedic tradition. However that may be AUROBINDO by his doctirne of *Ātman* places the soul outside the reach of karma by insinuating an all-powerful Divine Controller between that soul and the principle of karma. He saves the autonomy of the soul, along with the omnipotence of the Divine, but does it perhaps at the expense of the tradition.

As many historians have pointed out, and as we mentioned in our discussion in Part II, the law of karma is a principle which is regarded by the Indians without exception as an unseen (*adṛṣṭa*) principle which "holds sway even over the material atoms and brings about objects and events in accordance with moral principles."[446] Just as the Gods of the *Veda* were subject to *Ṛta* so also, from its first appearance in the *Brāhmaṇa's*, karma's wholly impersonal, super-human and superdivine character became well known and widely accepted.[447]

The same super-human and super-divine power may also be attributed to *saṁsāra*, karma's twin. Consequently, we may conclude that, with the exception noted (AUROBINDO), God is not all powerful with respect to these two principles, karma and rebirth. Some comments :

(1) The criticism is not unlike those seen previously in Part I. In our discussion of the limitations of God as seen for example by Saint Thomas, we discovered both logical and moral limitations: God couldn't make yesterday occur today, nor could He create evil. On the latter point Thomas had said that while God couldn't cause evil He could nonetheless permit it, and for various reasons.

The Indian argument that would lead to the denial of the omnipotence thesis, while not unlike the Western argument in that both end up apparently at the same conclusion, is nonetheless strikingly different. Thus both arguments put God in the position of permitting an evil deed to be punished. But the Thomistic implication behind "permission" is that if God wanted to, God could hold off the punishment. Thus my permitting you to drive my car implies that if I wanted to I could tell you not to drive it and I could prevent you from driving it: "permission" entails "possible prevention." But

Īśvara or *Indra* or *Viṣṇu* are all apparently as much bound by the principle of karma as are Jones and Devadatta.

(2) A second important difference stressing the limitations on God's power between India and the West, is that salvation can be taken as an act, oftentimes, of God's will in the Christian, Moslem, and Jewish sects, and the *Bible* and *Q'uran* abound with many such salvation stories. Not so for the Indian tradition, save for a few relatively minor exceptions like the *dvaitists* led by *Madhvācārya*, the 13th century Vedāntist.[448] Thus while the Europeon God can apparently eternally save whom He will by an act of will, the Hindu God has no such power. He can help as Kṛṣṇa helps Arjuna in the *Gītā*, but He cannot by an act of will produce *jīvanmukta* in whom He will. Thus *mokṣa* like karma is not in God's control either. If God is caught in the net of *māyā*, as all beings with qualities apparently are, then *saguṇa Brahman*, whether seen as Īśvara, Viṣṇu or what-have-you, is as much subject to the unseen principles of *karma* and *saṁsāra* in the cosmic universe as is man.

(3) But the omnipotence thesis for the Indian can still be salvaged despite these problems. A possible way out for the Indian with his God now reduced simply to a rather super superhuman, is for him to argue, as we did for Thomas in Part I, that among the list of possible doings, there must first of all be acts which are actually do-able. Just as lifting an unliftable stone is not an example of something that can be done because it's not a do-able thing, it's not an act at all, much less a possible act, so also granting *mukti*, halting the workings of karma, or preventing the rebirth are not do-able things for they are not acts or possible acts. Two interpretations of this are possible:

(a) Halting the working of karma is self-contradictory, like lifting the unliftable. But the problem with this is that halting karma is not surely explicitly self-contradictory. And granting *mukti* is surely not contradictory in any very apparent sense, else many Christians, Jews and *dvaitists* are dead wrong.

(b) Within the Indian conceptual scheme, there are certain kinds of to-be-dones that are acceptable (because of that scheme) as to-be-dones. The principles mentioned above, particularly rebirth and karma, are so fundamental as primitives in that scheme, that to treat them as acts or to-be-dones, like e.g. changing a river's course, or halting an enraged elephant, is to miss the point of their status in the system. They are not deniable, changeable or falsifiable. They are as basic as the laws of logic themselves to the Indian conceptual scheme. Therefore to speak of their dislodgment or alteration by God is to miss the point of their function in that scheme. This follows quite naturally from our discussion of the principle of karma as an assumption or pragmatically grounded convenient fiction in Part II above, and that followed our general scheme throughout Part II of treating A_1, A_2, A_3, and A_4 as assumptions with all the rights and prerogatives of assumptives.

(4) However these arguments for karma and rebirth may go, and *mukti* presents a special problem as I have indicated, both will be treated at greater length in our discussion of re-birth below.

b. The Omniscience Thesis

There are many references to the all-knowingness as well as the all-powerfulness of Brahman in one of His aspects,[449] as Īśvara. But despite the presence of such numerous references, the classical Indians do not seem to have gotten into the free-will and omniscience controversy that plagued our Western philosophers in Part I. Not only is God regarded as omniscient in these ancient texts, there are, reportedly, *jīvan muktas* who can through *siddhi* see into the future as well. Our concern, right now however, is with God's omniscience and the Indian tradition's ability to deny this omniscience. We shall have, I am afraid, little success in that regard.

One commentator, E. A. Solomon, exhaustively traces the concept of divine and human omniscience in the classical Indian texts and systems. According to Solomon the doctrine of divine omniscience was present as early as the *Vedas*, where omniscience is attributed to Agni and Varuṇa, and the *Upaniṣads*, where the characteristics of Ultimate Reality are attributed to the human soul and the latter is looked upon as potentially omniscient.[450] All the Indian schools, save for a few obvious exceptions like the *Cārvāka* and the *Ajñānavādins*, supported the doctrine of omniscience (*sarvajñatva*), as applied to both God, in the theistic systems, and the *jīvan mukta*. One objector to human omniscience was the great *Mīmāṁsaka* philosopher of the 7th century A.D., Kumārila, who argued that no man can become *sarvajña* through only one *pramāṇa* namely, *pratyakṣa*. But he does not challenge the possibility of a man becoming *sarvajña* by all six *pramāṇas*.

The important point for our purposes here, again, is the *sarvajñatva* of God and not man. And in all the systems that acknowledge a personal God *Nyāya-Vaiśeṣika*, *Yoga*, and theistic *Vedānta*, for example, that God is regarded as omniscient.[451]

Speaking of omniscience in Buddhism, EDWARD CONZE argues that the *Mahāyāna* stressed omniscience as a human goal, and that Buddha, (whose name from the Sanskrit—$\sqrt{budh}$ connotes both *to wake up* and *to know*) as omniscient became a standard to be aimed at by all mankind:

> "This is one of the reasons why the Mahāyāna stressed Omniscience as a goal for all."[452]

Thus according to the Mahāyānists, Buddha was omniscient in the most literal sense of that term, knowing accurately all the details of every aspect of existence.

The Pali Canon on the other hand invests Buddha with what we might call "selective omniscience", as opposed to the strict omniscience of the Northern School:

> "Not all Buddhists seem to have believed that strict Omniscience on the part of the Buddha would be necesary to invest his religion with the required authority. If he knew everything that was essential to salvation, that would be sufficient to make him into a trustworthy guide. In some passages of the Pali Scriptures, as a matter of fact, the Buddha expressly disclaims any other kind of Omniscience."[453]

But while according to SOLOMON and CONZE, the Hindu and Buddhist texts are capable of investing God and Buddha with the power of omniscience, either strictly or selectively, nothing is said specifically about limitations on God's or Buddha's knowledge with regard to future events. Selective omniscience is not presented sufficiently to enable us to make a determination in this regard.

The dilemma, consequently, that if God knew the future He could stop the evils He saw, and that if He didn't know the future, He wouldn't be perfect, never really arises for the classical Indians. Perhaps it should, but they don't seem to have been concerned about it. I think the reason is apparent. The *jīvan mukta* as well as God are not bound to time or time's events as freed or liberated souls. Hence events in time are of no concern to them, particularly future events. And for certain *Vedāntins*, when the unreality of the space-time world is manifested, there is even greater reason for letting the illusion go on its merry, old, unreal way, unhindered, disregarded, and philosophically ignored.

However, contemporary Indian philosophers are willing to consider the relationship between Divine Omniscience and the state of man in the world. One of the pitfalls engendered by God's omniscience is recognized and duly noted by S.S. SURYANARAYANA SASTRI in his paper, "Omniscience."

> "If the Lord knows all, He knows the future too; if He knows it, it is predetermined and there is no freedom for us to choose and act whether for elevation or otherwise".[454]

Thus the following dilemma ensues : If God is omniscient, a problem of human free will obtains; if God is not omniscient, a problem of Divine perfection obtains. The *advaitin*, according to SASTRI, is apparently committed to holding that the future, which is "in the womb of *māyā*," and evolves according to the *adṛṣṭa* of the *jīvas*, can be known by Īśvara, since *māyā* is under the control of Īśvara. But to escape the fatalism thereby implied, the *advaitin*, it would seem, must give up the concept of Divine omniscience :

> "The moot questions (raised by the *advaitin*) are still left unsolved, what place there is for voluntary effort to affect a course of evolution which may now seem inevitable, and whether the possibility of such change does not limit the Lord's knowledge".[455]

SASTRI concludes that the conception of omniscience is neither "intelligible nor reconcilable with the demands of human freedom." Hence the way is open, for SASTRI at any rate, to deny the omniscience of God.

Another conclusion reached by SASTRI, again within the *advaitin* context, is that while omniscience as knowledge is real, "there is nothing to know."[456] Thus SASTRI seems to be saying that for the God who truly knows, and for those traditions, like *advaita*, which regard all but *Brahman* as *māyā*, there are no future events because there are no real events. Hence, future events are not objects of knowledge because "there is nothing to know." But then it might legitimately be argued, as we did when a similar issue was raised in Part I, that one commits a category mistake *par excellance* when one bothers to ask this (transcendental) question; Can God know the Future? Thus one cannot accuse God of imperfections, for ignorance of the future is no ignorance—thus because I don't see the pink bats that you see when you're in your cups, is no limitation on my part but rather it is one on yours. Consequently, from this level of experience and for many Indian philosophers lack of omniscience in this sense as herein described is no real lack. Hence the omniscience thesis is also salvagable for the Indian.

c. *The Ethical Thesis*

The singular goodness of God can be theoretically attacked by those Indians who maintain that *saguṇa Brahman* possesses evil as well as good characteristics. Whether this conclusion follows from arguing that God as *saguṇa Brahman* possesses all conceivable properties, as is indeed possible unless one wants a "limited" God, or from arguing that God as destroyer (Śiva) as well as preserver (*Viṣṇu*) of the universe possesses properties consonant only with those two separate aspects of its nature, is no matter of concern. The point is that the conclusion that God is not purely all good can be reached in this way. (See discussion of God's awful nature below in Part III c, also).

One of the chief sources for this argument in the Indian literature is the *Bhagavad Gītā*. Speaking to the problem we are concerned with and the *Gītā*, FRANKLIN EDGERTON has observed :

> "Every theistic religion has its difficulties with the problem of evil. In describing the manifestations

> of God in the universe, the Gītā, quite naturally, tends to emphasize the good side of things; but at times it does not shrink from including the evil also. Since *all* comes from God, it seems impossible to deny that origin to anything [including evil]."[457]

EDGERTON illustrates his point by quoting *Gītā* VII.12 where Kṛṣṇa (Viṣṇu) says :

> "Whatsoever states of being there are be they of the nature of goodness, passion, or darkness, know that all of them come from Me alone".[458]

Another passage illustrating even more aptly the evil-and-good-rounded character of God comes in the famous revelation of His person that Kṛṣṇa makes to Arjuna in Chapter XI. The terrible and awe-inspiring picture of God that emerges is enough to scare the theological wits out of any Sunday-school teacher. Kṛṣṇa shows Himself, Arjuna looks and cries :

> "When I see Thy mouths terrible with their tusks, like Time's devouring flames, I lose sense of the directions and find no peace. Be gracious, O Lord of gods, Refuge of the worlds !"
>
> "(All) are rushing into Thy fearful mouths set with terrible tusks. Some caught between the teeth are seen with their heads crushed to powder".
>
> "Devouring all the worlds on every side with Thy flaming mouths, thou lickest them up. Thy fiery rays fill this whole universe and scorch it with their fierce radiance, O Viṣṇu."[459]

The picture of this terrible side of God, should convince us that the denial of the ethical thesis does indeed seem possible in the Indian systems which accept this particular *smṛti* as authoritative. We might well ask, however, if evil can be accounted for by these "imperfections" in God then how is it that the evil that befalls me does befall me ? Is God responsible ? And further, why does so much evil befall me ? We are pointing away now from the ethical thesis, toward karma and the rebirth solution. There is a sense, in other words, in which the denial of the theological theses, and the existence of evil in the world for me, all rest upon the principles of karma and rebirth. Hence any complete treatment of solutions to T.P.E. must await our treatment of the rebirth solution below. Even in God as we have seen, His power, knowledge and goodness or the lack thereof, may be taken, when God is seen as Iśvara, as karma related.

However that goes, a puzzling dilemma emerges with respect to the God who has qualities. For if *saguṇa Brahman* possessed all qualities, evil must be accounted among them, and therefore God is evil. And if God possessed only some qualities, not the bad ones, then He is limited because He fails to have all the qualities. Hence, since *saguṇa Brahman* must have either all qualities or only some qualities, He is imperfect,, for He is either wicked, or He is limited. This is a curious dilemma which the supporters of the theory of *saguṇa Brahman* must apparently be willing to live with. The paradox that leads to this dilemma we might denominate "the *saguṇa* paradox." It can be illustrated very simply in the following way. Supposing there is an infinite set of properties, p_1, p_2, p_3, . . . Suppose further that there is a Deity that we wish to describe as morally perfect in that It possesses only those properties that are morally good. Let's assume that only the odd numbered properties p_1, p_3, p_5 are these morally good properties, and that p_2, p_4, and p_6 are morally bad properties. Suppose further that we wish to describe this Deity as qualitatively unlimited, hence perfect in what He has as properties, i.e., this God possesses all possible properties of any infinite list of properties, p_1, p_2, p_3 . . . But we've already seen that this cannot be the case, i.e., that there are certain wicked properties that God, because of his moral perfection, cannot have. Therefore if God is morally perfect, He must be limited in his properties. And if He is limited in His properties, then He is limited in His being, i.e., in what He is; and this limitation is an imperfection. Hence if God is morally perfect, He must be ontologically imperfect. It could also be demonstrated, that if God is ontologically perfect in the sense of possessing all ontologically possible properties, then He must *pari passu* be morally imperfect. Both of these conclusions follow from the *saguṇa* paradox. A way out of the *saguṇa* paradox would be to argue, of course, that morally bad properties possess no real being, i.e., that they are ontologically privative in nature. Recall our discussion in Part I.

In a sense, this paradox of *saguṇa Brahman* is not unlike the Creator paradox mentioned above in Part I, where God had either to create man perfect or imperfect; we saw that this led to some curious tangles as well. Both the *saguṇa* paradox and the Creator paradox follow from attributing certain perfections to God (having all qualities, and having the power to create perfection, respectively) which, when one tries to cash-in on those perfections leads one up the merry old path to undesirable conclusions; hence the paradoxes.

An interesting argument by Aśvaghoṣa in his *Buddhacarita* will illustrate how both the *saguṇa* paradox and the creator paradox can be combined with real force to challenge the notion that a perfect Īśvara could have created an imperfect world. It is one of the few single instances of a recognition of T.P.E. in the Indian texts, and it comes from a *Mahāyāna* Buddhist source of the first or second century A.D. Lord Buddha is said to have argued thus with one Anāthapiṇḍika and attacked the idea of an all powerful God :

> "If the world had been made by Īśvara there should be no change or destruction, there should be no such thing as sorrow or calamity, as right or wrong, seeing that all things, pure and impure, must come from him. If sorrow and joy, love and hate, which spring up in all conscious beings, be the work of Īśvara, he himself must be capable of sorrow and joy, love and hatred, and if he has these, how can he be said to be perfect?"[460]

In conclusion, I might simply say that the upholders of *saguṇa Brahman* perfection must be willing to put up with these internal problems relating to God's qualities or properties. But again the problems are not insuperable for the Indian just as they were not insuperable for the Westerner. One can salvage the ethical thesis together with the assumption of the unlimited nature of the Divine qualities simply by arguing that immoral properties have no being, and are not really qualities at all, which brings us to an examination of the evil thesis.

2. Indian Analysis of the Evil Thesis

From our discussion in Part I, we can recall that the evil-is-illusion solution argued variously that evil was privation, non-being, illusory or non-existent. This same conclusion has been reached by many Indian commentators who have also held that evil in the world is mere appearance, illusory or unreal.

The contention that evil is unreal is bandied about primarily by *Vedāntins* like Śaṁkara,[461] or at least the position has been attributed to him. One must be careful with epistemological dualists like Śaṁkara, however, for one cannot always be sure out of which side of their philosophical mouth, the noumenal or phenomenal, they are speaking. But for many contemporary *Vedāntins*, evil is indeed unreal. Thus Kali PRASAD states :

> "The point is that, according to Vedānta, the so-called contradictions, discords, and evils were never such, were never real at all, not even in the moment of their so-called being".[462]

And he continues :

> "As long as there is evolution Māyā is necessarily there, for it is the principle of dynamism and individuation. That is why the world, the Saṁsāra, is known as Māyā that is; not something evil, but something which has to be experienced—Bhoga—for the eventual emancipation of the soul from the thraldom of ignorance or Avidyā. From the point of view of the Absolute, however, Māyā does not exist at all".[463]

The "points of view" throughout are of course significant as we shall see. A word or two about this attack on the evil thesis.

(1) I am not convinced that Indians, even, are prepared to say that suffering is unreal. Surely one can grant them that it is not metaphysically, ultimately, absolutely, really, real. Everything said is talked about from some point of view, and all we are saying is that from the absolute point of view, evil may be "unreal," whatever that means. But from the "other" point of view evil, suffering, waste, terror, and fear are real

enough. Having said that, one can surely justify, as I think the Indians must, the truth of the evil thesis.

(2) If evil is wholly unreal, then rebirth and karma are wholly unreal. If they are wholly unreal then a concern for or interest in release or *mokṣa* is a waste of time. But I don't know *any* Indians, save the *Cārvākas*, who will admit to this last thesis. The frenetic *mokṣa* activity or at least the daily, monthly, and yearly rites within Hinduism itself are proof positive that no one believes that *moṣka* activity is a waste of time. Therefore there is a sense in which evil is real, and a sense in which karma and rebirth are real as well. The dogma of unreality is betrayed by the activity and concern of the faithful.

It is important therefore that the phenomenal and the noumenal talk be kept clear and separate; when one Indian philosopher speaks out of the philosophical side of his mouth, we must be careful to distinguish from which side he speaks, and not have expectations raised by one side carried over for resolution to the other. The upshot is again, that the evil thesis as it relates to the phenomenal, talked-about world of qualities and things, of suffering and pain and waste and horror, is a perfectly justifiable thesis for generating T.P.E.

In conclusion then I think it can be said that the results of our oddly negative approach to an analysis of the theses of T.P.E. has shown two things : First, all the theses needed to generate T.P.E. have been attacked directly or indirectly (by silence if nothing else) in the Indian tradition; second, that within and without that tradition sufficient defense of these assumptions or theses is available such that we can say that the theses necessary to generate T.P.E. are all present in the Indian tradition.

We turn consequently to two possible solutions to the Indian T.P.E. for an examination and analysis of these solutions within the Indian context. The first, the necessary solution, we mention only briefly, and then focus our main efforts for the remainder of this book on the second : The rebirth solution.

CHAPTER IX

Two Indian Solutions to T.P.E.

1. *The Necessity of Evil* : *The Necessary Solution*

In Part I this solution expressed a logically or metaphysically necessary relation that held between certain contrary or contradictory (we were never sure which) predicates, such that if certain ones obtained then their opposites must obtain as well. For the present, the chief exponents of this view are ALAN WATTS and ANANDA K. COOMARASWAMY. WATTS, in his *The Way of Zen* comes out flatly asserting about evil in the world and Hinduism :

> "For Hindu thought there is no Problem of Evil. The conventional, relative world is necessarily a world of opposites. Light is inconceivable apart from darkness; order is meaningless without disorder; and, likewise, up without down, sound without silence, pleasure without pain".[464]

This position, even the language, is familiar to us from Part I. COOMARASWAMY tells a similar story, relying on the meaning of "a real creation," and the dualism thereby entailed :

> "However the ultimate truth of "dualism" may be repudiated, a kind of dualism is logically unavoidable for all practical purposes, because any world in time and space . . . must be one of contraries, both quantitative and qualitative, for example, long and short, good and evil . . ."[465]

COOMARASWAMY then turns to a species of T.P.E. and answers it, like WATTS, with a version of the necessary solution :

> "For anyone who holds that "God made the world," the question, Why did He permit the existence in it of any evil, or that of the Evil One in whom all evil is personified, is altogether meaningless; one might as well inquire why He did not make a world without dimensions or one without temporal succession".[466]

The question we raised with regard to this solution in Part I was two-fold : First, does this inability to create a world without evil because there is good imply a limitation of God's potency?, thereby taking us back once more to the problems regarding God's all powerfulness. Second, granted that evil was necessary because there is good, why is there so much evil? i. e., why is there hard evil or dysteleological or gratuitous evil? And here the necessary solution can answer : Because there is so much good ; or it can fall back, as I think the Indians do, on the rebirth solution. In other words, there is so much suffering because there is so much sin. And that sin and that suffering, in the face of God's various powers, can only be explained by the rebirth solution. This was an answer of course that was not open to us in Part I. There, when gratuitous evil was spoken of, it seemed terribly difficult to balance it by its opposite, i.e., by pointing to nebulous piles and mountains of good. The retreat from the necessary solution, therefore, led to the problem of gratuitous evil. And the presence of gratuitous evil did not in Part I seem answerable by the theists we examined; recall JOHN HICK's sudden withdrawal into the mystery solution, faith, and irrationality when faced with extraordinary evil. The Indian is not necessarily driven there, not at this stage of the argument anyway. For he can speak about the many accumulated and diverse past evils suddenly and cataclysmically surfacing to produce the gratuitous and dysteleological evils that drove HICK and others into their various mystery solutions.

Thus, the necessary solution carries us back to the rebirth solution once again, and like the attack on the theological theses above, a final word on it must await our treatment of the rebirth solution in the following section.

Conclusion

There may indeed be other more viable solutions than the rebirth solution to T.P.E. In fact we shall find two more solutions yet to be named, in our examination of ŚAṀKARA and RĀMĀNUJA below in Part III c. But for the Indian, at least, solutions to T.P.E. of the type examined here, would all seem to lead or rest upon or give-way to the more powerful rebirth solution. The reasons for this giving-way are, I think, two-fold:

1. The rebirth solution is simply a more powerful solution since it is not subject to the singularly crushing criticisms of the type levelled against the others, viz., it can explain and justify gratuitous or hard evil, which the others as we saw in Part I, could not do. Whether it can do this without leading us into greater difficulties, or indeed whether it can really do this at all, of course, remains to be shown.

2. The rebirth solution is, as we saw in Part II, an indigenous segment of the Indian philosophical tradition, insofar as the doctrine of rebirth is a part of that tradition. Hence the rebirth solution is more powerful because it is blessed with orthodoxy. It is on the essentially *pakka* stature of the doctrine of rebirth in general that my contention rested that Indians in the classical and medieval tradition were never really bothered by T.P.E. as other Western theists were. The problem never achieved the horrendous magnitude for the Indians, though they have theoretically admitted as we saw in Ch. VIII to all the necessary ingredients that would lead to T.P.E.; i.e., they could admit to all the major assumptions, it would seem, from the theological theses, to the ethical thesis, to the evil thesis, necessary to generating T.P.E. They differed from their Western counterparts, however, in one very significant respect : They assumed the doctrine of rebirth. We now turn, climactically, I trust, to a discussion of the rebirth solution.

2. *Transmigration and Reincarnation*
The Rebirth Solution

We have been a long time indeed in getting to the main point. But the sparrings and joustings, the distinctions and the clarifyings, the dashed hopes and realized fears, all part of the foregoing panoply of philosophic materials in Parts I and II, ought now to pay off. If they do not, then we have been about a useless business.

In what follows, I want to do three things:

a. Briefly review the literature regarding the high hopes

many philosophers and other thinkers have had regarding the solution of T.P.E. by the rebirth solution. These high hopes are from Western writers or contemporary Indians, there being nothing quite like it, as we have argued, in the classical and the medieval Indian literature. Perhaps this lends weight once again to our original contention in Part I that T.P.E. is indeed a European problem and not an indigenously Indian one, and the argument from silence would seem to support this contention.[467] The argument from silence, a purely methodological research device, would probably run as follows: If the Indians had been concerned with T.P.E., they would have said so. They don't say so. Hence they weren't. However, in their *bhāṣyas* on the *Brahma sūtras* as we shall see below, Śaṁkara and Rāmānuja do take up T.P.E., but only incidentally, and only in order to answer a far more important question for them: Did *Brahmā* make the world?

b. Just as quickly say something about the counter-blast from Western writers regarding the rebirth solution as a solution of T.P.E., and show wherein these attempts to refute the rebirth solution miss the mark; at least show how they miss the mark as far as Indians are concerned.

c. Finally, present in some detail Indian arguments by Śaṁkara and Rāmānuja to support the goodness of the Creator in the face of the world's evil. Our task will be simply to analyze a series of three closely argued contentions that while there is evil in the universe, God is not responsible for it. Among the three arguments used will be the rebirth solution; and the criticism we have of that solution will be vented at that time.

a. The Rebirth Solution Will Solve P.E.

A number of writers, Indian and European, have contended that the rebirth solution will solve P.E. We can give some precision to their claims, following our analysis in Part I, by distinguishing in the rebirth solution, reincarnation from transmigration, and by distinguishing in P.E. the three kinds of evil or the three types, viz. S_pE, S_b E and H.E. Further, within transmigration theory following our analysis in Part II, we can distinguish two theories of souls, at least for the Indian setting, viz., $Soul_{HP}$ and $Soul_{HI}$.

It will be apparent as we proceed with the modern defenders of rebirth that for all of them that doctrine is a transmigration doctrine of rebirth, and that the transmigration doctrine it upholds is attached to a $Soul_{HP}$ theory. Further, the P.E. with which they seem generally concerned is T P.E., and the kind of evil they are by and large engaged with is human evil (H.E). Consequently, our main concern will be with determining whether the rebirth solution as a transmigration doctrine with $Soul_{HP}$ can indeed solve TPHE.

(1) MAX WEBER

In his *The Sociology of Religion* (first published in Germany in 1922) MAX WEBER lays out what he conceives to be the Indian solution to P.E. He begins by claiming, contrary to what we have found in the classical texts, that

> "All Hindu religion was influenced by it [the problem of theodicy] in the distinctive way necessitated by its fundamental presuppositions; even a meaningful world order that is impersonal and supertheistic must face the problem of the world's imperfections."[468]

Two comments on this introductory remark before we move into his presentation of the rebirth solution.

1. Just where the problem of theodicy springs up WEBER does not say. What form it takes, and in what texts or persons it appears, he does not tell us. But more importantly,

2. Just how the Indians can produce or manufacture a theodicy, given the assumptions he finds the Indians making, is not clear. That is to say, since a theodicy must seemingly involve a personal God (WEBER had read his Leibniz), and since one assumption that he imputes to the Indians is that they do have an impersonal Brahman undergirding their entire system, then how can he cross these personal and impersonal categories and still make any theodical sense? Following a brief review of the Indian doctrine of souls, where they can go and under what conditions or circumstances they can go, a discussion which illustrates rather aptly our assumptions A_1, A_2, A_3 of Hindu rebirth theories presented in Part II above, following all this, WEBER leaps into his

main thesis, rebirth as a solution to P.E.

> "The most complete formal solution of the problem of theodicy is the special achievement of the Indian doctrine of *karma*, the so-called belief in the transmigration of souls. The world is viewed as completely connected and self-contained cosmos of ethical retribution. Guilt and merit within this world are unfailingly compensated by fate in the successive lives of the soul, which may be reincarnated innumerable times in animal, human, or even divine forms. The finiteness of earthly life is the consequence of the finiteness of good or evil deeds in the previous life of a particular soul. What may appear from the viewpoint of a theory of compensation as unjust suffering in the terrestrial life of a person should be regarded as atonement for sin in a previous existence. Each individual forges his own destiny exclusively, and in the strictest sense of the world."[469]

WEBER goes on to say, quite rightly, that given the rebirth doctrine there can be no sin in the Augustinian sense as offenses against others, for any evil one does is clearly to one's own detriment (recall our discussion of karma, A_4 in Part II, where we argued that morality becomes essentially personal, private and selfish, where helping others might be to postpone their release from the karma they have a need to work off and expiate) and not theirs.

From his discussion of rebirth as a solution to P.E. WEBER draws what I think are a total of five conclusions, conclusions with which the defender of the rebirth solution must be prepared to live :

1. The first is mentioned above, viz., there is no sin or doing evil to others as much as doing evil to oneself. For in the end the doer is the one who suffers. Thus suppose I kill a man. His suffering is temporary, and besides, if he dies in a proper moral state, he might be rewarded by a better birth next time around, while I am sunk into a lower birth as a consequence. This need not follow necessarily for the man who suffers, for what happens to him may also be interpreted as a just punishment for his previous misdeeds. More on this below.

2. In the doctrine of metempsychosis, the bifurcation between a sacred, all powerful and holy God, and a mass of morally inadequate creatures is wholly lacking. Weber seems to be saying that the doctrine of rebirth itself, if mechanical and wholly impersonal (as we mentioned, this was one of the interpretations of A_4 above in Part II, *pace* Śrī AUROBINDO), totally removes God from the picture. As Lord Buddha's own last words imply, one can, without the Gods as helpers or hinderers, work out one's salvation with diligence because one does it by and for ones self. From this it follows :

3. That there is no bisection of the creation into dichotomous camps of light and darkness, pure and the impure spirits, clear spirit on the one hand as opposed to dark and dreadful matter on the other, as in "spiritualistic dualism."[470] What emerges is, of course, a metaphysical monism, with two contrasting elements soon to be reduced to one :

4. The contrasting elements are the restless, churning transitory events with the "serene and perduring being of eternal order—immobile divinity resting in dreamless sleep."[471] But while WEBER sees the doctrine of rebirth leading to a kind of grand *advaitic* synthesis he fails to take into account those pluralistic systems which hold to A_4, the karma thesis, and the rebirth solution as well, but which don't end up in a metaphysical monism. Further, one could criticize WEBER's conclusion 2, for it is the case with certain theistic Hindu religions that hold to rebirth, that God as Viṣṇu or Śiva or any other multitude of named deities help in the salvation and release of the soul from *saṁsāra*. Consequently, Weber's conclusion 3 surely doesn't follow, for again with those pluralistic, theistic religions there will always be a gulf between those souls who are churning about in the creation on the wheel of birth and death, and those that have been released; and insofar as the round is beginningless, as many Indians contend (see c below), the gulf will remain.

5. One suspects that WEBER, therefore, is not speaking sociologically in drawing these conclusions, i.e., he is not speaking historically nor predictively, but only logically in showing what the inevitable ideal or logical result would be, given in A_4 and rebirth in general :

"Only Buddhism has deduced from the doctrine of trans-

> migration of souls its ultimate consequences. This is the most radical solution of the problem of theodicy, and for that very reason it provides as little satisfaction for ethical claims upon god as does the belief in predestination".[472]

The Buddhism that WEBER has in mind is Theravāda, presumably. And $Soul_B$ theory as we have seen, can certainly produce no "satisfaction for ethical claims" upon God since there is no God.

If one accepts the rebirth solution and A_4, according to WEBER, then one must be prepared to accept certain consequences along with it : a metaphysical monism, a $Soul_B$ theory, and reincarnation, if our interpretation of his conclusions are correct. That none of this need necessarily follow is apparent from our discussion, however. One important point to be gleaned from this entire presentation, though, is this : If one accepts the rebirth solution and the karma thesis in solving T.P.E., one must be prepared to accept certain other consequences as a result. What these consequences might be we shall note in c below, and what other implications in turn might be forced upon us will be analyzed in turn in our conclusion in Chapter X which closes this entire study.

I have spent considerable time with MAX WEBER for the simple reason that he sets a pattern more or less for the other defenders of the rebirth solution that follow. They can all be treated a bit more circumspectly as a result, since they more or less repeat or embellish what WEBER has already said :

2) CHRISTMAS HUMPHREYS

The well-known exponent and scholar of Buddhism, CHRISTMAS HUMPHREYS, in his book *Karma and Rebirth* defends the rebirth solution (as reincarnation not transmigration) as a solution to the "problem of Good and Evil," and the implications for T.P.E. are obvious enough. Thus of the origin of evil, HUMPHREYS says there can be no Original Sin ·

> "Evil is man-made, and is of his choosing, and he who suffers, suffers from his own deliberate use of his own free will. Cripples, dwarfs and those born deaf or blind are the products of their own past actions..."[473]

Thus with respect to the above remark, it is quite plain that metaphysical evil in the Augustinian sense is sheer illusion for the rebirth theorist like HUMPHREYS. Recall our discussion on LEIBNIZ, sin, metaphysical evil and God, and all the terrible, horrendous, tangles these led to in Part I above. In one fell swoop the rebirth solution sweeps all that into the dust bin. If one pushes further and asks : Yes, but who started it all ?, the Indian answer in general is that there was no "start." More of this in b and finally c, below.

Of the "law" of karma HUMPHREYS says :

> "Once the Law is reasonably understood it solves a large proportion of the problems which cloud our present mind, and certainly in the East, where karma is as obvious as the law of gravity, these problems do not arise. In the first place it explains the inequities and inequalities of daily life. Only karma "can explain the mysterious problem of Good and Evil, and reconcile man to the terrible apparent injustice of life."[474]

HUMPHREYS goes on to detail the other items that the law of karma can explain. Quoting from HENRY CLARKE WARREN'S, *Buddhism in Translations*, he says that karma explains heredity, wherein one could be, to put it fancifully, one's own grandfather :

> "Karma explains heredity. 'Karma' expresses, not that which a man inherits from his ancestors, but that which he inherits from himself in some previous state of existence."[475]

Further, karma explains war and hatred.[476] Thus in wiping out problems of original sin, in solving this Buddhist puzzle, and in "explaining" heredity and why it pays to be good, the principle of karma is not merely a convenient fiction, as ELIOT DEUTSCH maintained in Part II, but at the very least a very real force in the universe.

HUMPHREYS takes up two objections to rebirth that might be worth mentioning. Our concern hasn't been in this book to prove *saṁsāra* and its four assumptions, but rather to take it and them, as we did in Part II, as just that : assumptions. For this reason, also, the need has not arisen to defend the doctrine against attacks. Assumptions can't be defended save on the ground of convenience alone. But the second of the two objections that HUMPHREYS raises draws him and us back into $Soul_B$ theory, and a difficulty with it which for P.E. purposes might seem to be quite real. The objections are :

First, that rebirth can't be possible for we don't remember our previous lives. HUMPHREYS answers the objection rather opaquely by stating that the brain, the organ of memory, is new in each life, but that in the *ākāśa* a record of previous lives may, under the appropriate circumstances, be read.[477] His answer is obscure and need not detain us anyway, but presumably he is denying that previous lives can't be recalled.

Second, he plunges into an objection based on SoulB theory. If one identifies the self with memory as LOCKE apparently did (recall Part II above), then when memory goes that self also goes. So how, the objection concludes, can I be responsible in this life for a lost self in some previous life? This complaint oddly enough is linked to $Soul_B$ theory since the continuity of self as mere patterns or traces of desire, is presumably broken from life to life, just as it is from moment to moment.

HUMPHREYS states:

> "The second objection usually raised is the injustice of our suffering for the deeds of someone about whom we remember nothing. The answer is the same. It is the inner mind, the reincarnating entity, which draws from the universal memory the lessons it would learn. The man who has forgotten . . . who complains is, though he has a new brain, the man whose deeds he suffers."[478]

HUMPHREYS seems to be letting a Hindu $Soul_{HP}$ theory complete with mind and memories, get in the way of his Theravāda Buddhist doctrine. He wants to explain evil; he seems to believe that he can't do it with $Soul_B$ because SoulB has no enduring self, qua mind and memory, from life to life. But a problem crops up for him when he argues that the past life is not remembered because a new brain is present in the present life. This becomes a problem of identity like $P.I._{4P}$ mentioned in Part II, where the self is identified with certain memories. He doesn't really solve the problem at all then, by resorting to that rather vague talk about "inner mind" and "universal memory". For if the self is identical with memories, and those memories are brain-specific, and the old brain is replaced by a new brain, and those old memories are gone, then that old self is gone—hence $P.I._{4P}$ is not solved: HUMPHREYS has a $Soul_B$ theory that he has apparently then suffused with $Soul_H$ elements. In mixing Buddhism with Hinduism, he has failed to explain evil (and, for us, solve T.P.E.). He has failed to make "responsibility" from life to life meaningful, consequently he has failed to render a justification for evil such as the second objection mentioned above demands, and he ends up with a problem of personal identity to boot.

(3) SWAMI DESHIKANANDA

DESHIKANANDA, I would suggest, is rather typical of present-century *Vedāntin* Hindus who have discovered that T.P.E. can be solved by the rebirth solution,[479] or solutions closely tied to it. I don't wish to dwell on his comments but simply note them and then move on to more problematic matters. The SWAMI says of T.P.E. :

> "The only scientific explanation for the solution of this problem is that offered by Vedānta. It is the law of karma.'[480]

He then adds in what I take to be $Soul_{HP}$ fashion, though unhappily he never clarifies his position directly:

> "Evil exists because we ourselves are the cause for it and have sown its seeds . . ."[481]

4) WILMON HENRY SHELDON

The critics have leaped upon WILMON HENRY SHELDON, *emeritus* Sheldon Clark Professor of philosophy at Yale University, because SHELDON has been one of the few really able philosophers to support the hypothesis of the rebirth solution as a viable possibility in solving T.P.E. SHELDON is respectable, well-philosophized and with established credentials, but more than this, he presents in a rather clear way the best possible case for rebirth. In his *magnum opus*, *God and Polarity, A Synthesis of Philosophies*, SHELDON discusses ways of retaining the perfections of God (our theological theses) consonantly with the evil in the world (our evil thesis);

> "Another hypothesis is possible. It may not be verifiable, it may not be probable, but if it is possible, we have no proof that God is in any way limited."

That "other hypothesis" is used to explain the facts of evil:

> "Start from the facts. Many people, many animals, suffer untold miseries without any apparent fault of their own. It is the injustice of it that rankles. Now why do we think these sufferers are punished far beyond their deserts? Because we have no evidence of their having done wrong in anything like the degree of their pains. And in the case of very young children, they couldn't have done so."[482]

Thus from this beginning SHELDON observes that the rebirth solution is an "open possibility," even though it may be false, and even though it will be rejected by "scientific" minds:

> "It is, so far as compelling proof goes, an open possibility. If it is a true hypothesis, it at once removes the apparent injustice of so much suffering—or rather, it makes the removal possible."[483]

It is, SHELDON continues, the apparently undeserved pain and suffering of creatures (our "hard" evil of Part I) that leads men to question God's power and nature. The choice left open then, to the theist is a choice between a God with certain imperfections like MILL's deity mentioned in Part I or the "wild, unprovable, unscientific notion" of reincarnation (he is really speaking of transmigration). Hence to avoid the following conclusion which is the heart of T.P.E.,

> "So God must be partly evil; or, rather, since He is perfect in goodness He must be lacking in power."[484]

SHELDON turns to the rebirth solution as a possibility and a real alternative to a finite, imperfect deity:

> " ...... for aught we know every single iota of suffering is deserved. True, we cannot at present prove that

> it is deserved, is the result of grievous sins in some former incarnation. The possibility remains. It cannot be ruled out. Perhaps then God permits person A to cause misery in person B because B deserves punishment for sins committed in a former life. Perhaps *all* the miseries of men and animals are to be justified in this way.[485]

The type of rebirth solution proposed is Soul$_{HP}$ or Soul$_{P}$ transmigration. SHELDON's possibility is criticized by Western critic's, and it is to a few of these critics that we turn next.

In conclusion let me say that my intention in this section has been simply to demonstrate what a number of Western and Indian philosophers have had to say about the explanation of evil by the rebirth solution as both relate to T.P.E. It is to be noted once again that all the defenders of the rebirth solution are contemporary, and that by and large the stake they have in the matter would seem to be either to defend rebirth against non-rebirth doctrines like Christianity, this is the case with not a few of the Indians mentioned above, especially DESHIKANANDA and COOMARASWAMY, or to really solve T.P.E. by the rebirth solution as with the Western critics especially WEBER and SHELDON.

The great champions of rebirth are of course the Indians. They take rebirth for granted and hence, because it is such an important assumption in their conceptual scheme, it is rarely mentioned *per se* in discussing philosophical issues: Classical Indian philosophers are nobly silent, in general, about their assumptions, and rebirth is one such assumption.

Western philosophers, on the other hand, see rebirth as just plain nonsense, not worthy of serious attention; the theory is usually considered as unverifiable nonsense, a woolly-headed and fuzzy-minded fiction. The Bridie Murphie scandals are what one gets into if one dips too deeply into such goings on: Western philosophers, consequently, are warily silent, in general, about rebirth and the rebirth solution to T.P.E.

Some Westerners have spoken up in recent years, however, as we have seen above, and others have begun to treat rebirth seriously enough to warrant giving it (even) critical rebuff. Again, much of the time, one can't tell if the opponents are chastising a reincarnation theory or a transmigration theory (if it makes any difference), and for the simple reason that it is not clear which theory the rebirth proponents are advancing (recall the confusions above with HUMPHREYS). However, the debate is in the open now, and we turn next to two of the critics of the rebirth solution (it's very difficult to find any more, though we, ourselves, shall have a plunge at criticism in c below), who have felt the theory at least important enough to shout it down.

b. *The Rebirth Solution Will Not Solve T.P.E.*

A number of writers have contended that the rebirth solution will not solve T.P.E. I would suggest that the paucity of criticism of the solution to T.P.E. as mentioned above, is based more on the seeming sheer unbelievability of the rebirth doctrine itself, than on an inability of the theory to cope with T.P.E.; that is to say, when most Western critics mention possible solutions to T.P.E., the rebirth solution is automatically excluded, and this because of the feeling that rebirth is outlandish or superstitious skulduggery; to treat it any differently, even to mention it as a possible solution, would be to take it seriously, and that is anathema. At least it was. The literature seems to be opening more and more now to rebirth as a metaphysical theory worth considering on its own merits and as a solution to T.P.E. The present study is, of course, just such an undertaking.

But the theory does have its critics.

(1) ALAN WATTS

WATTS had previously (cf. note 464) been a defender of rebirth as a solution to T.P.E., and to a certain extent, for WATTS, the popular theory of rebirth, by which he must mean transmigration, still works:

> "Popular Hinduism and Buddhism explain such tragedies as the individual's Karma, as his own doing, inherited from a former life. The syphilitic baby is therefore paying a price for some evil that he has done in a previous incarnation."[486]

This sounds much like SHELDON, and the WATTS of old. But

then WATTS mentions what he regards as serious limitation of the theory:

> "But this is not so much an explanation as an indefinite postponement of explanation. Why and how does the reincarnating individual first go wrong?"[487]

It is not clear from reading WATTS whether he believes that this difficulty is serious enough to warrant giving up the rebirth solution. I suspect it is; but WATTS doesn't say how he personally feels about this formerly acceptable theory. The criticism seems to be essentially this : Granted that my suffering in this life can be partly explained by misdeeds I did in my previous existence; and granted that those deeds can in part also be explained by another previous life before that one (I say "partly", for many of the evils I suffer now are the results of causes in the present life, i.e., things I do, or that you do, etc., now); but somewhere there must have been a start, a time when I was pure and innocent, a golden age, perhaps, when God first created me, pure and lily-virtuous. Call this assumption the golden-age assumption. It destroys the effectiveness of rebirth as a solution to P.E. for it of necessity drags God back into the picture as a creator or first mover, and as we have seen *via* the good Baron d'HOLBACH in Part I, God as the cause of me, and me as the cause of evil, raises moral problems with God that lead immediately to T.P.E.

The golden age assumption is found in the work of two other authors, and we turn next to them and their criticism of SHELDON.

2) EDWARD H. MADDEN and PETER H. HARE

MADDEN and HARE mention one principal criticism, in this case within the context of SHELDON's defense of rebirth as a hypothetical possibility that rests quite plainly on the golden age assumption:

> W. H. SHELDON has suggested that it is at least possible that sufferings undeserved by deeds in this life are punishment for evil deeds in an earlier incarnation. This suggestion, however, is not very helpful, even if we were to take the reincarnation hypothesis

> seriously. Even as a mere possibility the hypothesis provides only temporary relief because it immediately has the problem of explaining the original moral evil. We ask at once why God permitted all the moral evil in earlier incarnations for which we are now being punished . . . "[488]

The key phrase is "original moral evil" for by it the golden age assumption is made. Thus they argue in effect, there had to be an origin; a first human evil act that would lead to evil consequences and that would perpetuate the soul or at least keep it going for another birth. The golden age assumption thereby entails three sub-assumptions.

1. There was a beginning of human action, a first human act so to speak.

2. That first human act was either in itself wicked or there was a later human act after that one that was wicked. Thus Adam named the animals and those acts were good. But subsequently he ate of the forbidden fruit and that was bad.

3. Prior to that first wicked human act, or in the context in which it was made, the garden of Eden, for example, God had created a perfect paradise into which he set man who was as perfect a creation *as possible* but still perfect else God becomes sullied with man's evil.

All three sub-assumptions combine to form the golden age assumption, and all three speak of beginnings, firstnesses, and perfect origins: All three assume beginnings. The way out of this net spread by the critics for the proponents of the rebirth solution is for those proponents simply to deny the golden age assumption. This is precisely what the Indians by and large do, and we shall see their counter assumption, viz., beginninglessness of *saṁśāra*, at work next in c.

The beginningless response to the golden age assumption is a regress response but it is not a vicious regress. It is not vicious for the simple reason that at each stage the nature of existence can be explained by previous existences—there is no case of a no-explanation-until-the-regress is-completed-and-it-can't-be-completed conclusion. That would indeed be a vicious regress. Here, on the contrary, at each stage we have an answer to the question, Why do I suffer the evil that I do when God is so perfect? There is no postponement of an answer until the incompletable series is completed. The answer, however vague, is there: Because of karma, my karma.

MADDEN and HARE launch into a second but trivial objection to the rebirth solution which I mention in our catalogue of objections here, simply because objections to, much less discussion of, this solution are so rare. They say

> "Among the further more obvious difficulties in the reincarnation hypothesis is the one of why God has systematically deluded Christians about why he is punishing them. Such delusion hardly argues for the existence of a God unlimited in goodness."[489]

This objection is trivial because it is answered within the context of the attack itself. All delusion is caused by human ignorance. That ignorance is, in part again, traceable to human failings in a previous existence. Therefore rebirth itself can explain and justify the delusions that Christians and others suffer under and it can do it rather neatly. This second objection is, consequently, not really a serious objection, but a request for clarification regarding the nature of the doctrine of rebirth (or "reincarnation" as MADDEN and HARE call it).

We turn finally, the above objections having been cleared away, to the strongest theodical defense, and perhaps the clearest rebirth defense, in the Indian literature. It emerges, not so much as a theodicy, however, largely because of its context; rather it appears as one of most powerful analyses of the rebirth solution that we possess from Indian philosophical literature.

C. *Indian Theodicy* : ŚAṀKARA *and* RĀMĀNUJA *on Brahma Sūtra II.* 1. 32-36:*

Whatever other differences the two major proponents of *Vedānta* may have, they reach a high accord in their comments on BĀDARĀYAṆA's *Brahma Sūtra* or *Vedānta Sūtra* II.1. 35-36.[490]

*A revised verision of this section has been published in *Philosophy East and West*, Vol. 21, Number 3, July, 1971.

This high accord centers on the proper treatment, handling, and solution of what we have called "the problem of evil" (P.E.), and in particular the theological problem of human evil (T.P.H.E., of. Part I of this book, above). P.E. and T.P.-H.E. are dealt with elsewhere in the *Brahma-Sūtra Bhāṣyas* by both Śaṁkara and Rāmānuja,[491] but nowhere else does their treatment reach the high pitch and sustained philosophic force as in the passages under discussion here.

The principle question taken up in the passages II.1. 32-36, is the question as to whether or not Brahman (God) created the world. The answer that both Śaṁkara and Rāmānuja give is in the affirmative. But the way to that answer provides us with some highly interesting jousts with P.E., and some entertaining answers to numerous insistent objectors along the way. Let me take the *sūtras*, one at a time, freely translate each of the five, and then attempt to explain what's going on as that going-on is understood by Śaṁkara and Rāmānuja. The programme of argument here calls for certain remarks by certain unnamed objectors supporting the thesis that God cannot be the cause of the world, and then replies by the opponents of this view, Śaṁkara and Rāmānuja period. In each case, the latter two Vedāntists build up the objector's position with reasonable arguments and then attack these arguments with reason and scripture (śruti and smṛti). One is reminded of the technique used by Thomas Aquinas.

Bādarāyaṇa opens now with the summary of the objector's argument:

> "Brahman cannot be the cause of the world because to cause or create involves motives or purposes (and if Brahman has either He is imperfect)."II. 1.32

The argument supporting the objector's conclusion is put by Śaṁkara into the form of a dilemma: "either God had a purpose or he didn't, a motive or not." If "purpose" is rendered "desire", I think the force of the objection can be seen in a number of interesting ways, and ways that relate back to what we called in Part I, Ch.II, "the paradox of perfection." For if God created the world, He did it for a purpose. If He had a purpose then He desired some goal. But if He desired something, then He was lacking something. But if He lacked something, then He's not perfect, i.e., wholly fulfilled. Hence, in line now with the paradox of perfection, if the theological theses (cf. Part I, Ch. II) are extended to include God's having goals, purposes, or desires, they must apparently on the interpretation of what it is to cause, i.e., create, something, then those theological theses (the omniscience thesis, the omnipotence thesis, and the ethical thesis that God is all-good), together with what we might call "the creator thesis", i.e., the thesis that God desires to make a world, men, etc., gives us an inconsistent set. ŚAṀKARA summarizes this objection, which he and RĀMĀNUJA will shortly attempt to answer, as follows:

> "Now, if it were to be conceived that this endeavor of the Highest Self is useful to itself because of its own desire, then such supposition would contradict the scriptural statement about the Highest Self being always quite contented."[492]

Thus that horn of the dilemma leads to a contradiction.

But suppose Brahman created without a purpose. This way, too, there is a problem. For to act without purpose is in effect not to *act* at all. And if creating is an act, then one could not create without some purpose. A contradiction results: If one tries to create without purpose, then one cannot create, for to create means to act purposefully. God ends up purposelessly purposing, a contradiction. Again ŚAṀKARA states this horn as follows:

> "If on the other hand, one were to conceive no such purpose (behind such endeavor), one would have to concede that (in such a case) there would not be any such endeavor . . ."[493]

In summary then, if God creates with purpose then this exposes a glaring inconsistency in the nature of God. On the other hand if God tries to create (endeavor, desire, act) without desire, endeavor, or action, this proves contradictory and impossible. But must we be hung on these horns? No. BĀDARĀYAṆA slips between them followed by a host of Vedāntins. Before rushing after them, let me comment briefly on this argument:

We argued previously in Part I with respect to the paradox of perfection that certain properties attributed to

God formed a practically inconsistent set of predicates, and the creator thesis re-emphasizes this problem. Thus the creator thesis relates to the benevolence thesis (that God desires the good) and the beneficence thesis (that God does the good) of the ethical thesis (that God is all-good) regarding the predicates attributed to God. The creator thesis is more specific than the ethical thesis since it spells out in what particular way God wants and does the good, i.e., He wants a world, and in wanting what He does not have, what He lacks, He shows His imperfection. Both our commentators must step a narrow line in what follows, first between having God as the cause of the world while avoiding the conclusion that the creator thesis leads to; and second having God as the cause of the world while avoiding the conclusion that God brought evil into it as the cause of it: The latter puzzle is, of course, T.P.E.

> "But as with men at times, so with God, creation is a mere sport." II 1.33.

Sport (*līlā*) is understood here to be a third sort of activity; it is therefore neither purposive nor purposeless, those words being inapplicable to what God's sport is really like. ŚAṀKARA uses the example of breathing—it is not an act of will but follows simply "the law of its own nature."[494] Thus *līlā* prompts creation out of sheer joy, an overflowing from God's great and wonderful sportive nature. We have here a new solution of sorts to T.P.E. It amounts to saying that while evil exists in the creation, it cannot be due to its "creator," since what He did was not really an act of creation at all; the creation is a kind of playful over-flowing of His joyful inner nature call this "the evil-in-the-world-is-not-from-God-who-did-not create-it-but-merely-sported-it solution" or "the *līlā* solution." RĀMĀNUJA speaks to the *līlā* solution with an entertaining example:

> "We see in ordinary life how some great King, ruling this earth with its seven *dvīpas*, and possessing perfect strength, valour, and so on, has a game at balls, or the like, from no other motive than to amuse himself . . ."[495]

Moreover it is not in creation alone that *līlā* is evidenced, but in the world's ultimate destruction as well:

> "...there is no objection to the view that sport only is the motive prompting Brahman to the creation, sustentation, and destruction of this world which is easily fashioned by his mere will." [496]

I. A comment on this solution; it becomes attempted solution number twenty-two, if the reader is still counting. The Vedāntists actually don't need the *līlā* solution to counter objections to T.P.E. All objections can be handled, as we shall note, rather neatly by the rebirth solution mentioned previously in Part I. For, as we shall show, all superhuman, human, and subhuman suffering or evil, seen in T.P.E. as TPS_pE TPHE or TPS_bE respectively, can be dealt with adequately with the rebirth solution, with one or two slight additions involving the non-beginningness of the world.

2. *Līlā* solves nothing as far as T.P.E. is concerned, for while *līlā* may be a purposeless act, it is surely an activity about which we can ask; Who did it? That is to say, labeling *līlā* as merely motiveless, goalless sport, sensible enough in itself, does not rule out asking, Whose intention was it to engage in this motiveless activity? God is not responsible for the purposes in *līlā*, for supposedly there are none, but He is surely responsible for the act that brings *līlā* into existence. Let me make this clearer. Suppose I'm going to play a game. Suppose the game I play is like observing a work of art, an aesthetic activity, in which there are no goals, purposes, or ends, but just activity for activity's sake, enjoyment without repercussions (e.g., I'm not doing it to win a prize, raise my blood pressure, impress my peers, work up a sweat, etc.) But while I have no desires raised and satisfied in the aesthetic or game activity itself, I did have an antecedent desire raised ahead of time and it was only realized when I subsequently played the game. If we distinguish between the play as activity, aesthetic in itself, and the play as a something-to-be done, a goal in itself, then we can see that the former is consequentless and goalless at the time the activity is going on, and since there is no motive being satisfied, it is like *līlā*—play without purpose; but the latter, involving a decision to play, the getting the ball, the going to the museum, the bringing about of the act of play, aesthetic indulgence, or *līlā*, surely has a goal or aim—viz., goalless or aimless activity. I am not responsible for the pur-

poses in *līlā*, for there are none. But I am responsible for the act that brings *līlā* about. Thus I may be responsible and to blame for what happens after *līlā* is over, or after separate acts of *līlā* have been made.

3. I bounce a ball on the wall. My neighbours are annoyed. They say "Why did you bounce the ball?" I say, "I had no purpose." They say, "But your bouncing keeps our baby awake, disturbs our studying, frightens our wife, angers our mother-in-law, cracks our walls." Now, can I say, "I am not to blame, I was only playing", and we all know there are no purposes in playing? That would be silly. What am I responsible for? The bouncing. Does the bouncing bother anyone? No. It's the noise from the bouncing that bothers. Could I conceivably argue that I'm not responsible for the noise? Nonsense. In the act of play, from my point of view, what I do is without purpose. From my neighbour's point of view, what I do has results that are all too evident.

4. I pull the wings and legs off a baby bird, as RICHARD BRANDT has said "Hopi" children do in their play. Someone says, What are you doing? and I say, playing. I haven't excused my act, only described it. Granted that in a game the purpose is lost in the game, i.e., the game's purpose is lost in the game, to say this is not to excuse what results from the game, but simply label a certain sort of activity, and rule out silly question like, "Why are you playing a game?" Thus to describe God's activity as *līlā* is to describe the play act from two possible points of view. From God's point of view, it is a description of a purposeless, aimless, play, without motives, without intentions. But from the neighbour's point of view, from the suffering bird's point of view, *līlā* is fraught with effects and consequences that are undesirable to say the least. *līlā* cannot be used to justify the results that follow from the act; *līlā* merely describes the act. The *Vedāntists* have mistaken the description of *līlā* for a justification of *līlā*.

5. While one cannot ask, why are you playing that game, after one has been told that a game is being played, one can, nonetheless, ask, "why are you playing that game that way ?" If I move the King two places in a "chess" game (and I'm not castling) and you say, don't you know the rules of chess, your question would be quite legitimate. If the game has rules

and one violates the rules, one can ask, "what game are you playing?" If God plays a game of creation, and seems to violate rules for playing the creation game, we might very well ask, "Doesn't He know the rules of the game of creation?" I assume this question is at the very heart of T.P.E. And philosophers are notorious for having all sorts of legitimate suggestions for better rules and better ways of playing the creation game.

6. Some games one plays in a sportive mood can be won or lost. Chess and most card games can be played to such a conclusion. Some games, like bouncing a ball on my neighbour's wall, are not playable to a winning or losing conclusion. But all games can be played better or worse, with greater facility or less, more joy, commitment, playfulness, indulgence, and what-have-you, or less. "A man full of cheerfulness on awakening from sound sleep dances about without any motive or need but simply from the fulness of spirit, so is the case with the creation of the world by God."[497] But such a joyful man can dance poorly or well, better this time than last. To leap out of bed and dance on the sides of one's feet, clumsily, is no good at all. One can learn to express one's sportive feelings better than that. Practice in expressing joy is possible and necessary to true joyfulness, anyway. If I leap out of bed, overflowing with *gemutlichkeit* or *freude*, and then trip all over my feet in expressing my feelings, I'm not going to be very joyful for very long. One expresses one's joy and sorrow, and one's feelings in general, in appropriately tried and tested ways: at the piano, singing in showers or cars, kissing and hugging friends or one's self; one can get better at such expressions, just as one can improve one's self in other purposeless or goalless activities like games. It is therefore legitimate to ask, "When Brahman, through *līlā*, expressed His joy, why didn't He do it better?" If He is perfect He could, and if He's good He would want to—so why didn't He? We are back again with T.P.E.

7. Śaṁkara's example of breathing is curious, but the same question raised above can be applied to it. Some people are poor breathers—"shallow breathers" my physician calls them. They breathe at the very top of their lungs; their respiration, in place of the normal sixteen per minute, runs twenty-five to thirty: They must breathe faster, for only

one-fourth to one-third of their full lung's capacity is being used. They are bad breathers—but they can be taught to breathe better. Looking at the creation, one could ask of Brahman, "Why didn't He learn to breathe out or in better?" Once more, we are back to T.P.E. Thus the *līlā* ploy solves nothing.

Finally RĀMĀNUJA brings in as we have seen another dimension to the *līlā* story that will make T.P.E. stand out even more strongly. He says from above in part :

> "...that sport alone is the motive prompting Brahman to the creation, sustentation, and destruction of this world.."[498].

The other dimension is the dissolution (*pralaya*) of the universe, for Brahman in his trinitarian role of Brahmā, Viṣṇu, and Śiva, is of course the exhaler, Brahmā, the sustainer, Viṣṇu, and the inhaler or destroyer, Śiva, of the universe. Thus if Brahman's play involves not simply creating and maintaining the universe, (that was essentially all that was discussed in T.P.E. here and previously in Part I) but also if Brahman is the great destroyer as well, and that is play, too, then Brahman's putative sins are far grander than any Western theologian had dreamed. The *Vedāntist* has his work cut out for himself, indeed.

But as I've tried to indicate, the *Vedāntists* have another theodical card to play, that seems to get them out of the problems raised by *līlā*.

> "Discrimination (treating beings unequally) and cruelty cannot be attributed to God, for He is aware of beings' Karma; and the Scriptures say so" (II. 1.34).

The objector, as interpreted by ŚAṀKARA, opens his case by saying :

> "It is not reasonably sustainable that the Lord is the cause of the world, because there would result the predicament of (the fault of) discrimination and cruelty (attaching themselves to the Lord)..."[499]

In our discussion of evil in Part I we referred to evils *caused* by man, and evils *endured* by man, as sin and suffering, respectively: AUGUSTINE's ancient distinction. The objector tells us here, that both sin and suffering could be attributed to God if God indeed were the Creator of the world. The objector then continues using another example of evil, call it "cosmological evil," that we have seen in RĀMĀNUJA's commentary above. ŚAṀKARA's objector says:

> "Similarly by his inflicting misery and by destroying all his creation, faults of such pitilessness and cruelty, as would be abhorred even by a villain, would attach themselves to the lord".[500]

And then the objector concludes again that the Lord cannot be the cause of the world. The cyclic act of absorptive destruction is on a scale so vast that, aside from rather curious cosmologies such as those of Empedocles, the Stoics, and FREDERICH NIETZCHE, it has no strict parallel in the West—unless one count Armageddon or the Flood or the Last Judgment as envisioned by ALBRECHT DURER. This mythical vision of destruction and de-evolution, this horrendous cosmological display of the Lord's ferocious and destructive side, comes closest to what LEIBNIZ called "metaphysical evil," and as was mentioned in Part I, what AUGUSTINE on a humanly smaller scale called "original sin." Both metaphysical evil and original sin intend an imperfection inherent in the basic cosmic stuff or material, respectively, in the universe and man, because of the fact that though each was created by God, each fell short of the perfective majesty of God: Each may be good but, as AUGUSTINE and LEIBNIZ are at pains to try to bring across, each is nonetheless imperfect. We had argued that problems arose here because of a confusion between metaphysical imperfection and moral imperfection, such that given the first, the second doesn't necessarily follow in the way AUGUSTINE and LEIBNIZ thought it did. But the objectors ŚAṀKARA serves up to us don't have that problem. They aren't caught in any such confusion since their point is not so much that the creation is good or bad (they don't say) but that it has to be destroyed. Since nearly all Hindus accept the cyclical theory of history and cosmology, there would indeed seem to be a problem : The Lord does destroy the creation, men, animals, Gods, the whole glorious and inglorious works. Hence we have with this cosmic or metaphysical evil, a T.P.E. of human evil

(TPHE) of superhuman evil (TPS_p E) and subhuman evil (TPS^b E). Thus the objector's case.

The form this evil takes comes closest as I said to metaphysical evil doctrines in the West, but only because the scale, the sheer quantity of each, is the same. But Indian attitudes toward the quality of the creation is far different, particularly for those cosmogonies that see nature, man, animals, and the Gods as all created from a similar substance. Thus both ŚAṀKARA and RĀMĀNUJA argue at 1.4.26 that the creation is Brahman since Brahman is the material cause of the creation; ŚAṀKARA uses the analogy of clay and the pots made from the clay, and in 1.4.27 he uses the example of the spider (*Brahman*) and its thread (world) to make his cosmogonic point. RĀMĀNUJA is more cautious in these passages, realizing as he does that the evil in the creation could be attributed to Brahman if the connection between them is too close, and especially in I.4.26 and 27, this threat seems more than obvious to him. He agrees in the latter commentary that Brahman has the entire universe for Its body, but the universe is the result of Brahman modifying (*pariṇamayati*) Itself "by gradually evolving the world-body." Both authors agree that Brahman is modified in some way, but the question remains, Has It been modified sufficiently to escape P.E. with respect to the creation?

Creation *ex nihilo*, the cosmogenic theory most prevalent in Western metaphysical theories stressing as it does the absolute separation between creator and creation, avoids a "pantheism" true enough, but leaps faith-first into the nasty tangles that AUGUSTINE and LEIBNIZ get into : If the creation is imperfect, how can you still call it good and, how could a perfect Creator create an imperfect universe ? This gulf between man and God inherent in most Western theological cosmogonies, is reflected in the theological dogma regarding the utter transcendence of God, the absolute dependence and depravity of man, and the agonizing sense of guilt and the necessity for atonement that pervades most classical Western religions. Indian religions, perhaps because of their cosmogonic theories, do not have these particular hang ups.

Thus far from II.1.34, we have two objections to the Lord's being the cause of the world: first, that the Lord would be responsible for evil in the world, and second, the Lord would be responsible for the destruction of that world. Call the first the discrimination and cruelty argument, and the second the destruction argument. Both arguments as we have seen lead to T.P.E. in all three of its formulations. RĀMĀNUJA expands on the discrimination and cruelty arguments in an interesting way, expertly displaying the two parts of this argument. Call the first part the discrimination argument. Objectors, according to RĀMĀNUJA, would say :

> "But the assumption of his having created the world would lay him open to the charge of partiality, insofar as the world contains beings of high, middle and low station—Gods, men, animals, immovable beings.."[501]

The discrimination argument is frequently expressed in the form, "Why was I born poor ? blind ? a *śūdra* ? lame ? with such and such defect ?, when other persons I know are not poor, blind, *śūdras*, lame, or defective." In other words, if the Lord is impartial and just, why are there such terrible inequalities in the creation ? Doesn't God play favorites ? Therefore isn't He partial, unjust, and therefore imperfect ?

The second part of this argument, the cruelty argument, is familiar to us from fore-going pages. RĀMĀNUJA states it simply, that God would be open to the charge

> ". . . of cruelty, insofar as he would be instrumental in making his creatures experience pain of the most dreadful kind . . ."[502]

The arguments thus presented by the imagined objectors of both ŚAṀKARA and RĀMĀNUJA come down then to the discrimination argument, the cruelty argument and the destruction argument. All three lead to T.P.E. as we have seen, for all three embroil the perfect majesty of the Lord with injustice, cruelty on a micro-scale, and cruelty on a macro-scale, respectively. But all three are apparently neatly handled by ŚAṀKARA and RĀMĀNUJA and with the same counter-argument, i.e., the rebirth solution. ŚAṀKARA says :

> "The Lord should rather be looked upon to be like "rain". Just as rain is the general cause which makes rice and barley grow, while the different

> potentialities inherent in their seeds, are the cause of the disparity between such rice and barley, even so in the creation of Gods and men, etc. the Lord is but the general common cause only [see below], while for the inequality between Gods and men, etc. they have their own different individual actions as the cause . . ."[503]

And RĀMĀNUJA[504] explains further that it is because of *karman* that different potentialities inhere in men, and that whatever happens to men is due to their own previous actions. Quoting "the reverend PARĀŚARA," he says :

> "He (the Lord) is the operative cause only in the creation of new beings; the material cause is constituted by the potentialities of the beings to be created".[505]

RĀMĀNUJA adds, that "potentiality" here means *Karman.* There then follows from both ŚAṀKARA and RĀMĀNUJA references to the scriptures.

The key to the Lord's escaping complicity to cruelty and evil lies in that phrase "operative cause" for RĀMĀNUJA, or "general common cause" for ŚAṀKARA. It can best be understood by returning to ŚAṀKARA's rain and grain analogy. Seen in this light, the Lord emerges as the beneficent and benevolent gentle rain that dropeth from the heavens, watering the just and the unjust alike. In philosophical parlance, God looks like a necessary but not a sufficient condition for growth of evil in the world, hence He seems blameless; for the true motivating or dynamic forces of creation, maintenance and destruction in the universe are the transmigratory souls which are karma-driven, returning lustfully and thirstily to the source of their longings, the trough of the wicked world. Some comments are in order on I.i.34.

1. It is easy to see how the discrimination argument and the cruelty argument can be handled by the rebirth solution. The conditions of birth, and the evils and goods attendant upon it, can all be laid to *karma* and the various cosmic processes operating seemingly independently of the Lord. What ill befalls you, that you deserve. It's true God can't help you—the *karma* must be played out. It's also true that this seems to severely limit God's power: For if there is indeed

a cosmic force, *karma*, and cosmic results of this force, *saṁsāra*, operating independently of the will of God, then God's power would seem to be curtailed. But just as Saint Thomas's God could not raise an unraisable stone, so also it might be countered here, Brahman cannot make the universe unjust. And surely to alter karmic laws for one's own purposes would be unjust. Thus the rebirth solution might account for the arguments of discrimination and cruelty, while producing at the same time some puzzles regarding the conjunction of God's love and mercy (let no man suffer) with God's justice (let no man suffer purposelessly). The rebirth solution however callously employed, can thus be used to explain and justify the most abominable cruelty. But can it justify cosmic cruelty, i.e., can it satisfy the destruction argument ?

2. Why must the entire universe be dissolved. Why must the *Kali-Yuga*, with all its attendant woes and ills be followed by even greater woes and ills issuing in the supreme cataclysmic climax ? Two answers are open to the theological cosmologist turned theodicist :

a. The world is so supremely wicked at this point, so thoroughly filled up with wanton, unregenerate, unrealized souls, that *mokṣa* for any of them is impossible, and the *līlā* must consequently end: It may therefore be good of God to stop all that wickedness.

Thus the Lord is in complete control, He sees the way things are, and by an act both merciful (to end their suffering) and just (they deserved this end) He throws the switch and dissolution occurs. Here again rebirth would or could solve the destruction argument.

b. The Lord has no choice. The cosmic process is automatic such that after the required number of years have passed, the *Kali Yuga* arrives and the process of disintegration and dissolution and destruction must occur whatever God's feelings in the matter.

One is reminded of Plotinus, of course (cf. Chapter I). The process of manifestation is such that the farther away from the One the creation evolves, the more non-Being it has, the more instability it contains, the more evil it manifests, until like a ball on a rubber band, having expanded to its greatest permissible length, it suddenly springs back to its source. This answer throws us once again into the old puzzle about limitations on God's powers mentioned in Part I and also above in 1 here. For it would seem that universal cosmic processes are at work such that God could not suspend them. This may mean a limitation of His powers, or it might again simply be a case of God being unable to do anything contrary to His nature without involving Himself in self contradiction. The cosmologists must, it seems, worry over this problem if the rebirth solution is to answer the problem raised in the destruction argument. If the Lord is responsible for the end and the end contains evil, then it would seem *prima facie* that the Lord is responsible for evil. How responsible ? Indians themselves as we have seen, differ as to whether or not the law of karma and presumably other cosmic laws are God-controlled or not. The *Nyāya-Vaiśeṣika* and AUROBINDO maintain that the law of karma is in varying degrees apparently under the guidance and control of God since *adṛṣṭa* alone is unintelligent and cannot consequently produce the proper effects. But in Jainism, Buddhism, the Sāṅkhya, and the Mīmāṁsā "the law of karma is autonomous and works independently of the will of God."[506] But this produces a curious dilemma (the *saguṇa* paradex, again) for the Indian theodicists : If God is in control of the law of karma then He is involved with the suffering and misery dispensed through or by way of the law: Thence T.P.E. with its attendant puzzles. And if God is not in control of the law of karma and it works independently and antonymously of God, then either God is not all powerful, or we are involved with T.P.E. (since an impersonal force is somehow one of the conditions for suffering and misery), or both. But the theodicist welcomes neither conclusion. We shall return to these points later in this work.

3. This brings us to ŚAṀKARA's analogy: God is like rain, the help rain gives is, in Thomas's language, merely permissive and not causative (in the sense of being responsible). But we've seen what happens to an argument like the permissive argument in St. Thomas : To permit evil when you have the power and nature to stop it is immoral. Some comments :

a. God is not like rain for the analogy can be twisted all to pieces from the simple fact that rain is not all powerful, all knowing and beneficent, nor benevolent—it's just wet.

b. Rain is the occasion for seed growth, but rain doesn't know that this seed contains, let's say, ergot; that more that 1% ergot in seed grain or wheat flour can cause tissue damage and death due to alkaloid poisoning in animals and humans. But these are things that the Lord presumably knows. To know this, to have the power to prevent it, and not to prevent it is surely curious, if not immoral.

c. If God is an "operative" or "general common cause," what does this mean ? To say that God is a necessary condition, like rain or water to seed growth, won't do. For if we make God's will, hence God, a full-fledged necessary condition for evil, then God is morally responsible for evil, just as rain is physically responsible for growth. But while we can't blame rain for the seed's growth even with physiological ergotism as the outcome, we can blame God who unlike the rain could have prevented the evil because of His peculiar moral properties. To make God a causal factor at all, in whatever sense, would lead to His implication with, His responsibility for (in the strictly personal-human sense), and thence His blameworthiness in the resulting situation.

4. But if God is either implicated in the end (hence blameable) or merely a pawn in the hands of uncontrollable cosmic processes (not all-powerful), it would seem He is also involved in both these ways in the beginning of the creation or the origin of the universe. Thus, suppose that we grant that the rebirth solution takes care of the three arguments advanced above so that my life today with its constituent suffering is the result of my previous life. There is a kind of sense to this, and despite the puzzles even a sort of justice to it such that one must come to admire the ingenuity and boldness of the rebirth solution face to face with T.P.E. But what about the origin of evil, i.e., in particular, what about a pure unsullied soul at the beginning, in the golden age, at the start of it all ? What then brought about evil ? I couldn't be responsible for that, because I wasn't there before event number one, to make my fall the product of *karma* and rebirth. Thus RADHAKRISHNAN puts the objection :

> "Many passages in the *Upaniṣads* tell us that "In the beginning there was Being only, one without a second." There was no *Karma* which had to be taken into account before creation. The first creation at least should have been free from inequalities."[507]

So where did they come from ? God ? But this objection, a familiar one surely after our bout with the same puzzle in Part I, is parried by the *Vedāntists* in the *sūtra* that follows:

> "If it is objected, that in the beginning there could have been no differences, and the Lord must then be responsible for the differences (good and evil) that came, then we counter, there is no beginning". (II.1.35).

RADHAKRISHNAN, speaking to this conclusion, says :

> "The world is without beginning. Work and inequality are like seed and sprout. They are caused as well as causes".[508]

And ŚAMKARA agrees that the objection stated in 4 above would indeed stand as valid, if it were not for the beginninglessness of the world. Using the seed and sprout example mentioned previously, he concludes that action and creation are like the seed with its sprout that gives rise to seed again, and so on :

> "But transmigratory existence being beginningless, there need not be any objection for action and the variety of creation, to act, alternately as cause and effect of each other, like the seed and the sprout . . ."[509]

But now a fundamental difference between ŚAṀKARA and RĀMĀNUJA emerges. RĀMĀNUJA quoting the *śruti* argues that the flow of creation goes on through all eternity and that the souls have always existed though subsequently their names and form were developed :

> "The fact of the souls being without a beginning is observed, viz., to be stated in Scripture . . ."[510]

He then quotes Scripture, and selects one in particular that makes his point about the eternal and pluralistic nature of souls:

> "Moreover, the text, "Now all this was then undeveloped. It became developed by form and name." (*Bṛ Up.* 1.4,7) states merely that the names and forms of the souls were developed, and this shows that the souls themselves existed from the beginning".[511]

Of course, none of this could be said by ŚAṀKARA, who we shall see has problems precisely because he cannot speak of eternal and plural souls. RĀMĀNUJA concludes :

> "As Brahman thus differs in nature from everything else, possesses all powers, has no other motive than sport, and arranges the diversity of the creation in accordance with the different Karman of the individual souls, Brahman alone can be the universal cause".[512]

In summary RĀMĀNUJA can hold that God and individual souls are distinct and have existed from eternity. ŚAṀKARA as we have said with his strict *advaita* position cannot maintain such an apparent pluralism, however hedged about and qualified RĀMĀNUJA might subsequently decide to make it. But this internal disagreement does not alter the fact that the beginninglessness of the world argument seems to take care of the objections to the rebirth solution mentioned above in 4. The whole matter is developed further in the last *sūtra* we shall discuss.

> "The beginninglessness of *saṁsāra* is proved by reason, and found in Scripture."(II.1.36)

RĀMĀNUJA advances no arguments here, and very briefly summarizes what he has more or less said already. ŚAṀKARA devotes nearly six times the space that RĀMĀNUJA does to expanding on a point he had raised in II.1.35. In that earlier *sūtra bhāṣya*, ŚAṀKARA had said that we would be involved in a circularity if we assumed that there was a beginning with no prior human actions, and that the Lord was guided in his dispensings of good and evil to living beings by their prior actions (the argument he attacks is self contradictory to boot), for then work depends on diversity in life conditions, and the latter in turn would depend on work. In the *bhāṣya* on *sūtra* 36, ŚAṀKARA delivers what I take to be five separate arguments to establish the beginninglessness of *saṁsāra*, or at least five arguments can be wrung without violence from the following statement. I mark the arguments with Arabic numerals:

That transmigratory existence is beginningless is reasonably sustainable. i. If it were to have a beginning, then it having come into existence capriciously without any cause,

ii. the predicament of persons who have attained *Final Release* being again involved in transmigratory existence, would take place,

iii. as also the predicament of "fruit" arising without any action having taken place, because (under such supposition) there would be no cause for the disparity between pleasure and misery (to come into existence).

iv. .... Without action, a physical body would not result, nor would action result in the absence of a physical body, and hence it would all result in the fault of mutual interdependence. If on the other hand, transmigratory existence is understood to be beginningless then it would all be reasonably sustainable.

v. That, transmigratory existence is beginningless, is understood both from the scriptures and *Smṛtis*.[513]

Let me take these arguments in order and look closely at them. The general form of all of them is essentially *reductio*: Thus, accepting a beginning of the world, you have to accept: i. capricious or chance creation, ii. released persons become unreleased, iii. effects arising without any causes, iv. physical-body-effects arising without action-causes in particular, and action-effects arising in the absence of physical-body-causes in particular, and finally, v. the wrongness of *śruti* and *smṛti*. But all of i. to v. are, ŚAṀKARA says, patently absurd, so our assumption must be wrong; hence *saṁsāra* has no beginning. But does all this really follow? Suppose a beginning:

i. Why must we admit to "capriciousness" (Apte, the translator of this passage, introduces the word; I don't find it in ŚAṀKARA's text), and why must it be causeless? If it happens by chance then chance causes it. What is wrong with chance causes? But why resort to such subterfuge? God could perfectly well cause the world. By an act of His super will He could bring it into being *ex nihilo*, or out of His own superabundant Self. It's true this gets us into T.P.E., but it certainly does not lead to the absurdity ŚAṀKARA claims it must lead to if we accept the beginning-hypothesis. Our possibilities are not limited, to think so is to commit the myopic fallacy. There is a cause according to our counter argument, chance or God, hence ŚAṀKARA's narrowed possibility doesn't apply.

ii. There is nothing to guarantee that liberated souls must perforce return to *saṁsāra.* It is true that nothing guarantees that they won't on the information we have been given here to work on. But if we do have a cause, God, then He could guarantee that liberated souls don't return. To assume they must or will is a species again of the myopic fallacy. To believe they might could be equally well entertained under either a beginning-hypothesis or a beginningless-hypothesis. If chance rules the universe they might return, but with chance ruling could one even speak of liberated souls? i.e., there might be none at all. If God rules, they need not return, unless God Himself is capricious and in that case we are back to chance once again.

iii. The third argument, of course, is predicated on the assumption that the first beginning moment of *saṁsāra* must be an effect of some action. But we have seen that it could be the effect of God's action. To assume as ŚAṀKARA does that first human moments *must* be the effect of previous human moments is absurd and without support. When the first gibbering primate came out of the trees and silently walked erect, he was then surely the *first* silent and erect non-arborial primate: the first human being. ŚAṀKARA's whole hangup here, of course, is that he holds strenuously to a *satkāryavāda* theory of causation and a *pariṇāma* theory of cosmogony. These assumptions are attackable and presenting a counter model, e.g., with the gibbering primate above, would be one such approach. This counterargument to ŚAṀKARA will be expanded on in iv.

iv. Granted that physical bodies and action are dependent in one direction, i.e., action causes physical bodies, there is nothing to guarantee mutual interdependence. To assume it, as ŚAṀKARA does, is to beg the whole question loudly and mightily. For we can argue that physical bodies don't cause action, e.g., the first action at least, for that first action could be caused by God in an act of creation *ex nihilo* let's say, and surely God is not a physical body. Thus there is no reason to fall into the net that ŚAṀKARA has spread before us; we simply question his presuppositions. With respect to iii. and iv., I think it is obvious that they both rest on the same causal assumptions such that if either iii. or iv, can be successfully attacked, and I'm not saying we have done that, then iv. and iii., respectively, must needs fall as well.

v. Scripture and *Smṛti* are notorious in being many things to many people. It is curious that although ŚAṀKARA and RĀMĀNUJA both do quote scriptural sources to display their proof for 36, neither quotes the same passages. RĀMĀNUJA quotes selections to back up his *Viśiṣṭādvaita*, while ŚAMKARA, of course, carefully steers away from such verses. Thus quoting scripture in the end can prove nothing when passages can be selected to support such diverse views on the soul as those of ŚAMKARA and RĀMĀNUJA.[514]

This ends our discussion of the *sūtras*.

Conclusion

Whatever their basic difference may be both ŚAMKARA and RĀMĀNUJA are agreed on the basic issues regarding T.P.E. These are essentially three:

1. They both agree that *līlā* absolves God from blame for the evils and sufferings in creation. Who after all can blame a child for acts done in joy and playful exhuberance? But the problems resulting from our analysis of play, its putative purposelessness, and its *prima facie* innocence, were too enormous to permit the *līlā* solution as a solution to T.P.E.

2. The rebirth solution can account for all the evil, human, superhuman, and subhuman, around us today (cf. the cruelty argument and the discrimination argument). Final cosmic dissolutions can be accounted for (the destruction argument) by a form of the rebirth solution that stresses the downright unregenerate state of the creation immediately preceding and even during that dissolution. Thus the rebirth solution manages to meet these three arguments that promised peril for the Lord and that would make T.P.E. a genuine puzzle.

But the price may be high. We are involved once again with problems about the goodness and powerfulness of God who saw what was coming (if He could) but permitted it anyway. If this is justice, perhaps we have need of less of it. Thus while the problem of extraordinary or gratuitous evil can be explained by a reference to previous karma, this cannot, the plain man might feel, justify that evil (cf. our discussion of children suffering) in Part I. The *Vedāntist* may counter with, There really is no extraordinary (unearned or chance evil) but all is deserved and all is paid back by the law of karma. Most persons might object, and on two grounds:

a. The doctrine is seemingly callous for it attempts to not only *explain* evil by the rebirth solution, but also to *justify* it at the same time by calling it "right". One is reminded of early Puritan attitudes to poverty and the poor—the poor you have always with you and their suffering is the will of God. Whether the will of God or the will of karma, the position might seem to the plain man somewhat callous. Another objection follows hard upon this one:

b. The doctrine may lead to quietism and a certain passiveness of spirit that many would find personally and socially immoral. Thus if people suffer because of their previous bad deeds, then if the law of karma is seen as the universal arbiter, and is just and right, any attempt to assuage the sufferings of others will be seen as an abridgment of their needs, their right to suffering and cleansing. Hence the right thing to do would be to wink at the human plight, and go about my own merry old selfish moral business. The position might seem to the plain man as leading to such a quietistic conclusion. Further, not only are there problems with man and the world resulting from accepting the rebirth solution but we have seen that there are theological problems quite outside the rebirth solution that seemingly implicate the divine in the touchy position of having perfections while permitting evil He could prevent, or preventing an evil creation from having so darned much extraordinary evil. Once again, we can ask, as we did in Part I previously, Granted that evils must needs come, why is there so much? Why is it so hideous ? Why is it so seemingly senseless? Again, of course, the *Vedāntist* has a ready reply to all such challenges.

3. They both agree, furthermore, that God cannot be responsible for the beginning of creation for the simple reason that *saṁsāra* has no beginning. This raises at least one simple

prima facie puzzle now, not with rebirth and karma that He cannot control as in 2 above, but with a beginningless creation He could not start. The whole notion of beginninglessness needs analysis here, and I want to mention two minor problems connected with it:

a. The *Vedāntists* speak about a final destruction, or if not *final* ultimate dissolution, then a series of penultimate ones. How, it might be asked, can you have a dissolution and then a creation without involving yourself in a beginning? If the *Kali Yuga* will end in violence and suffering because all deserve it, then isn't the golden age which preceded it a time of "beginning" in some sense of that word? And if a beginning in some sense of that word, then how about God and evil in some sense of those words? And if a beginning and God and evil in some sense of those words, then how about a T.P.E. in some sense of that word (Recall our discussion between JOHN STUART MILL, Sir William HAMILTON and HENRY MANSEL in Part I).

b. If the *Vedas* mention, as they do in their various cosmogonic moods (e. g. RV. X. 190; 129), origins of the Universe, then are these rather straightforward metaphysical myths to be subjected to procrustean therapy just to save a nasty puzzle? Thus if the mythology of creation does indeed say that there was a beginning, in some sense of that word, in non-Being, or *Puruṣa*, or in an act of Indra or Brahmā, and if you are inclined to take your *śruti* seriously, then isn't the better part of philosophic valor to admit to beginnings and face the philosophic music, rather than to hedge about on what on earth "beginning" might mean such that stretching it a bit, one can come to face oddities like T.P.E.? Again, the plain man might be affronted by this Vedāntic ploy in what must otherwise be seen as a series of brilliant theodical moves to solve T.P.E. in *B.S.* II. 1. 32-36.

In conclusion, I don't believe any of these problems resulting from the premise set of T.P.E. or from the implications of the rebirth solution are insuperable. We have seen replies to the objections resulting from the problems raised with the theological paradoxes of perfection in Part I, and we have seen that the Indians can mount similar replies with respect to the problems arising with respect to karma and *saṁsāra*. Thus we must conclude that if there is a theological problem of evil, one perfectly respectable response to it, despite a few minor philosophical puzzles for the plain man, would be that provided by *Vedāntists* like Śaṁkara and Rāmānuja.

CHAPTER X

Conclusion to Part III

In as succinct a manner as possible, I want to conclude this study of the relation between the theological problem of evil and the doctrine of rebirth. In what follows I want to do three things:

I. Consider the question with which we have all along been concerned, viz., can the rebirth solution solve the problem of evil?

2. Consider some of the difficulties to be faced, not by the rebirth solution, but rather by the problem of evil itself, as formulated by the theological theses and the evil thesis.

3. Consider some additional benefits that result as a consequence of adopting the rebirth solution, benefits which relate directly to as well as beyond the theological problem of evil.

1. Can the doctrine of rebirth solve the problem of evil ?

The answer to this question depends on making clear what "rebirth" means and which problem of evil is meant. Taking "rebirth" to mean "transmigration," where the soul that moves from place to place, or body to body, is a soul capable of personal identity, and taking the theological problem of evil as the problem of evil to be focused upon, then I think it can be said that the doctrine of rebirth solves the problem of evil:

a. Unlike the Western theories taken up in Part I, theories which attempted to solve the theological problem of evil, we have seen that the doctrine of rebirth is capable of meeting the major objection against which those Western attempts all failed: the problem of dysteleological, extraordinary, or hard evil. Thus no matter how terrible and awe-inspiring the suffering may be, the rebirth theorist can simply attribute the suffering to previous misdeeds done in previous lives, and the puzzle over extraordinary evil is solved with no harm done to the majesty and holiness of Deity.

b. Unlike the Western theories, the doctrine of rebirth can justify superhuman, subhuman, as well as human evil, since, for the Indians at least, their soul theory can be extended to all three realms. Thus, e.g., AUGUSTINE, LEIBNIZ, JOHN HICK, and others, were unable to give a satisfactory account of suffering on the animal level. Their theories were, we argued, incomplete for this reason, and since completeness was one of the criteria for the adequacy of a solution, along with consistency and common sense, we were forced to reject their theodicies outright. The rebirth solution, on the other hand, neatly handles the problem of animal suffering, and the same could be said, *pari passu*, for superhuman suffering. Hence the rebirth solution is complete with respect to all three realms of beings.

c. Further, the rebirth solution is able to satisfy all three of the criteria for adequacy mentioned above. Thus the formal criterion of consistency is met, for there is no logical contradiction in the rebirth solution; the practical criterion of completeness is met, for as we've seen above, the rebirth solution is able to justify suffering in the triple world of the Gods or angels, human beings, and the beasts; finally, the subjective criterion of common sense is met, for relative to the conceptual scheme we have investigated in India, the rebirth solution follows from a perfectly orthodox doctrine, *saṁsāra*, together with a doctrine about the beginninglessness of the soul. Thus, satisfying these three criteria for adequacy, the rebirth solution can be seen as an adequate solution of the theological problem of evil for all three types of evil. Since the rebirth solution is adequate for the solving of the theological problem of evil, this undoubtedly explains why the problem was never of much concern to the classical Indians, and why also theodicy, as a philosophical way of life, was practically unknown to them.

2. Some problems for the theological problem as a set of premises.

Whatever problems arise with respect to the problem of evil, arise primarily within the premises necessary to generate the theological problem of evil. Certain paradoxes develop, the paradoxes of perfection and the *saguṇa* paradox, which, we argued, while not involving logical inconsistencies, entail nonetheless a practical inconsistency that makes the premise set, the theological theses together with the evil thesis, a strange set indeed. Most theologians, as we have seen, are not bothered by these inconsistencies; they have selected to run with the problem of evil as generated, and hunt for a solution to it amidst the theologies, myths, and philosophies of the world. Thus we must add to what we have said at the beginning of this summary above in 1, that *if* there is a theological problem of evil, and we have strenuously defended the notion that there is, then the doctrine of rebirth will adequately solve it.

3. Some additional advantages to accepting the rebirth solution to the theological problem of evil.

There are some advantages to accepting the rebirth solution to the theological problem of evil, over and above the fact that it may explain and justify such things as extraordinary evil on the divine, human, and subhuman planes. I list six possible theoretical benefits :

a. As a consequence of adopting the rebirth solution, a number of other solutions proposed by Western theists and rejected by us in Part I as inadequate, now become acceptable as solutions to the theological problem of evil. I refer primarily to the aesthetic solution, the discipline solution, and the man is free solution in their reduced form, together with their eight or ten unreduced forms, from Part I. With rebirth as an assumption, these rejected solutions now become quite acceptable. The principle reason for this change is obvious, for under the rebirth solution, hard or extraordinary evil is no longer a threat to our solutions. And since the problem of extraordinary evil was the chief cause for rejecting the above solutions, these solutions now become acceptable. Evil emerges as purposive, designed by me, caused by me, and ultimately leading all out of *saṁsāra*.

b. Under the rebirth solution there are no one-chance-only shots at salvation for the theist. The anxiety caused by the feeling that I must make it (Heaven, *mokṣa*, Freedom) now or never in this life, laudable in itself perhaps in a time given over to maximum efforts of all sorts, is erased once and for all.

c. The threat of eternal damnation is removed as well. For some theists, even in this secular age of ultimate concern for militarism and MIRVS, it may come as a welcome relief to discover that damnation is simply a temporary state.

d. Under the rebirth solution and the principle of karma, there is no (moral) pure chance that can befall man in the sense that some evil acts will go unpunished or some good acts unrewarded. All are gathered under one universal, all-embracing "law" such that whatever I do has just repercussions, and is or will be significant and important not only to me but to the creation as a whole. My significance as a man is considerably broadened, through the continuity of my lives from the past into the future, and my importance as a real person, as compared to the person in the one-life theories, is given "a new depth and meaning" (as they say).

e. Next we return to the question taken up in our opening investigation of the *Upaniṣads* in Part II, Chapter V, viz., why is that yonder world (Heaven) not filled up ? This seems a fitting question to take up in our study of the relation of the rebirth solution to the theological problem of evil, for it is the query that prompted the Indians initially in two of their greatest and oldest *Upaniṣads* to search out the nature and implications of *saṁsāra*. The *answer* to the question, fraught with puzzles in itself, to be sure, probably consoles no one any more. But just maybe, in these latter days when man is busy breeding himself into near extinction, the question might be asked again. Thus, face to face with a terrestrial overcrowding, the worried theist might turn his thoughts to the problem of a heavenly overcrowding. If he does, then haply the true-believer in rebirth has an answer that may, just may, set the worried theist's heart at rest : There is no filling up in that yonder world, for all are reborn again into this world. But this answer, while perhaps consoling the nervous theist, should give no surcease to the elbowed and harried demographer.

f. Finally and more significantly, for these days of ecological nervousness, it may be welcome news indeed to discover the continuity present throughout all of the creation.

The environment seen through the eyes of the rebirth believer is far different than the environment seen through the eyes of the alienated, separated, isolated, non-believer. Nature is no longer a wild beast to be conquered, exploited, dominated and subdued, but a part, in principle, of one's self, to be known, understood, and embraced.

NOTES

[1] Aiken, Henry David, "God and Evil: A Study of Some Relations Between Faith and Morals," *Ethics*, LXVIII, 2, Jan. 1958, 79.

[2] Hume David, *Dialogues Concerning Natural Religion*, 201.

[3] Lactantius, *On the Anger of God*, Ch. 13, Tr. by William Fletcher in *The Writings of the Ante-Nicene Fathers*, VII, 1951, quoted in John Hick, *Evil and the God of Love*, p. 5, fn. 1. I have relied on Hick's excellent book extensively in this section.

[4] Greene, William Chase, *Moira, Fate, Good and Evil in Greek Thought*, 298.

[5] Republic 379 c, Paul Shorey, Translator in *The Collected Dialogues of Plato*, Ed. Edith Hamilton and Huntington Cairns, 626. *Cf.* 364 b, c; 380 b, ff., 391 d, e.

[6] Augustine, Saint Aurelius, *Divine Providence and the Problem of Evil*, Tr. Robert P. Russell in *The Fathers of the Church*, V.

[7] Augustine, *The Free Choice of the Will*, Tr. Robert P. Russell in *The Fathers of the Church*, Vol. LIX.

[8] Augustine, *Confessions*, Tr. Vernon J. Bourke in *The Fathers of the Church*, Vol. XXI.

[9] Augustine, *The City of God*, Tr. Gerald G. Walsh and Grace Monahan in *The Fathers of the Church*, Vol. XIV.

[10] Augustine, *Faith, Hope and Charity*, Bernard M. Peebles in *The Fathers of the Church*, Vol. iv.

[11] *Op. Cit.*, 239-240.

[12] *Ibid.*, 287.

[13] *Ibid.*

[14] *Ibid.*, 287-288.

[15] *Ibid.*, 288.

[16] *Op. Cit.*, 72.

[17] Cf. *Contra Adimantum Manich* 26, quoted in *Confessions*, Op. Cit., 165.

[18] *Ibid.*, 170.

[19] *Ibid.*, 173.

[20] *Ibid.*

[21] *Ibid.*

[22] *Ibid.*, 175.

[23] Dostoievsky, Fyodor, *The Brothers Karamazov*, Tr. Constance Garnett, 546-48. Cf. also Book V, Ch. 3-5, *passim.*

[24] Kazantzakis, Nikos, *Zorba the Greek*, Tr. Carl Wildman , 247.

[25] *Op. Cit.*, p. 226.

[26] *Ibid.*

[27] *Ibid.*, 227.

[28] *Ibid.*, 228.
[29] *Ibid.*, 227, italics mine
[30] *Ibid.*, 222-23.
[31] *Op. Cit.*, 166.
[32] *Op. Cit.*, 393.
[33] *Ibid.*, 448-49.
[34] *Op. Cit.*, 168.
[35] *Ibid.*, 184.
[36] *Ibid.*, 183.
[37] *Ibid.*
[38] *Ibid.*, 169.
[39] *Ibid.*, 61.
[40] *Op. Cit.*, 376.
[41] *Confessions, Op. Cit.*, 121.
[42] *Ibid.*, 44.
[43] *Ibid.*, 165.
[44] *Op. Cit.*, 213-214.
[45] *Ibid.*, 222.
[46] *Ibia.*, 408.
[47] *Op. Cit.*, 392.
[48] *City of God*, 410.
[49] *Ibid.*, 408.
[50] *Op. Cit.*, 376.
[51] *Ibid.*, 254.
[52] *Ibid.*, 376.
[52]a *Ibid.*, 379.
[53] *Ibid.*, 378.
[54] *Ibid.*, *Isaiah* 5.20.
[55] *Ibid.*, 393.
[56] *Ibid.*, 380.
[57] *Ibid.*, 391.
[58] *Ibid.*, 453.
[59] *Ibid.*, 377.
[60] Plotinus, *The Enneads*, Tr. by Stephen MACKENNA, 67.
[61] *Ibid.*
[62] *Ibid.*, 69.
[63] *Ibid.*, 72.
[64] *Ibid.*, 70.
[65] *Ibid.*, 72.
[66] *Ibid.*
[67] *Dionysius the Areopagite on the Divine Names and the Mystical Theology*, Tr. C. E. Rolt.
[68] *Ibid.*, 110-11.
[69] *Ibid.*, 113.
[70] *Ibid.*
[71] *Ibid.*, 117.
[72] *Ibid.*, 118-19.

[73] *Ibid.*, 118-25.

[74] *Ibid.*, 126.

[75] *Ibid.*, 127.

[76] *Ibid.*

[77] *Ibid.*

[78] *Ibid.*, 128.

[79] *Ibid.*

[80] *Ibid.*

[81] *Ibid.*, 129.

[82] *Ibid.*, 128.

[83] *Summa Theologica*, Pt. I, Q. 47, Art. 2, *Basic Writings of Saint Thomas Aquinas*, Anton C. PEGIS, Ed., I, 461.

[84] *Ibid.*

[85] *Ibid.*, Q. 48, Art. 1., p. 465.

[86] *Ibid.*, Q. 48, Art. 2, p. 467.

[87] *Ibid.*

[88] Cf. also *Summa Theologica*, Part I, Q. 19, Art. 9 for more on the privation theme, and also Q. 14, Art. 10.

[89] *Ibid.*, 467.

[90] *Ibid.*,

[91] Cf. Stephen TOULMIN, *An Examination of the Place of Reason in Ethics*: Limiting questions are ultimate questions such as "Why ought one to do what is right?", "What holds the world up?" ... they are of particular interest when one is examining the limits and boundaries of any mode of reasoning... "(p. 205) I am suggesting that the following are limiting questions as well: "Why is there evil at all?" "Why was anything created?"

[92] *Ibid.*

[93] *Op. Cit.*, 96.

[94] *Ibid.*, 151.

[95] G. W. LEIBNIZ, *Theodicy*, 61.

[96] *Ibid.*

[97] *Ibid.*, p. 67.

[98] *Ibid.*, p. 128.

[99] *Ibid.*

[100] *Op. Cit.*, Q. 25, Art. 6, p. 269.

[101] *Ibid.*

[102] *Op. Cit.*, 136.

[103] *Ibid.*, 138.

[104] *Ibid.*, 130.

[105] *Ibid.*

[106] *Ibid.*, 135.

[107] *Ibid.*, 144.

[108] *Ibid.*, 147.

[109] *Ibid.*, 154.

[110] *Ibid.*, 137.

[111] *Ibid.*, 132.

112 *Ibid.*, 276.
113 *Ibid.*, 196.
114 *Op. Cit.*, 160.
115 *Op. Cit.*, 281.
116 *Ibid.*, 287.
117 J. W. N. SULLIVAN, *Beethoven, His Spiritual Development*, 43.
118 *Op. Cit.*, 216.
119 *Ibid.*, 378.
120 *Ibid.*, 169.
121 *Ibid.*, 281.
122 MILL, *Three Essays on Religion*, 40, fn. *
123 *Ibid.*, 25.
124 *Ibid.*, p. 28-29.
125 *Ibid.*, 33, 34.
126 *Ibid.*, 31.
127 *Ibid.*, 37.
128 *Ibid.*, 38.
129 *Ibid.*
130 *Ibid.*, p. 39-40.
131 *Ibid.*, 177-78.
132 *Ibid.*, 41, 65.
133 *Ibid.*, 178.
134 *Ibid.*, 181.
135 *Ibid.*, 194.
136 *Ibid.*, 256.
137 ROYACE, Josiah, *The World and the Individual*, I, 380.
138 *Ibid.*, 381.
139 *Ibid.*, 378.
140 *Ibid.*, 396.
141 *Ibid.*, 396-97.
142 *Ibid.*, 397.
143 *Ibid.*, 399.
144 *Ibid.*, 400-1.
145 *Ibid.*, 404.
146 *Ibid.*, 387.
147 *Ibid.*, 405.
148 *Ibid.*, 411.
149 *Ibid.*, 379.
150 *Ibid.*, 386.
151 *Ibid.*, 409.
152 *Ibid.*, 410.
153 *Ibid.*, 381.
154 *Ibid.*
155 *Ibid.*, 388.
156 *Ibid.*, 410-11.
157 *Op. Cit.*, 186.
158 *Ibid.*, 4.

[159] *Ibid.*, 300.

[160] *Ibid.*, 301.

[161] *Ibid.*, 371.

[162] *Ibid.*, 18.

[163] *Ibid.*, 19.

[164] *Ibid.*, 197.

[165] *Ibid.*, 202.

[166] *Ibid.*, 220.

[167] *Ibid.*, 223.

[168] *Ibid.*, 237.

[169] *Ibid.*, 254.

[170] *Ibid.*, 375.

[171] *Ibid.*, 295.

[172] *Ibid.*, 297.

[173] *Ibid.*, 293-94.

[174] *Ibid.*, 294.

[175] *Ibid.*, 297.

[176] *Ibid.*, 363-64.

[177] *Ibid.*, 370-71.

[178] *Ibid.*, 371.

[179] *Ibid.*

[180] *Ibid.*, 377f., 382f.

[181] *Ibid.*, 377

[182] *Ibid.*, 397.

[183] *Ibid.*, 46.

[184] *Ibid.*, 377f., 382f.

[185] *Ibid.*, 398.

[186] *Ibid.*, 371.

[187] TOULMIN, *Op. Cit.*, 202.

[188] *Op. Cit.*, 345-346. Cf. also C. C. J. WEBB, *Problems in the Relations of God and Man*, 268; J. S. MILL, *Three Essays on Religion*, "Nature", 58; One author even says animals don't suffer: Dom Illtyd TRETHOWAN, *An Essay in Christian Philosophy*, 41, 92.

[189] *Ibid.*, 349-50.

[190] *Ibid.*, 352.

[191] Conditions for adequacy will be carefully laid down in that chapter.

[192] *Op. Cit.*, 83-84.

[193] For the problem of divine analogy cf. George BERKELEY, *Alciphron* IV, 16-22; Peter BROWNE, *Divine Analogy*, Ch. 8; and a recent discussion on both/by Jean-Paul PITTION and David BERMAN, "A New Letter by BERKELEY to BROWNE on Divine Analogy," *Mind*, Vol. LXVII, No. 311, July 1969. BROWNE takes the position later defended by Sir William HAMILTON and Henry MANSEL, and BERKELEY takes the position John Stuart MILL was later to defend against HAMILTON and MANSEL.

[194] *Confessions*, *Op. Cit.*, 167.

[195] Augustine, "Enchiridion."

[196] *Summa Theologica*, Pt. I, Q. XXV, Art. 3.

[197] John Hick, *Op. Cit.*, 172.

[198] J. L. MACKIE, "Evil and Omnipotence," *Mind*, Vol. LXIV, No. 254, April, 1955, 210.

[199] E.g., Monroe C. BEARDSLEY and Elizabeth Lane BEARDSLEY, *Philosophical Thinking. An Introduction*, 106-107; John HICK, *Philosophy of Religion*, 40; HICK, *Evil and the God of Love, Op. Cit.*, 4; Max WEBER, "Religious Rejections of the World and their Directions," *From Max Weber: Essays in Sociology*, 275; Edward H. MADDEN and Peter H. HARE, *Evil and the Concept of God*, 3; J. L. MACKIE, "Evil and Omnipotence," *Op. Cit.*; H. J. PATON, *The Modern Predicament, A Study in the Philosophy of Religion* 357; John HOSPERS, *An Introduction to Philosophical Analysis*, 461-462; This version of the argument is found as we saw in ch. I. from Epicurus to MILL.

Those philosophers who hold out for the necessity of three theological theses, the ethical thesis, the omnipotence thesis, and the omniscience thesis, are e.g., James W. CORDMAN and Keith LEHRER, *Philosophical Problems and Arguments: An Introduction*, 340; G. E. LEIBNIZ, *Theodicy, Op. Cit.*, 377; Henry David AIKEN, "God and Evil: A Study of Some Relations Between Faith and Morals" in *Ethics* LXVIII, 2, Jan. 1958, 79-82; Terence PENELHUM, "Divine Goodness and the Problem of Evil", *Religious Studies*, II, 2, Oct. 1966, 95-107; Augustine in *Divine Providence* as we have already seen.

[200] BRADLEY, A. C ., *Shakespearean Tragedy*, 23.

[201] *Ibid.*, 35.

[202] *Ibid.*, 39.

[203] BRIGHTMAN, Edgar Sheffield, *A Philosophy of Religion*, 316, where BRIGHTMAN attacks a solution put forward by evolutionists like WHITEHEAD that good comes ultimately out of evil.

[204] *Op. Cit.*, 4.

[205] *Ibid*, 5.

[206] LOVEJOY, *Arthur O. The Thirteen Pragmatisms and Other Essays*, 102.

[207] ELIOT, Sir Charles, *Hinduism and Buddhism, A Historical Sketch*, Vol. I, p. LXXIX.

[208] *Op. Cit.*, 16, cf. 17, 20: "...the difficulty with evil (is) a good reason for rejecting religion..."

[209] *Evil and the God of Love, Op. Cit.*, p. IX.

[210] *Op. Cit.*, 91.

[211] *Op. Cit.*, 136.

[212] *Ibid.*, 138.

[213] *Op. Cit.*, 6.

[214] Monroe C. BEARDSLEY and Elizabeth Lane BEARDSLEY *Op. Cit.*, 111.

[215] See the BEARDSLEY's , *Op. Cit.*, 111f.

[216] *Op. Cit.*, 341.

[217] *Op. Cit.*, 467.

[217a] *Op. Cit.*, 43.

[218] J. L. MACKIE argues that God's traditional properties, though

he chooses only two, omnipotence and goodness, are logically incompatible with the world's evil. With P. E., MACKIE believes,

> "...it can be shown, not that religious beliefs lack rational support, but that they are positively irrational, that the several parts of the essential theological doctrine are inconsistent with one another...' (*Op. Cit.*, 200).

and that,

> "The problem of evil...is a problem only for someone who believes that there is a God who is both omnipotent and wholly good. And it is a logical problem...God is omnipotent; God is wholly good; and yet evil exists. There seems to be some contradiction between these three propositions, so that if any two of them were true the third would be false." (*Ibid.*)

Cf. Terence PENELHUM "Divine Goodness and the Problem of Evil," *Op. Cit.*, 95-96 and Nelson PIKE "Hume on Evil" *Philosophical Review*, LXXII 2, 1963, 180-97 for a discussion denying that P. E. need be treated in the logical or *a priori* manner in which MACKIE treats it.

219 Cf. MILL in Ch. I, above.

220 William T. BLACKSTON, *The Problem of Religious Knowledge*, 161.

221 Nels F. FERRE, *Evil and the Christian Faith*, 85-86.

222 WITTGENSTEIN, Ludwig, *Philosophical Investigations*, 47.

223 *Ibid.*, 49.

224 BODE, Boyd H. "Russel's Educational Philosophy," *The Philosophy of Bertrand Russell*, 627.

225 *Op. Cit.*, 30.

226 MACKIE had four: 1. "Good cannot exist without evil" (*Op. Cit.* 203). 2. "Evil is necessary as a means of good" (*Ibid.* 205). 3. "The universe is better with some evil in it than it could be if there were no evil" (*Ibid.*, 206) and 4. "Evil is due to human free will' (*Ibid.*). These four headings are not unlike our necessary, discipline, aesthetic, and man is free solutions, respectively.

227 *Philosophical Book*, III: 17, 1966.

228 *Op. Cit.*, 388.

229 *Op. Cit.*, 386.

230 G. E. MOORE, *Principia Ethica*, 216 .

231 *Op. Cit.*, 379.

232 *Op. Cit.*, 43.

233 *Ibid.*, 155.

234 *Op. Cit.*, 197.

235 WHALE, J. S. *The Christian Answer to the Problem of Evil*, 43.

236 FERRE, Nels F. S. *A Philosophical Scrutiny of Religion*, 267.

237 LEWIS, C. S. *The Problem of Pain*, 117-31.

238 FARRER, Austin, *Love Almighty and Ills Unlimited*, 71-94.

239 BERTOCCI, Peter. *Introduction to the Philosophy of Religion*, 397.

240 *Op. Cit.*, 390.

241 PATON, H. J. *The Modern Predicament, A Study in the Philosophy of Religion*, 358.

242 PLANTINGA, "The Free Will Defense," *Philosophy in America*

204-20, *passim.*

[243] MARITAIN, Jacques. *God and the Permission of Evil*, 37.

[244] *Op. Cit.*, 194.

[245] D'HOLBACH *Good Sense or Natural Ideas Opposed to Supernatural*, 44-45.

[246] SPINOZA, *Short Treatise on God, Man and His Well-Being*, H. WOLF, Pt. ii, Ch. IV, p. 75.

[247] RUSSELL Bertrand, *Mysticism and Logic and Other Essays* (London: George-Allen and Unwin, Ltd., 1917), p. 10.

[248] McCLOSKEY H. J., "God and Evil," *The Philosophical Quarterly*, April 1960, 100.

[249] *Op. Cit.*, 187.

[250] *Op. Cit.*, 94.

[251] *Op. Cit.*, 72.

[252] McTAGGART J. M. E., *Some Dogmas of Religion*, 171.

[253] *Op. Cit.*, 65.

[254] *Ibid.*, 177.

[255] *Op. Cit.*, 203.

[256] *Op. Cit.*, 377.

[257] *Op. Cit.*, 171.

[258] *Enchiridion, Op. Cit.*, IV, 13-14.

[259] *Op. Cit.*, 254.

[260] JAMES, William, *The Will to Believe and Other Essays in Popular Philosophy*, 189.

[261] *Ibid.*, 190.

[262] STACE Walter, "The Problem of Evil," in *Philosophy, Religion, and the Coming World Civilization*, 130.

[263] FARRELL P. M., "Evil and Omnipotence," *Mind*, LXVII, 267, July, 1958, 401.

[264] Cf. Mackie, "Evil and Omnipotence," *Op. Cit.*; and Antony FLEW in the same journal (Jan., 1962) and MACKIE (April, 1962). MACKIE and FLEW have both argued, in part, that God could have created man such that man would always have acted rightly.

[265] *Philosophy of Religion, Op. Cit.*, 41

[266] *Ibid.*

[267] *Op. Cit.*, 305.

[268] HICK, John, *Evil and the God of Love, Op. Cit.*, 311.

[269] *Op. Cit.*, 257.

[270] MILL, *An Examination of Sir William Hamilton's Philosophy*, 126.

[271] *Ibid.*, 128.

[272] *Ibid.*, 125.

[273] *Ibid.*

[274] *Ibid.*, 127.

[275] *Ibid.*

[276] *Ibid.*, 105.

[277] *Ibid.*, 107, fn.

[278] BUTLER Joseph, *Works*, I, 162.

[279] *Op. Cit.*, 141.

[280] TILLICH, Paul, *Systematic Theology*, I, 372-74.

[281] *Ibid.*, 373.

[282] *Op. Cit.*, 43.

[283] AIKEN, *Reason and Conduct*, 185.

[284] *Op. Cit.*, 220.

[285] The Cassandra paradox resulted when an all-good, (emotionally stable, yet compassionate and feeling deity) was also regarded as omniscient. If the deity is omniscient, there is a clash between Its emotional stability and the horrors It envisions. If It is not omniscient, a characteristic quality of deity is excluded.

[286] The paradox of omnipotence resulted when one tried to answer the following questions: Can an omnipotent being make things which He cannot subsequently control? and, Can an omnipotent being make rules which, subsequently, He cannot break?

[287] The paradox of divine fatalism resulted from attributing both omniscience and omnipotence to deity, for deity then becomes limited by what He knows He will do in that future. If He knows, therefore, He is not free, and if He does not know, this would seem to circumscribe one of the qualities traditionally ascribed to deity.

[288] As the most popular philosophic doctrine in Hinduism, *saṁsāra* has a vast literature. For our purposes the following have been found useful as secondary sources: BASHAM, A. L., *The Wonder That Was India*, HIRIYANNA M., *Outlines of Indian Philosophy* (London :George Allen and Unwin, 1932); DANDEKAR, R. N., "The Role of Man in Hinduism," in *The Religion of the Hindus*, Ed. Kenneth W. MORGAN (New York: Ronald Press, 1953); ZIMMER, Heinrich., *The Philosophies of India* (New York: Bollingen Foundation, 1951); RADHAKRISHNAN, S., *Indian Philosophy*, Two Volumes (London: George Allen and Unwin, 1951); COOMARASWAMY, Ananda K., "On the One and Only Transmigrant," *Journal of the American Oriental Society*, Suppl. 3, 1944.

For my primary sources I will be using RADHAKRISHNAN S., and C. A. MOORE, *A Source Book in Indian Philosophy* (Princeton University Press, 1957), hereafter, "S. B."; *Hindu Scriptures*, Nicol MACNICOL, ed. (London: J. M. Dent and Sons, 1938); EDGERTON, Franklin, *The Beginnings of Indian Philosophy* (London: George Allen and Unwin Ltd., 1965) and *The Bhagavad Gītā* (Harvard University Press, 1944); *Śatapatha Brāhmaṇa* in *Sacred Books of the East*, ed. MAX MULLER (Delhi: Motilal Banarsidass, 1963) hereafter, "S.B.E"; *The Thirteen Principal Upaniṣads*, Tr. Robert E. HUME (Oxford University Press, 1934).

[289] Cf. RADHAKRISHNAN, *Op. Cit.*, I, 115.

[290] *S. B.*, 32.

[291] *S. B.*, 32.

[292] *Hindu Scriptures*, Ed. Nicol MACNICOL, *Op. Cit.*, 25.

[293] *Ibid.*, 12.

[294] *Ibid.*, 10.

[295] For disagreement on this point, however, see A. A. MACDONELL *Vedic Mythology*, 166, and his discussion of *R.V.* X. 16 and X. 58; and also

KUNHAN RAJA in "Pre-Vedic Elements in Indian Thought" and DEUSSEN's counter to this kind of disagreement as described in RADHAKRISHNAN *Op. Cit.*, I, 115-16.

296 *Op. Cit.*, 84.

297 *SBE.*, *Op. Cit.*, Ed. MAX MULLER XII, 148.

298 See the indexed references e.g., under "Reincarnation" in HUME's *The Thirteen Principal Upanishads*, 581-82. All translations here are from HUME.

299 HUME, *Op. Cit*, 140.

300 *Kaṭha Upaniṣad* II. 7, *Op. Cit.*, 352.

301 *BU.*, 6.2.2. in Hume, *Op. Cit.*, 1.

302 Hell, The Heaven of the Fathers, and the Heaven of the Gods; cf. MACDONELL, *Op. Cit.*, 165-174.

303 *CU* V. 3.3. Hume, *Op. Cit.*, 230.

304 *CU* V. 10.8, *Ibid.*, 233.

305 *CU* V. 10.7, *Ibid.*

306 II. 22 in EDGERTON's translation, *Op*, *Cit.*, 11.

307 SMART, Ninian, *Doctrine and Argument in Indian Philosophy*, 159. SMART goes on to detail empirical and religious arguments for rebirth, as well as cataloguing objections against it; for other arguments see DEUSSEN *The Philosophy of the Upaniṣads*, 314-315.

308 *Philosophies of India*, *Op. Cit.*, 236.

309 DASGUPTA, Surendranath, *A History of Indian Philosophy*, I, 75.

310 *Ibid.*

310a POTTER, Karl H., *Presuppositions of India's Philosophies*, 131,

311 *The Questions of King Milinda*, T. W. RHYS DAVIDS, 111.

312 *Ibid.*, 112.

313 *Ibid.*, 64.

314 Chapter XVII, Quoted in *Buddhism in Translations*, WARREN, Henry Clarke, 238.

314a *Ibid.*, 239.

315 ELIOT, Sir Charles, *Hinduism and Buddhism*, I, 199.

315a CONZE, Edward, *Buddhist Thought in India*, 133.

CONZE's entire discussion regarding the Buddhist's problems with the doctrine of *anātman* is readable and illuminating, Cf. Ch. 2, *passim.*

316 The STCHERBATSKY, *The Central Conception of Buddhism and the Meaning of the World "Dharma"*, 26.

317 *The Religion and Philosophy of the Vedas and Upanishads*, XXXII, 535.

317a CONZE says, "If indifference to a personal creator of the Universe is Atheism, then Buddhism is indeed atheistic." (*Op. Cit.*, 39). But later CONZE adds, " 'If Atheism is the denial of the existence of a God, it would be quite misleading to describe Buddhism as atheistic." (*Ibid.*, 42). The issue needs doctrinal analysis, and we shall assume that Buddhism, as Theravada Buddhism, is atheistic in the first sense mentioned here, and that consequently T. P. E. cannot be a problem for the Buddhists.

[318] *The Collected Dialogues of Plato*, Ed. HAMILTON and CAIRNS, *Republic* 614b-615a, pp. 838-839.

[319] *Ibid.*, 617 d-e, p. 841.

[320] COOMARASWAMY, Ananda K., "On the One and Only Transmigrant," *The Journal of the American Oriental Society*, LXIV, 1954, Supplement, 19.

[321] *Ibid.*, 35.

[323] *The Bṛhadāraṇyaka Upaniṣad*, with the commentary of Śaṅkarācārya, Swami MADHVANANDA, 610.

[324] *Op. Cit.*, 36.

[325] *BU*, IV. 3.36, *Op. Cit.*, 694.

[326] *Op. Cit.*, 695-696.

[327] *Ibid.*, 20, n. 5.

[327a] Cf. *S. B.*, 443.

[328] *Ibid.*, 432.

[329] *Ibid.*, 427.

[330] *Ibid.*, 433.

[331] *Ibid.*, bhāṣya on *Karikā* XXI.

[332] *Ibid.*

[333] *Ibid.*, 434.

[334] *Ibid.*, 438.

[335] *Ibid.*

[336] *Sāṁkhya-Karikā* of *Īśvarakṛṣṇa, with Gauḍapādabhāṣya*, Ed. T. G. MAINKAR, 109.

[337] *Ibid.*

[338] MAHADEVAN, T. M. P. "The Upaniṣads" *History of Philosophy: Eastern and Western*, I, 67.

[339] Quoted in *S. B.*, *Op. Cit.*, 360; the commentary is by Vātsyāyana, a 4th century Naiyāyika.

[340] *Ibid.*

[341] *Ibid.*, 361.

[342] *The Vedānta-Sūtras* with the commentary of Śaṅkarācārya, George THIBAUT *SBE*, Vol. XXXVIII, III. 1.1, p. 102.

[343] *Ibid.*, 102-103.

[344] *Ibid.*, 103.

[345] HUME, *Op. Cit.*, *BU*, IV. 4.5, p. 140.

[346] *Ibid.*

[347] *Ibid.*

[348] *Ibid.*

[349] *Op. Cit.*, 114.

[350] All quotations from the *Essay* in this paper are from the edition by Alexander Campbell FRASER, I, 439-470, unless otherwise indicated.

[351] *Ibid.*, 439.

[352] *Ibid.*, 445.

[353] Not to be confused with the "identity of self" which follows as *Type four*.

[354] *Ibid.*, 439.

[355] *Ibid.*, 441.

[356] *Ibid.*, 442.

[357] *Ibid.*, 442.

[358] *Ibid.*, 443.

[359] *Ibid.*, 451.

[360] *Ibid.*, 449.

[361] LOCKE never seems to have bothered about puzzles and problems of personal identity beyond metempsychosis and talking parrots. In short, problems of the kind that bothered later philosophers in regard to this subject do not seem to have concerned the good doctor. For problem setting, beyond what is immediately practical, seemed foreign to him.

[362] "It is not possible to say what LOCKE thinks a person to be." (Richard I. Aaron, *John Locke*, 152). Cf. Antony FLEW, "Locke and the Problem of Personal Identity," *Philosophy*, Jan., 1951, 54-55, esp. FLEW is also concerned with the confusions regarding "person" in LOCKE's discussion.

[363] *Ibid.*, 448.

[364] *Ibid.*, 445.

[365] *Ibid.*, 94.

[366] We might mention other types of problems of identity besides those associated with the transmigrating Pythagorean that might be partially answered by this method of the *less strict* interpretation of "person".

One such problem is that mentioned by Thomas REID, which we might call "the problem of the brave officer". A boy steals from an orchard, is caught and flogged. He later becomes an officer who captures the enemy's standard in battle, and then goes on to become a general. The officer remembers the boy, the general remembers only the brave officer he once was, not the thief he had been. Thus "a man may be, and at the same time not be, the person that did a particular action" (*Essays*, I, 487).

On our interpretation, there can be no contradiction. For LOCKE could plainly answer that the boy and the general possess the same life, and are therefore the same with respect to life, but the consciousness differs and they are not the same according to this other criterion. Again there is no contradiction for we are employing two distinct criteria for identity.

In "The Late Mr. Elvesham," H. G. WELLS tells the story of a young student who is persuaded by an old man, a brilliant professor, to accept the professor's money and possessions upon the death of the old professor. When the two meet to celebrate the student's happy good-fortune, the old man slips a powder into the youth's drink and later the youth awakens in in the old man's body. He asks, terror-struck, "Was I indeed Elvesham, and he me?" (*Op. Cit.*, 364) and later, "But to exchange memories as one does umbrellas! I laughed, alas! not a healthy laugh, but a wheezing, senile titter" (*Ibid.*, 364), and later sums up his predicament:

"I take it he has transferred the whole of his memories ('with all the accumulated knowledge and wisdom of threescore and ten'), the accumulation that makes up his personality, from this withered old brain of his to mine, and similarly, that he has transferred mine to his discarded tenement. Practically, that is, he has changed bodies" (*Ibid.*, 367).

A similar fantasy is described in "The Swap" by Gerald HEARD. Two professors meet, one of them has a new "introspective" (literally method) he wishes the other to observe. The other agrees and after being seated and making a few passes, the transfer of consciousness occurs. "Yes, there sitting opposite him was himself" (*Ibid.*, 146). "Yes, there he was—his real self, sitting in front of him" (*Ibid.*, 147). HEARD identifies the "self", "the real self", with the body; but he admits, "There was the shock of what one had run into—of being right in someone else's body" (*Ibid.*, 146), so the "self" is identified with both mind and body; whereas, for WELLS, self is identified only with memory. Both problems of "Who am I?" could be treated, however, by the *less strict* method described above, by showing that "self" is ambiguous with respect to "body" or "life" or "memory, consciousness, or mind", and that any answer to a question of personal identity would have to take into account at least three different notions of "self".

367 The problems involved here with the exact relations between "self" and "consciousness" need not detain us. Cf. Joseph BUTLER, "Of Personal Identity" in *The Analogy of Religon*: "This wonderful mistake follows from the view that consciousness makes personality and thence personal identity..." (p. 308). The "wonderful mistake" was the fact, as BUTLER saw it, that consciousness of personal identity presupposes personal identity and can't, therefore, constitute it. "Wonderful mistake" or not, we assume it in our first premise, in order to show a different fallacy in Locke.

368 REID makes a "nice" (in the 18th century sense) distinction:

"The faculties of consciousness and memory are chiefly distinguished by this, that the first is an immediate knowledge of the present, the second an immediate knowledge of the past..." (*Op. Cit.* I, 489).

369 It has been demonstrated that certain types of idiots have a perfect memory of events two weeks previously and before, but that they have no remembrance of time events between that time (two weeks past) and the present. But the idiot of this sort does acquire memories; they are merely late in coming to consciousness.

370 Our arguments in I and II are an expansion of a sentence from REID:

"Is it not strange that the sameness or identity of a person should consist in a thing which is continually changing and is not any two minutes the same." (*Op. Cit.*, I, 491); and from Alexander POPE:

"The parts (say they) of an animal body are perpetually changed, and the fluids which seem to be the subject of consciousness are in a perpetual circulation: so that the same individual particles do not remain in the brain; from whence it will follow, that the idea of individual consciousness must be constantly translated from one particle of matter to another, whereby the particle A, for example, must not only be conscious, but conscious that it is the same being with the particle B that went before."

(*Martinus Scriblerus*, Works X, 333-334. Quoted in *John Locke and English Literature of the Eighteenth Century*, by Kenneth MACLEAN, 100-101).

371 *Op. Cit.*, 67.

372 *The Works of George Berkeley Bishop of Cloyne*, Ed. A. A. LUCE and T. E. JESSOP, Vol. I, par. 200, 26.

373 *Ibid.*, par. 194A, 26.

374 BERKELEY, George, *Common Place Book*, Ed. with G. A. JOHNSTON, 125.

375 *Ibid.*

376 *The Works of George Berkeley Bishop of Cloyne*, *Op. Cit.*, III, 299.

377 HUME, David, *A Treatise of Human Nature*, Ed. L. A. SELBY-BIGGE, 262.

378 BHATTACHARYA, H. D. "Personal and Impersonal Persistence," *The Philosophical Quarterly*, XVII, 3, Oct. 1941, 189-90.

379 *Ibid.*, 190.

380 *Ibid.*

381 III. 2.2., Hume, *Op. Cit.*, 375.

382 IV 4.5., *Ibid.*, 140.

383 AUROBINDO, *The Life Divine*, 708.

384 *Ibid.*, 709.

385 *Ibid.*, 710.

386 *Ibid.*, 714.

387 *Ibid.*, 727.

388 *Ibid.*

389 *Ibid.*

390 *Op. Cit.*, 72a, 54.

391 *Ibid.*, 70c, 53.

392 *Ibid.*, 81d, pp. 64-65.

393 *Ibid.*, 248d, 495.

394 *Ibid.*, 249b, 496.

395 *Ibid.*, 81b, 64.

396 *S. B.*, *Op. Cit.*, 252.

397 *Ibid.*, 254.

398 *Ibid.*, 254.

399 *Ibid.*, 256.

400 Cf. *Nyāya Sūtra*, *S. B.* 360-61; *Vaiśeṣika Sūtras*, *S. B.* 394-95; Śaṁkara, *Vedānta Sūtra Commentary*, *S. B.* 517, and 535-36, 538, etc.

401 Cf. the discussion regarding these views and others in KARL H. POTTER's, "Pre-Existence" in *East-West Studies on the Problem of the Self*, Ed. P. T. RAJU and Alburey CASTELL, 204-5.

402 *S. B.*, 417.

403 *Ibid.*, 417.

404 *Ibid.*, 417-18.

405 *Ibid.*, 418.

406 CHATTERJEE, Satischandra, "Early Nyāya-Vaiśeṣika," *History of Philosophy Eastern and Western*, *Op. Cit.*, I, 225.

407 *Op. Cit.*, 711.

[408] *Buddhism in Translations, Op. Cit.*, 234.

[409] *Ibid.*, 234.

[410] EDGERTON, *The Beginnings of Indian Philosophy, Op. Cit.*, 161.

[411] V. 10.7, HUME, *Op. Cit.*, 233.

[412] V. 11-12, HUME, *Ibid.*, 407.

[413] *Op. Cit.*, 30.

[414] *Ibid.*

[415] See a discussion of this in my "Ethical Theory in Theravāda Buddhism" in *The Journal of the Bihar Research Society*, XLVII, 1-4, 170-87.

[416] For a general discussion of this see my "Morality and Religion" in *The Aryan Path* (Bombay) Oct. 1963.

[417] POTTER, Karl H., "The Naturalistic Principle of Karma," *Philosophy East and West*, XIV 1, 40.

[418] *Ibid.*

[419] *Ibid.*, 43-44.

[420] DEUTSCH, Eliot, *Advaita Vedānta, A Philosophical Reconstruction*, 78.

[421] *Ibid.*

[422] *Op. Cit.*, 113a, 93.

[423] *Ibid.*, 113-e, pp. 93-94.

[424] *Ibid.*, 114b, 94.

[425] *Ibid.*, 248c, 495.

[426] *Ibid.*, 523a, 303.

[427] CONZE, *Buddhist Thought in India, Op. Cit.*, 48.

[428] *Ibid.*, 50.

[429] *The Questions of King Milinda, Op. Cit*, 71.

[430] *Ibid.*, 73.

[431] *Ibid.*

[432] CHATTERJEE Satischandra and DATTA Dhirendramohan, *An Introduction to Indian Philosophy*, 15-16.

[433] *Ibid.*, 15.

[434] WARREN, *Op. Cit.*, 214-215.

[435] *Ibid.*, 215.

[436] *Op. Cit.*, 25.

[437] CHATTERJEE and DATTA, *Op. Cit.*, 17.

[438] CHATTERJEE and DATTA, *Op. Cit.*, 15; DASGUPTA, *A History of Indian Philosophy*, I, 71-72; CLARK, Water Eugene, *Indian Conceptions of Immortality* (Cambridge: Harvard University Press, 1934), 22; BROWN William Norman, "Escaping One's Fate" in *Studies in Honor of Maurice Bloomfield* (New Haven: Yale University Press, 1920), p. 90; EDGERTON, *The Beginnings of Indian Philosophy, Op. Cit.*, 30; EDGERTON *The Bhagavad Gītā, Op. Cit.*, 131. For an extended discussion of the views, *pro* and *contra* regarding rebirth in general in Eastern and Western philosophy and literature, see the compendious *Reincarnation in World Thought*, Compiled and Edited by HEAD Joseph and CRANSTON S. L. (New York Julian Press, 1967). The literature explaining, defending, and purveying the doctrine of rebirth to the world is, as might be expected, enormous.

[439] *Op. Cit.*, 706.

440 *Ibid.*, 716.

441 *Ibid.*,

442 *Ibid.* 717.

443 *Ibid.*

444 See for example AUROBINDO where his 'evil as cosmic utility' is plainly a species of the discipline solution:

"One side of the truth of these things (evils in the world which are quite real) we discover when we get into a deeper and larger consciousness; for we find then that there is a cosmic and individual utility in what presents itself to us as adverse and evil. For without experience of pain we would not get all the infinite value of the divine delight of which pain is in travail..." (*Op. Cit.*, 365-366). And later his evil-in-the-greater-perfection notion is surel· the aesthetic solution all over again:

"All this imperfection is to us evil, but all evil is in travail of the eternal good; for all is an imperfection which is the first condition—in the law of life evolving out of Inconscience—of a greater perfection in the manifesting of the hidden divinity... (*Ibid.*, 366)

445 For Śaṁkara see *Brahma Sūtra Bhāṣya* II. 3.43, and for Rāmānuja, see *Brahma Sūtra Bhāṣya* I. 1.1: God "while producing the entire world as an object of fruition for the individual souls, in agreement with their respective good and evil deserts, creates certain things..." (quoted in RADHAKRISHNAN, *Indian Philosophy*, *Op. Cit.*, II, 675-76).

446 CHATTERJEE and DATTA, *Op. Cit.*, 15.

447 YEVTIC Paul, *Karma and Reincarnation in Hindu Religion and Philosophy*, p. 12.

448 For a brief but excellent summary of Madhva's system, see POTTER Karl H., *Presuppositions of India's Philosophies*, 249-50, See also the *Kauṣītakī Upaniṣad* III. 8 in HUME, *Op. Cit.*, 328, where the author of the *Upaniṣad* states that God causes those whom He wishes to lead downward (or upward) to perform bad actions (or good actions). Whether this leading upward or downward entails permanent freedom in any sense is not clear, but one must, given the general tenor of the rest of this Upaniṣad, assume not. The overwhelming opinion on this point would seem to be that of Śaṁkara, viz., that God may arrange favorable or unfavorable circumstances for me but that these are always in accord with my former efforts in a prior existence. Cf. Śaṁkara, *Sūtra Bhāṣya*, II. 3.43.

449 Cf. Śaṅkarācārya, *The Vedānta Sūtras*, *Op. Cit.*, I. 1.4 and 5, 46ff.

450 "The Problem of Omniscience (Sarvajñatva)" in *The Adyar library Bulletin*, XXVI, 1-2, May, 1962, 36-37.

451 *Ibid.*, 76-77.

452 CONZE, *Buddhism: Its Essence and Development*, p. 139.

453 *Ibid.*, 138.

454 SURYANARAYANA SASTRI S. S., "Omniscience," *The Indian Historical Quarterly*, XIV, 2, June, 1938, 289.

455 *Ibid.*

456 *Ibid.*, 292.

457 *The Bhagavad Gītā*, *Op. Cit.*, 147.

[458] *Ibid.*

[459] *S. B.*, *Op. Cit.*, 140.

[460] RADHAKRISHNAN, *Op. Cit.*, I, 456, n. 1.

[461] Cf. INGALLS Daniel H. H., "Bhāskara the Vedāntin," *Philosophy East and West*, XVII, 1-4, Jan-Oct. 1967, 63: "Śaṁkara denies suffering absolutely. To Bhāskara suffering is too real a thing to deny...he admits that it is real." Indeed, Śaṁkara admits that suffering is not real in *Brahma Sūtra Bhāṣya*, II. 2.10 in a dispute with the Sāṁkhyas.

[462] PRASAD Kali, "Vedānta Solution of the Problem of Evil," *Journal of Philosophical Studies*, V, 17, Jan., 1930, 63.

[463] *Ibid.*, 68.

[464] WATTS Alan, *The Way of Zen*, 35.

[465] COOMARASWAMY, "Who is Satan and Where is Hell?", *The Review of Religion*, XII, Nov., 1947, 36-47, 37.

[466] *Ibid.*

[467] For a fine discussion of the argument from silence and its place in historical-philosophical research cf. John LANGE, "The Argument from Silence" *History and Theory*, V, 3, 1966, 288-301.

[468] WEBER Max, *The Sociology of Religion*, 139.

[469] *Ibid.*, 145.

[470] *Ibid.*, 146.

[471] *Ibid.*, 146-47.

[472] *Ibid.*, 147.

[473] HUMPHREYS Christmas, *Karma and Rebirth*, 40.

[474] *Ibid.*, 39. The quotation is from another Hindu apologist, the great and original theosophist, Madame Helen P. BLAVATSKY.

[475] *Ibid.*, 40.

[476] *Ibid.*, 41.

[477] *Ibid.*, 59.

[478] *Ibid.*, 59-60.

[479] Cf. YATISVARANANDA, "God and the Problem of Evil," *Vedānta and the West* 9, 1946, 114-122; K. S. IYER, "Īśvara and the Problem of Evil," *Vedānta Kesari* VIII, 1921-22, 295 ff; P. J. CHAUDHURY, "The Problem of Moral Evil: A Vedāntic Approach," *Prabuddha Bhārata*, 54, 1949, 277-279; S. *Sengupta* "God and Evil," *Vedānta Quarterly*, 21 1956, 340-351; PRABHAVANANDA, "The Problem of Evil", *Vedānta and the West* 15, 1952, 1-8; G. D. RAO, "The Problem of Evil," *Vedānta Kesari*, 23, 1936-37, 384-387 where RAO uses a version of the discipline solution, but states it in such a way that it must involve multiple births to be truly effective.

[480] "God and the Problem of Evil" in *Prabuddha Bharata*, XLV, 8, Aug. 1940, 354-62, 356.

[481] *Ibid.*

[482] *Op. Cit.* 271.

[483] *Ibid.*

[484] *Ibid.*, 274.

[485] *Ibid.*, 274-75.

[486] WATTS Alan, *Beyond Theology*, 39.

[487] *Ibid.*, 39.

[488] *Op. Cit.*, 57.

[489] *Ibid.*

[490] *Brahma-Sūtra Śāṅkara-Bhāṣya, Bādarāyaṇa's Brahma-Sūtras* with Śaṅkarācārya's commentary, translated into English by V. M. Apte (Bombay: Popular Book Depot, 1960), 337-42; *The Vendānta Sūtras of Bādarāyaṇa, with the Commentary of Rāmānuja*, Tr. George Thibaut, Part III, *SBE*, XLVIII, 477-79; in addition to the above two commentaries, I shall be relying upon the translation and Sanskrit text in *The Brahma Sūtra, The Philosophy of Spiritual Life* Radhakrishnan, 361-365. All quotations from these three works will be identified by 'Ś', 'Rj' and 'Rk', respectively.

[491] E.g., *B. S.* II, i, 21-29, where the question is taken up as to whether or not Brahman's nature is compromised by the imperfect world.

[492] *Ś.*, 337.

[493] *Ibid.*

[494] *Ś.*, 477.

[495] *Rj.*, 477.

[496] *Ibid.*

[497] *RK*, 362.

[498] *Rj.*, 477.

[499] *Ś.*, 339.

[500] *Ibid.*

[501] *Rj.*, 478.

[502] *Ibid.*

[503] *Ś.*, 340.

[504] Cf. *Viṣṇu Purāṇa* I, 4. 51-52.

[505] *Rj.*, 478.

[506] Chatterjee and Datta, *An Introduction to Indian Philosophy, Op. Cit.*, 17.

[507] *Rk.*, 364.

[508] *Rk.*, 364.

[509] *Ś.*, 341.

[510] *Rj.*, 479.

[511] *Ibid.*

[512] *Ibid.*

[513] *Ś.*, 342.

[514] Cf. *Ś.*, 342 and *Rj.*, 479. And Radhakrishnan, the great synthesizer, quotes the scriptural selections from both these philosophers, *Rk.*, 364.

BIBLIOGRAPHY

AARON, Richard I., *John Locke*. Oxford University Press, 1955.

AIKEN, Henry David, *Reason and Conduct*. New York: Alfred A. Knopf, 1962.

. . . "God and Evil: A Study of Some Relations Between Faith and Morals," *Ethics*, LXIII, 2, Jan., 1958, 77-97.

AQUINAS, Saint Thomas, *Summa Theologica*, *Basic Writings of Saint Thomas Aquinas*, Ed. Anton C. PEGIS, Two Volumes, New York: Random House, 1945.

AUGUSTINE, Saint Aurelius, *Divine Providence and the Problem of Evil*, Tr. Robert P. RUSSELL, *The Fathers of the Church*, Vol. V, Ed. Ludwig SCHOPP, *et. al.*, New York: Cima Publishing Co. Inc., 1948.

. . . *The Free Choice of the Will*, Translated by Robert P. RUSSELL, *The Fathers of the Church*, Vol. LIX, Ed. Roy Joseph DEFERRARI, *et. al.*, Washington, D.C.: The Catholic University of America Press, 1967.

. . . *Confessions*, Tr. Vernon J. BOURKE, *The Fathers of the Church*, Vol. XXI, Ed. Roy Joseph DEFERRARI, *et. al.*, New York: Fathers of the Church, Inc., 1953.

. . . *The City of God*, Tr. Gerald G. WALSH and Grace MONAHAN, *The Fathers of the Church*, Vol. XIV, Ed. Roy Joseph DEFERRARI, *et al.*, New York: Fathers of the Church, Inc., 1952.

. . . *Faith, Hope, and Charity*, Tr. Bernard M. PEEBLES, *The Fathers of the Church*, Vol. IV, Ed. Ludwig SCHOPP, *et al.*, New York: Cima Publishing Co., Inc., 1947.

AUROBINDO GHOSE, *The Life Divine*, New York: The Sri Aurobindo Library, Inc., 1949.

BASHAM, A. L., *The Wonder That Was India*, New York: Grove Press, 1954.

BEARDSLEY, Monroe C., and Elizabeth Lane BEARDSLEY, *Philosophical Thinking, An Introduction*, New York: Harcourt, Brace and World, Inc., 1965.

BERKELEY, George, *The Works of George Berkeley, Bishop of Cloyne*, Ed. A. A. LUCE and T. E. JESSOP, Ten Volumes, London: Thomas Nelson and Sons, Ltd., 1950.

. . . *Common Place Book*, Edited with Introduction, Notes, and Index by G. A. JOHNSTON, London: Faber and Faber Limited, 1930.

BERTOCCI, Peter, *Introduction to the Philosophy of Religion*, New York: Prentice-Hall, Inc., 1951.

The Bhagavad Gītā, Translated and Interpreted by Franklin EDGERTON, New York: Harper Torchbooks, 1964.

BHATTACHARYYA, H. D., "Personal and Impersonal Persistence", *The Philosophical Quarterly*, III, Oct. 1941, 184-97.

BLACKSTONE, William T., *The Problem of Religious Knowledge*. Englewood Cliffs, N. J., Prentice-Hall, Inc., 1963.

BODE, Boyd H., "Russell's Educational Philosophy", *The Philosophy of Bertrand Russell*, Ed. Paul Arthur SCHILPP, Evanston: Northwestern University Press 1944, 621-42.

BRADLEY, A. C., *Shakespearean Tragedy*, London : Macmillan and Co., 1932.

BRADLEY, F. H., *Appearance and Reality*, Second Edition, London: Oxford University Press, 1969.

The Bṛhadāraṇyaka Upaniṣad, with the Commentary of Śaṅkarācārya, Tr. Swami MADHVANANDA, Mayavati, Almora, Himalayas: Advaita Ashrama, 1950.

BRIGHTMAN, Edgar Sheffield, *A Philosophy of Religion*, New York: Prentice-Hall, 1940.

Buddhism in Translations, Tr. Henry Clark WARREN, New York: Atheneum, 1963.

BUTLER, Joseph, "Of Personal Identity", *The Analogy of Religion*, Oxford, 1844.

BUTLER, Joseph, *Works*, Ed. GLADSTONE, Two Volumes, Oxford, 1896.

CHATTERJEE, Satischandra, and DATTA, Dhirendramohan, *An Introduction to Indian Philosophy*, University of Calcutta, 1950.

CHATTERJEE, Satischandra, "Early Nyāyavaiśeṣika," *History of Philosophy : Eastern and Western*, Ed. S. RADHAKRISHNAN, *et. al.*, Two Volumes, London: George Allen and Unwin Ltd., 1952.

CONZE, Edward, *Buddhism: Its Essence and Development*, New York: Harper Torchbooks, 1959.

. . . *Buddhist Thought in India*, London: George Allen and Unwin, Ltd., 1962.

COOMARASWAMY, Ananda K., "On the One and Only Transmigrant," *The Journal of the American Oriental Society*, LXIV, 1944, Supplement, 19-43.

. . . "Who is Satan and Where is Hell?" *The Review of Religion*, XII, 1, Nov., 1947, 36-47.

CORNMAN, James W. and KEITH, Lehrer, *Philosophical problems and Arguments: An Introduction*, New York: The Macmillan Company, 1968.

DASGUPTA, Surendranath. *A History of Indian Philosophy*, Five Volumes, Cambridge University Press, 1932-1955.

DESHIKANANDA, Swami, "God and the Problem of Evil," *Prabuddha Bharata*, XLV, 8, Aug., 1940, 354-362.

DEUSSEN, Paul, *The Philosophy of the Upaniṣads*, Edinburgh: T. and T. Clark, 1906.

DEUTSCH, Eliot, *Advaita Vedānta: A Philosophical Reconstruction*, Honolulu: East-West Centre Press, 1969.

Dionysius the Areopagite, *On the Divine Names and the Mystical Theology*, Tr. C. E. ROLT. New York: The Macmillan Company, 1951.

DOSTOIEVSKY, Fyodor, *The Brothers Karamazov*, Tr. Constance GARNETT, New York : The Modern Library, 1937.

EDGERTON, Franklin, *The Beginnings of Indian Philosophy*, London : George Allen and Unwin Ltd., 1965.

ELIOT, Sir Charles, *Hinduism and Buddhism, An Historical Sketch*, Three Volumes, London : Routledge and Kegan Paul, Ltd., 1921.

FARRELL, P. M., "Evil and Omnipotence", *Mind*, LXVII, No, 267, July, 1958, 399-403.

FARRER, Austin, *Love Almighty and Evils Unlimited*, New York : Doubleday and Co., 1961.

FERRE, Nels F., *Evil and the Christian Faith*, New York : Harper and Brothers Publishers, 1947.

. . . *A Philosophical Scrutiny of Religion*, London : Thomas Nelson and Sons, 1963.

FLEW, Antony, "Locke and the Problem of Personal Identity", *Philosophy*, XXVI, Jan., 1951, 53-68.

. . . "Divine Omnipotence and Human Freedom," *New Essays*

in Philosophical Theology, Ed. Antony FLEW and Alisdair McINTYRE, London : S. C. M. Press, 1961.

GREENE, William Chase, *Moira, Fate, Good and Evil in Greek Thought*, New York : Harper Torchbooks, 1944.

HEARD, Gerald, "The Swap," *The Great Fog and Other Weird Tales*, London: Cassell and Co., 1947.

HERMAN, A. L., "Ethical Theory in Theravāda Buddhism," *The Journal of the Bihar Research Society*, XLVII, 1-4, 1961, 170-87.

. . . "Morality and Religion," *The Aryan Path*, XXXIV, 10, Oct., 1963, 449-54; XXXIV, 11, Nov. 1963, 486-92; XXXIV, 12, Dec., 1963, 531-36.

HICK, John, *Evil and the God of Love*, New York : Harper and Row Publishers, 1966.

. . . *Philosophy of Religion*, Englewood Cliffs, N. J. : Prentice-Hall 1963.

D'HOLBACH, Baron Paul Henri, *Good Sense*, Tr. by J. P. MENDUM, New York : Wright and Owen, 1831.

HOSPERS, John, *An Introduction to Philosophical Analysis*, Second Edition, Englewood Cliffs, N. J. : Prentice-Hall, 1967.

HUME, David, *Dialogues Concerning Natural Religion*, Ed. Norman Kemp SMITH, Second Edition, New York : Social Sciences Publishers, 1948.

. . . *A Treatise of Human Nature*, Ed. L. A. SELBYBIGGE, Oxford : Clarendon Press, 1955

HUME, Robert Ernest. *The Thirteen Principal Upanishads*, Oxford University Press, 1949.

HUMPHREYS, Christmas, *Karma and Rebirth*, London : John Murray, 1948.

INGALLS, Daniel H. H., "Bhāskara the Vedāntin," *Philosophy East and West*, XVII, 1-4, Jan.-Oct. 1967, 61-67.

JAMES, William, *The Will to Believe and Other Essays in Popular Philosophy*, New York : Dover Publications Inc., 1956.

KAZANTZAKIS, Nikos, *Zorba the Greek*, Tr. Carl WILDMAN, New York : Simon and Schuster, 1952.

KEITH, Arthur B., *The Religion and Philosophy of the Vedas and Upanishads*, Two Volumes, Harvard Oriental Series, Vols. 31, 32, Cambridge : Harvard University Press, 1925.

LANGE, John, "The Argument from Silence," *History and Theory*, V, 3, 1966, 288-301.

LEIBNIZ, G. W., *Theodicy*, New Haven : Yale University Press, 1952.

LEWIS, C. S. *The Problem of Pain*, New York : Macmillan and Company, 1961.

LOCKE, John, *An Essay Concerning Human Understanding*, Ed., Alexander Campbell FRASER, Two Volumes, New York : Dover Publications, 1959.

LOVEJOY, Arthur O., *The Thirteen Pragmatisms and Other Essays*, Baltmore : The Johns Hopkins Press, 1963.

MACDONELL, A. A., *Vedic Mythology*, Varanasi : Indological Book House, 1963.

MACKIE, J. L., "Evil and Omnipotence," *Mind*, LXIV, 254, April, 1955, 200-12.

. . . "Review : John HICK's *Evil and the God of Love*," *Philosophical Books*, III. 17, 1966.

MACNICOL, Nicol, *Hindu Scriptures*, London : J. M. Dent and Sons, 1938.

MCCLOSKEY, H. J., "God and Evil," *The Philosophical Quarterly*, X, 39, April, 1960, 97-114.

MACLEAN, Kenneth, *John Locke and English Literature of the Eighteenth Century*, New York : Russell and Russell, Inc., 1962.

MCTAGGART, J. M. E., *Some Dogmas of Religion*, London : Edward Arnold, 1906.

MADDEN, Edward H. and HARE, Peter H., *Evil and the Concept of God*, Springfield, Illinois : Charles C. Thomas, 1968.

MAHADEVAN, T. M. P., "The Upanisads," *History of Philosophy Eastern and Western*, Ed. Sarvepalli RADHAKRISHANAN, Two Volumes, London : George Allen and Unwin, Ltd., 1952, I, 55-74.

MARITAIN, Jacques, *God and the Permission of Evil*, Milwaukee : Bruce Publishing Co., 1966.

MILL, John Stuart, *An Examination of Sir William Hamilton's Philosophy*, London : Longmans, Green and Co., 1889.

. . . *Three Essays on Religion*, London : Longmans, Green and Co., 1874.

MOORE, G. E., *Principia Ethica*, Cambridge University Press, 1959.

PATON, H. J., *The Modern Predicament : A Study in the Philosophy of Religion*, London : George Allen and Unwin Ltd., 1955.

PENELHUM, Terence, "Divine Goodness and the Problem of Evil," *Religious Studies*, Cambridge University Press, II, 2, Oct. 1966, 95-107.

PIKE, Nelson, "Hume on Evil", *Philosophical Review*, LXXII, 2, 1963, 180-97.

PITTION, Jean-Paul and BERMAN, David, "A New Letter by Berkeley to Browne on Divine Analogy," *Mind*, LXVII, No. 311, July, 1969.

PLANTINGA, Alvin, "The Free Will Defense," *Philosophy in America*, Ed., Max BLACK, London : G. Allen and Unwin, 1965, 204-20.

PLATO, *The Collected Dialogues of Plato*, Ed., Edith HAMILTON and Huntington CAIRNS, New York : Pantheon Books, 1961.

Plotinus. *The Enneads*, Tr. Stephen MACKENNA, Second Edition, New York : Pantheon Basic Books, Inc., n.d.

POTTER, Karl H., *Presuppositions of India's Philosophies*, Englewood Cliffs, N. J. : Prentice-Hall Inc., 1963.

. . . "The Naturalistic Principle of Karma," *Philosophy East and West*, XIV, 1, April, 1964, 39-49.

. . . "Pre-Existence, " *East-West Studies on the Problem of the Self*, Ed., P. T. RAJU and Alburey CASTELL, The Hague : Martinus Nijhoff, 1968.

PRASAD, Kali. "Vedānta Solution to the Problem of Evil," *Journal of Philosophical Studies*, V, 17, Jan. 1930, 62-71.

The Questions of King Milinda, Tr. from the Pali by T. W. RHYS DAVIDS, Delhi : Motilal Banarasidass, 1965.

RADHAKRISHNAN, S., *The Brahma Sūtra, The Philosophy of Spiritual Life*, Tr. with an Introduction and notes, London : George Allen and Unwin, Ltd., 1960.

. . . *Indian Philosophy*, Two Volumes, New York : The Macmillan Company, 1931.

Rāmānuja, *The Vedānta-Sūtra Commentary*, Tr. George THIBAUT, *The Sacred Books of the East*, Ed., F. MAX MULLER, XLVIII, Delhi : Motilal Banarsidass, 1962.

RANADE, R. D., *A Constructive Survey of Upaniṣadic Philosophy*, Poona : Oriental Book Agency, 1926.

REID, Thomas, "Mr. LOCKE's Account of Power," *Essays on the Powers of the Human Mind*, Three Volumes, Edinburgh: 1803.

Reincarnation in World Thought, Comp. and Ed. Joseph HEAD and S. L. CRANSTON, New York : Julian Press, 1967.

ROYCE, Josiah, *The World and the Individual*, Two Volumes, New York : The Macmillan Company, 1908.

RUSSELL, Bertrand, *Mysticism and Logic and Other Essays* London : George Allen and Unwin Ltd., 1917.

Śaṁkara, *The Vedānta-Sūtras Commentary*, Tr. George THIBAUT, *The Sacred Books of the East*, Ed. F. MAX MULLER, XXXIV, XXXV, Delhi : Motilal Banarsidass, 1962.

Śāṁkhya-Kārīkâ of Īśvarakṛṣṇa with Gauḍapādabhyāṣya, Critically Edited with Translation and Notes by T. G. MAINKAR, Poona : Oriental Book Agency, 1964.

SASTRI, S. S. Suryanarayana. "Omniscience," *The Indian Historical Quarterly*, XIV, 2, June, 1938, 280-92.

Śatapatha Brāhmaṇa, Tr. Julius EGGELING in *The Sacred Books of the East*, Ed. F. MAX MULLER, XII, Delhi : Motilal Banarsidass, 1963.

SHELDON, Wilmon Henry, *God and Polarıty : A Syntheses of Philosophies*, New Haven : Yale University Press, 1954.

SMART, Ninian, *Doctrine and Argument in Indian Philosophy*, London : George Allen and Unwin Dtd., 1964.

. . . "Omnipotence, Evil and Superman," *Philosophy* XXXVI, 137, April/July, 1961, 188-95.

SOLOMON, E.A., "The Problem of Omniscience (Sarvajñatva)," *The Adyar Library Bulletin*, XXVI, 1-2, May, 1962, 36-77.

A Source Book in Indian Philosophy, Ed. Sarvepalli RADHAKRISHNAN and Charles A. MOORE, Princeton University Press, 1957.

SPINOZA, Baruch, *Short Treatise on God, Man and His Well-Being*, Tr. A. WOLF, London : A. and C. Black, 1910.

STACE, Walter, "The Problem of Evil," *Philosophy, Religion, and the Coming World Civilization*, Essays in Honor of William Ernest HOCKING, Ed. Leroy S. ROWNER, The Hague : Martinus Nijhof, 1966.

STCHERBATSKY, Th., *The Central Conception of Buddhism and*

the Meaning of the Word "Dharma", London : Royal Asiatic Society, 1923.

SULLIVAN, J. W. N., *Beethoven : His Spiritual Develop̀ent*, New York : Vintage Books, 1927.

TILLICH, Paul, *Systematic Theology*, Three Volumes, Chicago : University of Chicago Press, 1957.

TOULMIN, Stephen, *An Examination of the Place of Reason in Ethics*, Cambridge University Press, 1961.

TRETHOWAN, Dom Illtyd, *An Essay in Christian Philosophy*, London : Longmans, Green and Co., 1954.

The Vendānta Sūtras with the commentary of Rāmānuja, Tr. George THIBAUT, *Sacred Books of the East*, Ed. F. MAX MŪLLER, XLVIII, Delhi : Motilal Banarsidass, 1962.

The Vedānta-Sūtras with the commentary of Śaṅkarācārya, Tr. George Thibaut, *Sacred Books of the East*, Ed. F. MAX MŪLLER, XXXVIII. Delhi : Motilal Banarsidass, 1962.

WATTS, Alan, *Beyond Theology*, New York : Pantheon Books, 1964.

. . . *The Way of Zen*, New York : Pantheon Books, Inc., 1957.

WEBB, C. C. J., *Problems in the Relations of God and Man*, London: James Nisbet and Co. Ltd., 1911.

WEBER, Max, *The Sociology of Religion*, Tr. Ephraim FISCHOFF, Boston : Beacon Press, 1963.

. . . "Religious Rejections of the World and their Directions," *From Max Weber : Essays in Sociology*, Tr. and Ed. Hans GERTH and C. Wright MILLS, New York : Oxford University Press, 1946.

WELLS, H. G., "The Late Mr. Elvesham, " *The Short Stories of H. G. Wells*, New York : Doubleday, Doran and Co., 1929.

WHALE, J. S., *The Christian Answer to the Problem of Evil*, London : S. C. M. Press, Ltd., 1936, 4th edition, 1957.

WITTGENSTEIN, Ludwig, *Philosophical Investigations*, Tr. G. E. M. ANSCOMBE, New York : The Macmillan Company, 1958.

YEVTIC, Paul, *Karma and Reincarnation in Hindu Religion and Philosophy*, London : Luzac and Co., 1927.

ZIMMER, Heinrich, *The Philosophies of India*, New York : Bollingen Foundation 1951.

INDEX AND GLOSSARY